Knowledge, Expertise and the Professions

It has long been recognised that specialised knowledge is at the core of what distinguishes professions from other occupations. The privileged status of professions in most countries, however, together with their claims to autonomy and access to specialised knowledge, is being increasingly challenged both by market pressures and by new instruments of accountability and regulation. Established and emerging professions are increasingly seen as either the solution or as sources of conservatism and resistance to change in western economies, and recent developments in professional education draw on a competence model that emphasises what newly qualified members of a profession 'can do' rather than what 'they know'.

This book applies the disciplines of the sociology of knowledge and epistemology to the question of professional knowledge. What is this knowledge? It goes beyond traditional debates between 'knowing how' and 'knowing that', and 'theory' and 'practice'. The chapters cover a wide range of issues, from discussions of the threats to the knowledge base of established professions including engineers and architects, to the fraught situations faced by occupations whose fragile knowledge base and professional status is increasingly challenged by new forms of control. While recognising that graduates seeking employment as members of a profession need to show their capabilities, the book argues for reversing the trend that blurs or collapses the skill/knowledge distinction. If professions are to have a future then specialised knowledge is going to be more important than ever before.

Knowledge, Expertise and the Professions will be key reading for students, researchers and academics in the fields of professional expertise, further education, higher education, the sociology of education, and the sociology of the professions.

Michael Young is Emeritus Professor of Education at the Institute of Education, University of London, UK.

Johan Muller is Emeritus Professor of Education in the School of Education at the University of Cape Town, South Africa.

Knowledge, Expertise and the Professions

Edited by
Michael Young and
Johan Muller

Routledge
Taylor & Francis Group

LONDON AND NEW YORK

First published 2014
by Routledge
2 Park Square, Milton Park, Abingdon, Oxon OX14 4RN

and by Routledge
711 Third Avenue, New York, NY 10017

Routledge is an imprint of the Taylor & Francis Group, an informa business

British Library Cataloguing in Publication Data
A catalogue record for this book is available from the British Library

Library of Congress Cataloging in Publication Data
Knowledge, expertise and the professions/edited by Michael Young and Johan Muller.
    pages cm
    1. Professions.   2. Expertise.   3. Knowledge, Sociology of.
    4. Education.   5. Professional employees – Education.
    I. Young, Michael F. D.   II. Muller, Johan.
    HD8038.A1K66 2014
    331.7'1 – dc23
    2013044858

ISBN: 978-0-415-71390-0 (hbk)
ISBN: 978-0-415-71391-7 (pbk)
ISBN: 978-1-315-88308-3 (ebk)

Typeset in Galliard
by Florence Production Ltd, Stoodleigh, Devon, UK

Contents

Contributors

Francis Carter is an architect and Senior Lecturer at the School of Architecture Planning and Geomatics, University of Cape Town (UCT), South Africa. His post-professional qualification is in higher education studies (MPhil, UCT), in which he began a review of principles for the pedagogic structuring of design knowledge evident in a variety of curriculum models.

Jennifer M. Case is a Professor in the Department of Chemical Engineering at the University of Cape Town, South Africa, with a special responsibility for academic development. She teaches in the undergraduate chemical engineering programme and her research on the student experience of learning has been widely published.

Jan Derry is a Reader in Philosophy of Education at the Centre for Philosophy, Institute of Education, University of London, UK. Her research interests focus on philosophical psychology, theories of knowledge and learning, and the nature of professional expertise and judgment.

Gerard Fealy is Associate Professor and Associate Dean for Research and Innovation at the UCD School of Nursing, Midwifery and Health Systems, UCD College of Health Sciences, Dublin, Ireland, Director of the National Centre for the Protection of Older People and a founding member of the European Association for the History of Nursing.

Gerald Grace has taught Education Studies at King's College London, the University of Cambridge and Durham University, UK, and Victoria University of Wellington, New Zealand. His early studies were concerned with the Sociology of the Teaching Profession. He is at present Director of the Centre for Research and Development in Catholic Education, at the University of London, Institute of Education, and is the Editor of the journal, *International Studies in Catholic Education*.

David Guile is Professor of Education and Work at the Institute of Education, University of London, UK, where he is also Head of the Department of Lifelong and Comparative Education, and a member of the ESRC-funded Research Centre Learning and Life Chances in Knowledge Economies and Societies. David's main research interests are using interdisciplinary perspectives to study professional, vocational and workplace learning. His most recent books are *The learning challenge of the knowledge economy* and *The knowledge economy and lifelong learning: Critical perspectives*, the latter edited with David Livingstone.

Hu Hanrahan is Professor Emeritus at the University of the Witwatersrand (Wits), Johannesburg, South Africa. A graduate of Wits University, he has served in the Siemens Chair of Communications Engineering, as Head of the Department of Electrical Engineering and as Dean of the Faculty of Engineering. He has contributed to policies, standards and processes for professional registration and accreditation of engineering education programmes, and is Chairman of the Washington Accord.

Ben Kotzee is Lecturer in the Jubilee Centre for Character and Values at the University of Birmingham, UK. He specialises in applying insights from contemporary epistemology to questions in the philosophy of education. He holds a PhD in Philosophy from King's College London and was previously Lecturer at Birkbeck College, University of London.

Martin McNamara is Dean of Nursing, and Head of the UCD School of Nursing, Midwifery and Health Systems, UCD College of Health Sciences, Dublin, Ireland.

Johan Muller is Professor Emeritus in the School of Education at the University of Cape Town and Senior Research Fellow at Higher Education South Africa. His research interests lie in the sociology of knowledge and of the curriculum. He has published in the sub-fields of schooling and higher education. His book *Reclaiming knowledge* was published by Routledge in 2000.

Yael Shalem is an Associate Professor of Education at the School of Education, University of Witwatersrand, Johannesburg, South Africa. Her research interests include professional knowledge, curriculum, teacher education and teacher work. She directed a teacher development project (Data Informed Practice Improvement Project, DIPIP) and is co-leading a professional knowledge project, based at the REAL (Researching Education and Labour) Centre at the University of Witwatersrand. She is the first of two Editors of *Retrieving teaching: Critical issues in curriculum pedagogy and learning*.

Nick Taylor holds a Masters degree in Geology and a PhD in Maths Education. He has been a teacher of maths and science, subject advisor for schools, policy researcher and Executive Director of the non-profit organisation JET Education Services. In 2012 he was appointed CEO of the National Education Evaluation Development Unit, South Africa's school inspectorate. Most recently he co-Edited *Creating effective schools*, published in September 2013 by Pearson.

Christopher Winch is Professor of Educational Philosophy and Policy in the Department of Education and Professional Studies at King's College, London.

He is the author of *The philosophy of human learning* (Routledge, 1998) and *Dimensions of expertise* (Continuum, 2010) among numerous other books and articles. He has worked in primary, further and higher education.

Michael Young is Emeritus Professor of Education at the Institute of Education, University of London, UK, and a Visiting Professor at a number of universities in the UK and overseas. His main research interests are in the sociology of the curriculum, professional knowledge and qualifications. His book *Bringing knowledge back in* was published by Routledge in 2008 and with Stephanie Allais he edited *Implementing national qualification frameworks*, published by Routledge in 2013. His book edited with David Lambert *Knowledge and the future school* will be published by Bloomsbury in 2014.

Acknowledgements

The editors would like to thank the British Academy for the grant awarded to Michael Young and Johan Muller to fund four seminars. This covered Michael Young and Johan Muller's travel and accommodation costs between Cape Town and London and the costs of some of those attending. Several of the contributions to the seminars became chapters in this book. They are also grateful to the National Research Foundation of South Africa (UID 85813) for a grant to support the work on the project undertaken by Johan Muller. The grant holders in each case acknowledge that opinions, findings and conclusions or recommendations expressed are those of the authors, and that neither the British Academy nor the NRF accepts any liability whatsoever in this regard. They would also like to thank Gyta Nicola (Institute of Education) for her help in organising the London seminars. Last, we are most grateful for the patience and quick response to our queries of our contributing authors.

Part One

Introduction and framing the issues

Outline of the book

Michael Young and Johan Muller

Part 1 of this book begins with a chapter by the editors outlining the current state of the sociology of the professions and provides an intellectual rationale for taking knowledge more seriously than is currently the case in much of the literature presently being produced. It is followed by a chapter by Gerald Grace, who sketches the broader moral compass of the professions, and asks whether the professions are still able to perform their Durkheimian duty as moral guardians of our contemporary society, and what it will take to restore some moral coherence to our market-fragmented world.

The two parts that follow present specific explorations into the dynamics of knowledge and professional judgment. The chapters in the book's second part all engage with contemporary philosophical work on theoretical and practical knowledge. The first chapter in Part 2, by Jan Derry, tackles a common misapprehension about the Russian social psychologist Lev Vygotsky, which depicts him as a kind of Cartesian rationalist because of his stress on theoretical knowledge. Using Robert Brandom's work, she shows us a far more nuanced and interesting Vygotsky and his possible contribution to a theory of professional knowledge and judgment. The second chapter, by Christopher Winch, continues his current work by unpacking in further detail the varieties of practical knowledge that must be given due consideration in the professional curriculum, showing too that there is no practical knowledge that is devoid of some conceptual content. Ben Kotzee next tackles the 'fluency theorists' who place exclusive stress on practical knowledge, and engages with the recent sociological work of Harry Collins on 'expertise', expanding his framework. Like Jan Derry, David Guile in Chapter 6 recruits the work of Brandom to approach the question of professional knowledge from the perspective of professional practice, and depicts it as a continuous process of successive recontextualisations. In the final chapter in Part 2, Yael Shalem addresses the question as to how professional judgments can be stabilised in a 'minor' or 'semi' profession like teaching, where a broadly accepted and stable knowledge base is not in place. She shows the value of a good educational theory in anchoring judgments rationally. All of the contributions in Part 2 attempt to refine the conceptual armoury we currently have to discuss, analyse and explain professional knowledge and how it works.

Part 3 of the book showcases five cases of professional knowledge in the curriculum or in practice. The first chapter by Hu Hanrahan tackles the question of engineering knowledge, presenting a picture of how it has changed over the years, and distilling from this socio-historical overview an account of how engineering knowledge varies between the engineering occupational positions across the theory–practice continuum. Francis Carter looks at struggles over time in the French architectural curriculum, and how theoretical considerations – in this case aesthetic ones – have managed to retain a measure of dominance despite the rising technical demands of contemporary science and technology. Jennifer Case takes us up to the present, examinining key contemporary debates in the engineering curriculum, and argues for a model of curriculum reform that will not undermine the demands of conceptual coherence. Martin McNamara and Gerard Fealy analyse the contemporary nursing curriculum and show why attempts to shore up the knowledge base of nursing as a profession have gone about it the wrong way. In the final chapter Nick Taylor looks at the mathematics teachers' curriculum in South Africa and shows that 'subject knowledge for teaching' – knowledge of mathematics itself – has to form the substrate to a strong professional identity, and an effective professional practice.

1 From the sociology of professions to the sociology of professional knowledge

Michael Young and Johan Muller

Introduction: professions and their knowledges

In a review of research on the sociology of work written two decades ago, Andrew Abbott (1993) commented that work on the professions was unusually dominant within the broader field of the sociology of work, and within that, 'theorizing dominates' (ibid.: 203). Notwithstanding this glut of attention, the sociology of professions remains a frustratingly under-specified area, and the demarcation criteria that have emerged to distinguish professions from other occupations – deployment of expert knowledge, technical autonomy, a normative orientation, and social and material rewards (Gorman and Sandefur 2011) – do not unambiguously distinguish between professions and other expert occupations. Nor do they take us much further than Glazer's depiction of 'their hopeless predicament' in analysing occupations that are variously described as minor (Glazer 1974), 'soft' (Becher and Trowler 1989) or semi-professions (Etzioni 1969). Opinion is divided on whether this matters or not. According to Evetts (2006, 2013), the bulk of researchers in the USA have 'moved on' (Evetts 2006: 134) and no longer seek demarcating criteria, since these do not help in understanding the power of some professional groups but not others, nor in understanding the 'contemporary appeal of the discourse of professionalism in all occupations' (ibid.).

For European researchers like Sciulli (2005), it decidedly does matter: how else do we distinguish between expert occupations like haute couture and cuisine, and professions like medicine or law? For Sciulli, it is important to see that:

> expert occupations (compared to professions) . . . do not bear fiduciary responsibility, and they also do not institutionalise either theory-based instruction or ongoing deliberation. They do not typically establish and then maintain collegial formations, as reflected in on-going behavioural fidelity to the threshold of procedural norms.
>
> (Sciulli 2005: 937)

What Sciulli is stressing here are the 'structural' or institutional features of professions. Yet here too, variation is so wide as to elude neat conceptual demarcation, and it is arguably growing wider still. Sciulli concludes, in a phrase that has resonance with the contributors in this volume below who draw on the philosopher Robert Brandom, that professions are 'reason-giving collegial formations' (Sciulli 2005: 958), but that too was already established by Abbott (1988).

The centrality of intrinsic normative commitments and responsibilities was established in what Gorman and Sandefur (2011) call the 'Golden Age' of the sociology of professions, by Parsons and Merton who, following Durkheim, emphasised the socially integrative function of professions. Although this was a diminution of Durkheim's contribution, it did foreground the relation between the internal normative commitments of professions and their broader macro social functions, a point taken further in the first chapter of this book by Gerald Grace. In reaction to the perceived conservatism of this functionalist description, a revisionist period followed, of Marxist, Weberian and later Foucauldian provenance, which put professional bona fides in question and, in an inversion of Parsonian optimism, pointed to the monopolistic and gatekeeping operation of professions and their broader ideological function. This phase of critique, with its shift of focus from professions as an occupation to professionalism as an ideology, also cast suspicion on the validity and value of expert and professional knowledge, a position that in science studies at least we have yet properly to emerge from, and one which made it difficult to establish the reality and efficacy of 'expert knowledge' (Collins and Evans 2009). Nevertheless, it was in this phase too that Abbott (1988) established the centrality of formal abstract principles for professional formations, as mentioned above.

The phase that followed re-interpreted the Parsonian values, and returned to the normative emphasis of the Golden Age (as in Friedson 2001), but in a 'more balanced and cautious' way (Gorman and Sandefur 2011: 138). There have been a wide variety of case studies, which seem to say more about the occupational niche in question than they do about what professions are and how they work. Evetts (2013) detects a shift in the occupational structure of professions, with corporations and organisations, both private and public, increasingly being the workplace location for all kinds of professions – the long established ones like doctors, lawyers, engineers and accountants, as well as the 'new boys on the block' such as social workers and teachers. This seems to have led to a shrinkage of autonomy and discretion in Evetts' view, fuelling the literature on 'de-professionalisation' and even 'proletarianisation'. This can be overstated, of course, and is not a major focus for European scholars, except in England.

There are two features that can be distilled from the contemporary work in the sociology of professions that are worth noting for the purposes of the present volume. The first is that, in the present discursive climate of the 'knowledge economy', 'knowledge work' and 'expert occupations', there is simultaneously concern about the increase in the riskiness of professional judgment, the threat that codification and standardisation poses to the autonomy and discretion of the traditional 'liberal' professional, and a residual suspicion about the probity and trustworthiness of all professions and professional judgment. Whether this reflects the views of an increasingly informed and sceptical public about the trustworthiness and value of the professions, or is a long hangover from the scepticism about knowledge that underlies public attitudes in an age that has distinct anti-intellectual overtones is hard to say. Second, the upshot has been that the nature of professional knowledge has escaped scholarly notice, and when spoken about at all, is spoken about in terms of professional expert judgment, and what professionals *can do* with the knowledge. What the *knowledge is that professionals have had to acquire to be experts* has, by and large, eluded scholarly attention.

The paradox we are left with is this: in an age where 'knowledge' as a qualifier is attached to a wide range of categories and actions, when expert occupations proliferate, and the legitimatory discourse of 'professionalisation' is deployed across the occupational spectrum, *knowledge itself*, and above all the sociological study of professional knowledge, goes virtually unremarked. In a nice twist to the paradox, 'knowledge' itself is increasingly used as a legitimatory qualifier for sociological work – but the knowledge itself is by and large passed over in silence (Young 2010).

The project we are pursuing by means of this volume is to put the sociological study of professional knowledge into the centre of scholarly focus in research on professions and their formation. This is not just a matter of restoring sociological balance. As educational sociologists, we (the editors) have also repeatedly come up against the intellectual lacuna left in discussions around the aims of higher education and the curriculum (Muller and Young forthcoming). We have noted in earlier work how the exclusive stress on the 'can do' side of the knowledge equation – on skills and competencies at the expense of knowledge; on skills in the design of national qualifications frameworks (Young and Allais 2013); and on outcomes in national school curricula (Young 2010; Muller 2007) – can distort the resultant educational achievements, and impair educational provision. It is the distinctive socio-epistemic properties of different kinds and bodies of knowledge that are put to use by members of professions in problem-solving and other kinds of knowledgeable practice that is our singular concern in this volume.

To say that, however, is not to make a strong split between knowledge and action; this would, in the case of professional knowledge, be particularly counterproductive. Indeed, as the various contributions to this book will show, there is a continuum between these, and it is easy to blur the lines. The distinctions we wish to refine are analytical. There is an interesting related body of work that focuses on 'knowledge engagement and learning' (Jensen, Lahn and Nerland 2012: 5), which has carved out new perspectives in understanding the knowledgeable nature of professional work. It starts, however, from our perspective and in terms of our central interest, just too far in the direction of 'can do' and the 'practice' of knowledge-based professions, and pays little attention to the 'specialised knowledge' involved in that practice. This perspective has obvious affinities with the work in this volume, and is represented by the contribution of David Guile, who makes a first stab at building a bridge between the two sets of interest. Other papers that reflect such bridge building are Afdal 2012, and Nerland and Karseth forthcoming, among others. We are mindful and appreciative of this work, but do not engage further with it directly in what follows; the opportunity will surely present itself in the future.

The difference in emphasis between the terms 'knowledge' and 'expertise' has resisted easy resolution, and this is critical when it comes to professions. This is so because professionals self-evidently have, and need, both specialised knowledge and practical expertise, 'know that' knowledge and 'know how' knowledge. On the other hand, while all professions involve some 'practical expertise', you can be an 'expert' in all manner of activities without your expertise being associated with a profession – brilliant poker players and winners at Mastermind-type quiz shows are examples that come to mind. This distinction is sometimes referred to as similar to distinctions between 'abstract', 'pure' or 'theoretical' knowledge, and 'applied' knowledge, and between theory and practice, but as we will show, the parallel is one of many that obscures more than it clarifies.

We will see, in the chapters by Winch and Kotzee in Part 1 of this book, that a marker in this debate was put down in a particularly graphic way by the English philosopher Gilbert Ryle (1946). Ryle was conducting a pointed argument with what is known as Cartesian rationalism, the view that the essence of all knowledge lies in its propositional content, and in his wake have come many educators who have railed against the 'content only' curriculum, and against the perniciousness, as Gradgrind in Dickens' *Hard Times* so memorably had it, of 'facts, facts, facts' (see Taylor and Vinjevold 1999 for a discussion). The Rylean point was that propositions, on their own, are inert. The learner must also know *how to do* something with the propositions. In this way Ryle launched his famous distinction between 'knowing that' and 'knowing how', in the process complicating the distinction between knowledge and practice.

But what does it mean to 'know how' to do something with a proposition? What exactly is that knowledge and how should it be described? Christopher Winch (2010), in an important recent book, helpfully describes two kinds of 'know how' knowledge, both of which, over and above propositional knowledge, he regards as integral to the 'systematically organised knowledge' that is the bedrock of school subjects and academic disciplines. These two are:

- Knowledge of the *inferential relations* between the propositions. It is not enough to know the propositions in themselves. Neophytes, to become adept, must also know what the reach and power of the propositions is, and how to make their way around and between them. This involves knowing which normative rules are non-negotiable and which admit of latitudes of discretion (are defeasible). This is facility with *existing knowledge*;
- Knowledge of the *procedures* in assessing, testing and acquiring new knowledge. For any field of knowledge, this is knowing how warrants work, what their scope and limits are, and how to put them to work in judgments that produce something novel. This is facility with *new knowledge*.

In an influential contemporary branch of philosophy, this is known as making your way around the 'space of reasons' – knowing how to play the game of giving and asking for reasons (see Jan Derry and David Guile in this volume). Conceptual knowledge in this account is that which can be offered as, and itself stands in need of, reasons. Understanding or grasping such propositional content is a kind of know-how, or practical mastery of the game of giving and asking for reasons: this entails being able to tell what is a reason, for what purpose, and being able to distinguish good reasons from bad. To be able to play the game is to be able to keep score on what you, and other players, are committed and entitled to. Evaluating a claim means understanding how it would change the score. The conceit of 'scorekeeping between players' usefully brings out the social nature of 'know that' and 'know how' knowledge and judgments based on them.

There is a position in philosophy – the intellectualist or Cartesian camp (see Stanley 2011; Stanley and Williamson 2001) – that maintains that all 'knowing how' is a kind of, or can be translated into, propositional knowledge, or 'knowing that'. On the other side of the spectrum, the 'fluency' theorists, like Hubert Dreyfus (2005) (see Ben Kotzee, this volume) seem to be suggesting that all knowledge possessed by expert practitioners is embodied, tacit and exercised in a fluent way without passing through cognition at all; all knowledge for them is 'know how'. Both intellectualists and fluency theorists have their defenders but are in the end not helpful for our specific problematic. That the Rylean position presents the midway position, has been persuasively argued by Winch (2010) in his chapter in this volume. To sum up the discussion thus far: there are two kinds of knowledge, 'knowledge that' and 'knowledge how'. Both are more interrelated than previously thought and both must be considered in accounts of professional knowledge.

Winch has been persuasive that all three kinds of knowledge ('know that' and the two kinds of 'know how') should be described in what he calls a (school) 'subject' (Winch, 2012). For Winch, a 'subject' is an example of 'systematically organised knowledge'. We can conclude that subjects are systematically organised ensembles of 'know that' and 'know how'. This is helpful as far as it goes, but we will need another distinction when considering professional knowledge or the professional, in contrast to the school, curriculum. Professional education students need access not only to 'knowledge that', of propositions of a subject, and 'knowledge how', how the propositions are used in a subject, they need knowledge of 'how' propositions may or may not be useful (or solve or suggest solutions to) specific problems in their sectoral 'field of practice' – a point we will return to (see also Winch this volume).

In what follows, we will first re-describe the distinction usually referred as 'pure' versus 'applied' knowledge in order to establish an initial point of departure for considering the nature of professional knowledge. We are not interested here in a related but different distinction between 'theory' and 'practice'. The distinction we are interested in is an antecedent one, and concerns the kind of knowledge that forms the substance of what gets taught in the professional curriculum, and what forms the cognitive substrate of all professional decisions and judgments. In the philosophy of technology, it is conventional (see Meijers 2009) to say that the 'pure'/'applied' distinction is too simple, which is easily granted. But how then should it be considered? We start with some theoretical clarifications:

1   According to Bernstein's (2000) schema, there are two kinds of theoretical knowledge. They are distinguished by the way that they *elaborate* – either 'hierarchically', that is to say, by means of an expanding conceptual edifice, which projects true law-like predictions of ever greater generality and universality: or 'horizontally', that is to say, by means of new theoretical languages, which break off to form a new theoretical stem, parallel and usually antagonistic to the parent stem or stems. What Bernstein did not do is to say further how specialists develop concepts *within* each new horizontally evolved theoretical stem, but we assume he thought this was obvious – they develop in principle in the same fashion as concepts do in hierarchical knowledge structures. (There may well be lateral filling out of conceptual implications, but this is embroidery rather than elaboration.) So, we may provisionally conclude that all attempts to make conceptual advances within knowledge structures are, in the Bernsteinian framework, *hierarchical* whether or not the knowledge structures are themselves hierarchical or horizontal. In what follows, we will not distinguish between conceptual cores that are more or less hierarchical; when we refer to 'conceptual cores' we include both kinds.

2   It is often asserted that professions are distinguished by their control over their knowledge base. From our point of view, in light of the clarifications above, we distinguish *two principal kinds of specialised knowledge* that together make up a professional knowledge base. It is sometimes assumed that only conceptual knowledge codified in disciplines is specialised knowledge – and therefore that the practical or 'know how' knowledge we referred to earlier is tacit and can be disregarded, another version of the misleading dichotomy we discussed above.

But a moment's reflection shows that this cannot be the case. The craft guilds that pre-dated the science-based professions such as engineering and medicine were jealous guardians of knowledge traditions that were anything but unspecialised. When Galileo wished to demonstrate that there were moons around Jupiter, a prediction he arrived at theoretically, he could only show it, and make it open to testing, because he had available to him precision-ground optical lenses that were the product of lens grinders' specialised knowledge. Today lens grinding is a machine operation, an aspect of optical engineering that draws on scientific developments first initiated by Newton, among others, in the seventeenth century.

If theoretical knowledge/conceptual edifices, as previously defined, could be regarded as knowledge specialised to *conceptual generality*, then lens grinding and other forms of medieval craft specialisation and their contemporary equivalents can be regarded as knowledge specialised to *purpose* – to attain a specific end or solve a contextually specific problem. So, on the one hand, there is knowledge *specialised to develop conceptually*, on the other, there is knowledge *specialised to a contextual purpose*. Prior to the mathematicization of the sciences in the seventeenth and eighteenth centuries (Collins 2000), links between these types of knowledge as in the case of Galileo were rare.

Yet this is the crux of the matter in the professions, particularly the science-based professions.

It is important to stress that this distinction between two distinct kinds of specialisation foregrounds a particular feature of knowledges, namely, the way they elaborate – their telos or their 'epistemic destiny'. In answer to the question, 'why elaborate the knowledge?', theoretical knowledge implicitly answers – to extend the generality and reach of the conceptual edifice; while for-purpose knowledge answers – to arrive at a more elegant or efficient solution to a technical problem.

These two forms of specialisation joined common cause in the seventeenth century to create in part the conditions for scientific take-off that has been called the Scientific Revolution (Gaukroger 2006; Cohen 2010). Each side co-opted parts of the other to its own purpose – scientific knowledge adopted technological solutions to refine instrumentation; for-purpose knowledge absorbed theoretical knowledge to advance its quest for ever more sophisticated technical solutions; both led to new sub-branches of specialised knowledge, and to new forms of the division of intellectual labour. For our purposes here, this means that contemporary for-purpose 'professional' knowledge has, embedded in it, conceptual cores of different sorts; and likewise, much contemporary theoretical knowledge has roots in technical solutions reached in advance of basic science to explain it. It is this irreversible twist in the braid of contemporary specialised knowledges that seems to cause the greatest problem in conceiving of distinctive components of the professional knowledge base.

3   Reference is sometimes made to 'systematic knowledge'. When we use it here, we mean to denote the different components of specialised knowledge that go to make up a curriculum leading to a professional qualification. Winch refers to this as a 'subject', a useful term not to be confused with a school subject; it distinguishes between a 'discipline' – the parent knowledge structure that is usually one principal reservoir from which the knowledge contents of the 'subject' are recruited, adapted ('recontextualised' as Guile says in his chapter), sequenced, and paced for learners. However, this does not distinguish either the different processes of re-contextualisation involved in developing school and university curricula and, more importantly for us, it does not distinguish the intra-subject re-contextualisation in say a physics curriculum from what we might call the professional re-contextualisation of physics involved in the engineering sciences, for example.

Whereas a subject such as physics or history involves 'know that' knowledge, and, as Winch argues, two kinds of 'know how', the systematic knowledge in a professional curriculum may, depending on the profession, require no less 'know that' knowledge, but, in addition, a new configuration of 'know that' knowledge *together with* practically derived and accumulated knowledge. This points to a far more complex recontextualisation than the simplification of 'application' or 'applied knowledge' might suggest. We return to this below.

The important point is that curricular 'subjects' optimally include both kinds of specialised knowledge referred to earlier. In fact, as Winch goes on to show, we can usefully distinguish further among distinct sub-types of specialised 'know how' that make up a curriculum. Nevertheless, there is also still an important sense in which 'subjects' making up a 'curriculum' – as a path towards a qualification that consecrates a particular blend of specialised knowledge expertise – can be said to be arranged according to either a conceptually or a contextually dominant *coherence principle* (Muller 2009; see Hanrahan in this volume). It is their dominant coherence principle that distinguishes between different qualifications such as degrees, diplomas, and certificates: they are designed to specialise the knowledge base and the resultant expertise of neophytes for different purposes and create and limit opportunities both for further study and future employment. Any curriculum accordingly reflects a leaning either towards conceptual or contextual coherence (Muller 2009).

Having described in general terms some of the intellectual debates that underlie the field of professional knowledge we now move towards a closer consideration of the debates in the sociology of knowledge between those who favour a 'knowledge' point of departure and those who favour an 'expertise', or as it is sometimes referred to, a 'practice-based' view. In order to stage this debate more graphically, we will contrast the views of Basil Bernstein and Donald Schön.

Donald Schön and Basil Bernstein – a comparative review

In contrasting two such different thinkers as Donald Schön and Basil Bernstein, it is important to note where they come from, and their very different projects. It is unlikely that many readers will be deeply familiar with the work of both. Schön became a Professor (at MIT) having spent the previous 15 years as a management consultant specialising in organisational learning. However, from the 1970s on, and following the publication of his book *Educating the reflective practitioner*, his work has had a profound and indeed increasingly global influence on professional development that extended from architecture and town planning to medicine, teaching and a range of other professions (Schön 1990). It is hard to come across a programme in initial or further Professional Development that does not somewhere mention Schön's idea of the 'reflective practitioner'. Whatever reservations we may have about his work for our purposes in this volume, there is no doubt that he grasped the predicament that neophyte members of any profession experience facing their first client, patient or student; they don't know what to do and nothing they have learned in their university degree seems to be of any help. It is a tribute to his insight that despite only engaging indirectly with the question of specialised professional knowledge, his work forms an essential starting point for us.

With regard to Basil Bernstein, we can do no more than acknowledge his place (with Pierre Bourdieu) as one of the two outstanding sociologists of education since Émile Durkheim. However, his international reputation, which has grown rather than diminished since his death in 2001, is based primarily on his work on school knowledge, language and pedagogy. It may therefore seem surprising that we should choose his work in establishing a sociology of professional knowledge. However, as we have already argued, the distinctive feature of professional knowledge is that it is specialised, and it is the sociology of specialised knowledge that was central to Bernstein's work, even if it was not until his last book (Bernstein 2000) that he linked this to the origins and future of professions. First, we examine the position of Schön.

Donald Schön's 'epistemology of practice'

Schön's starting point is that professional work is about judgement under conditions of uncertainty and complexity of modern society (see Yael Shalem's chapter in this volume). He concedes that some members of professions in every field succeed in coping well with these conditions but argues that this is despite what he identifies as fundamental 'flaws' in the mainstream model of professional education. Schön summarises the traditional model of professional education as including: (a) an underlying disciplinary or basic science component upon which professional practice is developed; and (b) an applied or 'engineering' component from which likely day-to-day procedures and problem-solutions facing the profession are derived. What he refers to as this 'technical rational' model will be familiar to many who have graduated in engineering or medicine (Schön 2001).

Schön raises two questions about this model. First, 'is it the right model?' in fields like engineering, where the conditions it assumes appear to at least broadly apply. Second, he asks what happens to 'professions' such as education, city planning and social work when the model is drawn on even though the conditions do not apply? In such occupational fields there are rarely stable contexts or agreed-upon systematic knowledge. Schön's alternative is developed in recognition that even in engineering and other science-based professions, real-world problems are rarely well formed; they are complex and ill-defined, and involve many different types of factors that are mixed up with technical issues. In such situations, traditional 'problem solving' approaches do not apply and, Schön argues, professionals have to act more like researchers and engage in forms of inquiry that they often cannot explain or describe. Underlying Schön's alternative is what he refers to as an 'epistemology of practice' (ibid.). It draws on a combination of ideas drawn from Dewey and Polanyi for whom, according to Schön, truth is tacit and located in the everyday practice of 'reflecting in action', which is common to all human beings. This position comes close to the anti-intellectualist stance that some derive from Ryle that we referred to earlier. However, it could also be seen as a nostalgic return to the practice of the medieval craft guilds but without their specialised focus. The irony is that the only way the specialised knowledge of professions can be recognised in Schön's approach is through the element of professional education and knowledge that his model excludes. He claims that while professional practitioners, such as physicians, managers and teachers, reflect-in-action as do we all, *their reflection is of a kind particular to the special features of professional practice.*

The professional, for Schön, builds up experience of certain types of situations and examples, and it is this store of experience that becomes the basis of his/her specialised knowledge. It is these stored experiences and the lessons to be derived from them, rather than any codified specialised knowledge, that form the basis of the professional's expertise and judgement. Progress or the development of new knowledge in such a model is limited to learning from one's mistakes – an attractive but highly individualistic, and in the end conservative, approach to being a member of a profession and one that had reached its limits with the craft guilds prior to the emergence of the science-based professions in the early nineteenth century. One is reminded of the doctors in many Victorian novels, where experience, a few somewhat dubious techniques and little more was all they had to draw on. The most Schön will concede to the idea of professional knowledge beyond individual experience is when he suggests that 'aspiring practitioners learn to see, in the unfamiliar phenomena of practice, similarities to the canonical problems they may have learned in the classroom' (Schön 2001: 16). The specific case, in other words, for Schön, always takes precedence over the power of generalisable knowledge.

Where does Schön leave us in relation to our aim of conceptualising professional knowledge? The enormous popularity of his work requires us to take it seriously and certainly his critique of the 'technical rational' model is persuasive. However, in relation to how we distinguish professional practice and judgement from everyday judgements, Schön has little to say. It is as if, despite the 'technical rationality' of the professional curriculum, some do become reflective professionals, even if we don't know exactly how. His form of judgment-based pragmatism has been superseded by Brandom and others (see Derry, this volume) and we are left with an experientialism without content or history. It is attractive because of its message that underlying the good professional is the good and self-reflective human being, and there are certainly far worse values for a doctor, lawyer or teacher to live up to. However, the idea of 'reflection in action' as a moral rule offers the sociologist far less than Durkheim's account of professional ethics, in which the idea of the professional as embodying society's morality is part of a theory of society as Gerald Grace discusses in his chapter. Part of the attractiveness of Schön's work is that it meshes with the anti-intellectualism of much that passes for research in the field of professional development. If reflection-in-action is generic to all professions, then professional developers do not need to worry about the specialist knowledge future professionals must acquire, whether they are engineers, actuaries, or teachers.

Schön's analysis is useful for reminding us that professions not only know things, they do things. However, they do things in a different way from the rest of us, and this is because of their specialised knowledge. It is on account of having this knowledge that today's professions do more for us than those of previous generations. Schön's unwillingness to go beyond experience and memory and engage with the specialised knowledge that is the defining feature of professional work limits the answers he leaves us with. We turn therefore to our second thinker, Basil Bernstein, far less well known, if at all until recently, in the fields of professional education and professional knowledge.

Bernstein's 'regions'

It was in his last book, and almost as an aside, that Bernstein made the following cryptic comment: 'The construction of the inner was a guarantee for the construction of the outer. In this we can find the origin of the professions' (Bernstein 2000: 85).

In one short sentence, parsed as how 'inwardness and commitment shape(s) the terms of practical engagement in the outer world' by Beck and Young (2005: 7), Bernstein encapsulates, in characteristic elliptical fashion, what might be the starting point for a sociology of professional knowledge. Earlier in this introduction we introduced Bernstein's classification of types of theoretical knowledge. They are based on a prior differentiation between theoretical and practical (or common sense) knowledge, or in his terms, vertical and horizontal discourses; all theoretical knowledge being a form of vertical discourse. However, he recognised in his later work that these binary categories, though of heuristic value, were not adequate to grasping what are the increasingly dominant forms of knowledge in modern societies. Professional knowledge is both 'theoretical' (that is, general and unvarying) and 'practical' (that is, purposive and contextual). Contemporary professions are about doing things, but doing complex things that cannot rely on experience alone, like crafts could for their expertise. Because professional practice is always in a context with a purpose outside itself, professional knowledge is always sectoral, not general, like the traditional disciplines; it relates to specific occupational sectors such as health, transport and education. Although he does not explicitly say so, it may be for this reason that Bernstein introduces the term 'regions'; it is the activity, in Bernstein's terms, in a 'field of practice' within a society that shapes a profession's specialised knowledge, so it will be *regional* – applicable to some fields and not others – not *general* – like physics, applicable to all physical phenomena, or sociology (at least for Durkheim), applicable to anything social. But specialised disciplinary knowledge is differentiated into domains such as mathematics, chemistry and economics, all of which have important roles in forms of professional knowledge such as chemical engineering and actuarial science. So Bernstein introduces another term, *singulars*, since each deals with a singular – that is, separate and bounded – class of natural or social phenomena.

Singulars thus refer to knowledge relations that emphasize 'inwardness' (as in the first quote in this section). More familiarly, inwardness refers to 'knowledge for its own sake', to the pursuit of truth when no external (regional or contextual) interests are involved. The nearest we get to the 'inwardness' of singulars are academic disciplines. In the terms we introduced earlier, singulars involve, as Winch has suggested, 'know that' knowledge and two forms of 'know how'.

Regions are sources of current and future professional knowledge. First, they bring together, or 're-contextualise', several disciplines in relation to a field of practice like construction or medicine. They do this in ways that enable professionals to reconceptualise real-world practices and processes in new ways related to new purposes. This means that professional knowledge will include 'know that' knowledge as the basis of the content to be selected from singulars (for example, engineers do not need to know all the content of physics) and the 'know how' involved in bringing them together and in transforming existing practically based 'know how'. Second, regions also bring into play the past consecrated and canonised body of specialised professional knowledge that represents the stable reservoir gleaned from earlier 'applied' research, which can, at times, augment not only the knowledge base of the profession, but add to new knowledge in one of the parent singulars.

This kind of specialised regional knowledge, which is not knowledge accrued from specific contexts, can, in stable professional fields like engineering, have its own proto-disciplinary form – for example, engineering science, with its own scientific literature and scientific communities that in the case of engineering, have global jurisdiction over the accreditation of engineers (see Hanharan, this volume). So, for example, engineering students learn about thermodynamics in at least two different formats: first in the science singulars (physics and chemistry) as the nearest scientists have got to the truth about heat and its relation to energy and work, and then again in engineering science, where thermodynamics is recontextualised in relation to problems such as the over-heating of nuclear reactors (See Hanrahan this volume; Smit 2012). It is this double movement in the professional curriculum, requiring a shift, with the same scientific concepts, from a singular to a regional mode, that can cause such headaches for students (see Case, this volume).

Bernstein's innovation is to conceptualise an old problem, the relationship between theory and practice, in a new way that also enables us to characterise this relationship as lying at the heart of professional knowledge. In the process, he extended the familiar *binary* distinction between 'theory' and 'practice' into a three-*fold* distinction:

- *Singulars*, which represent knowledge relations (or structures) oriented to inwardness – the rules, methods and boundaries that define a discipline (for example sociology or physiology).
- *Regions*, which combine disciplines, selecting, pacing and sequencing knowledge of muscles and joints from them in relation to specific purposes in a field of practice (for example, combining parts of physiology and physics and stable contextually derived knowledge to form biomechanics, which is part of the professional curriculum of physiotherapists).
- *Fields of practice* are the specialised practical contexts in which professionals practice – that is, exercise knowledgeable and reasoned judgments as professionals, by drawing on, often tacitly, their acquired stock of specialised professional knowledge (see Shalem, this volume; see also Stanley 2011: 184).

We can therefore analyse a profession's work, and the professional curriculum that aspiring professionals must follow to become qualified, as a region. Regions are never fixed and always 'face two ways' – towards their singulars and towards their field of practice. They will always express a tension between the demands of disciplines that are constantly searching for new, more general, knowledge, and the demands of fields of practice, which constantly face new, often more complex, practical problems. The latter may arise directly from clients or patients or customers; they may arise from, and become pursued in, sectoral research projects; they may also arise as demands from government to reduce the autonomy of a region and gain more control over their 'usefulness'. This is not to forget, of course, the 'interests' of the region, or the profession itself, which can, in the case of the mature professions at least, exercise considerable power.

The research tasks that Bernstein's approach points to are considerable if it is to be productive in developing a theory of professional knowledge, not least because it requires the sociologist to be at least familiar with the specialised knowledge of any profession to be studied to a competence Collins and Evans (2009) call 'interactional expertise'. Bernstein's distinction between singulars, regions and fields of practice, together with that between his types of theoretical knowledge, are the basic building blocks for a theory of professional knowledge.

Bernstein did not develop his idea of a 'field of practice'. However, this is a central issue for a project about professional knowledge that is not only influenced by singulars and regions but by the way practice is organised. The extent to which practice is codified, standardised or institutionalised will shape the form that professional knowledge in different fields takes (Nerland and Karseth 2013).

References

Abbott, A. (1988) *The system of professions: An essay on the division of expert labor*. Chicago: The University of Chicago Press.

Abbott, A. (1993) The sociology of work and occupations. *Annual Review of Sociology*, 187–209.

Afdal, H. W. (2012) Knowledge in teacher education curricula. *Nordic Studies in Education*, 3–4, 245–61.

Becher, T. and Trowler, P. R. (1989). *Academic tribes and territories*. Milton Keynes: Open University Press.

Beck, J. and Young, M. (2005) The assault on the professions and the restructuring of academic and professional identities: A Bernsteinian analysis. *British Journal of Sociology of Education*, 26(2), 1–26.

Bernstein, B. (2000) *Pedagogy, symbolic control, and identity* (2nd edn). New York: Rowman & Littlefield.

Cohen, H. Floris (2010) *How modern science came into the world: Four civilisations, one 17th-century breakthrough*. Amsterdam: Amsterdam University Press.

Collins, H. and Evans, R. (2009) *Rethinking expertise*. Chicago: The University of Chicago Press.

Collins, R. (2000) *The sociology of philosophies: A global theory of intellectual change*. Cambridge, MA: Harvard University Press.

Dreyfus, H. (2005) Overcoming the myth of the mental: How philosophers can profit from the phenomenology of everyday expertise. *Proceedings of the American Philosophical Association*, 79(2), 47–65.

Etzioni, A. (1969) *The semi-professions and their organisation: Teachers, nurses, social workers*. New York: Free Press.

Evetts, J. (2006) Short note: The sociology of professional groups: New directions. *Current Sociology*, *54*(1), 133–43.

Evetts, J. (2013) Professionalism: Value and ideology. *Current Sociology*, *61*(5–6), 778–96.

Friedson, E. (2001) *Professionalization: The third logic*. Chicago: The University of Chicago Press.

Gaukroger, S. (2006) *The emergence of a scientific culture: Science and the shaping of modernity 1210–1685*. Oxford: Clarendon Press.

Glazer, N. (1974) The schools of the minor professions. *Minerva*, *13*(3), 346–74.

Gorman, E. H. and Sandefur, R. L. (2011) 'Golden Age,' quiescence, and revival: How the sociology of professions became the study of knowledge-based work. *Work and Occupations*, *38*(3), 275–302.

Jensen, K., Lahn, L. C. and Nerland, M. (2012) (eds) *Professional learning in the knowledge society*. Rotterdam: Sense Publishers.

Meijers, A. (2009) (ed.) *Philosophy of technology and engineering sciences*, vol. 9. Amsterdam: Elsevier.

Muller, J. (2007) On splitting hairs: Hierarchy, knowledge and the school curriculum. In F. Christie and J. R. Martin (eds), *Language, knowledge and pedagogy*. London: Continuum, 65–86.

Muller, J. (2009) Forms of knowledge and curriculum coherence. *Journal of Education and Work*, *22*(3), 203–24.

Muller, J. and Young, M. (forthcoming) Disciplines, skills and the university. *Higher Education*, DOI 10.1007/s10734–013–9646–4 (accessed on 6 January 2014).

Nerland, M. and Karseth, B. (forthcoming) The knowledge work of professional associations: Approaches to standardisation and forms of legitimisation. *Journal of Education and Work*. Published online: 7 June, 2013. DOI: 10.1080/13639080.2013.802833 (accessed on 6 January, 2014).

Ryle, G. (1946) Knowing how and knowing that. *Proceedings of the Aristotelian Society*, *46*, 212–25.

Sciulli, D. (2005) Continental sociology of professions today: Conceptual contributions. *Current Sociology*, *53*(6), 915–42.

Schön, D. (1990) *Educating the reflective practitioner: Towards a new design for teaching and learning in the professions*. San Francisco: Jossey Bass.

Schön, D. (2001) The crisis of professional knowledge and the pursuit of an epistemology of practice. In J. Raven and J. Stephenson (eds), *Competence and the learning society*. New York: Peter Lang.

Smit, R. (2012) 'Engineering science and pure science: Do disciplinary differences matter in engineering education?' Presentation to the 23rd Annual Conference of the Australasian Association for Engineering Education, Melbourne, 3–5 December, 2012.

Stanley, J. and Williamson, T. (2001) Knowing how. *The Journal of Philosophy*, *98*(8), 411–44.

Stanley, J. (2011) *Know how*. Oxford: Oxford University Press.

Taylor, N. and Vinjevold, P. (1999) *Getting learning right: The report of the President's Education Initiative research project*. Johannesburg: Joint Education Trust.

Young, M. (2010) Alternative educational futures for a knowledge society. *European Educational Research Journal*, *9*(1), 1–12.

Young, M. and Allais, S. (2013) (eds) *Implementing NQFs across five continents*. London: Routledge.

Winch, C. (2010) *Dimensions of expertise: A conceptual exploration of vocational knowledge.* London: Continuum.

Winch, C. (2012) Curriculum design and epistemic ascent. *Journal of Philosophy of Education,* 47(1), 128–46.

2 Professions, sacred and profane

Reflections upon the changing nature of professionalism

Gerald Grace

Introduction

The argument of this chapter is that professions and professionals have a crucial role in society, which is 'to speak truth to power'. This was one of the roles of the first professions of priesthood, medicine and law but today the evidence suggests that professionalism is being reduced in scope to the demonstration of technical expertise and efficient performativity only.[1]

Historically, professionalism involved the demonstration of esoteric knowledge and expertise but it also involved commitment to codes of moral, ethical and social conduct. These commitments might, in certain circumstances, cause some professionals to be critical of, or even oppose, policies introduced by powerful authorities.

This analysis will be developed in three sections. In Section one the origins of the professions in the Middle Ages, in the culture of the sacred will be examined.

In Section two the transition of professionalism from the culture of the sacred to the culture of the profane by the nineteenth century will be discussed, with special reference to Emile Durkheim's classic text, *Professional ethics and civic morals* (1957/1992).

In Section three the contemporary situation of professionalism will be analysed, with special relevance to those professionals who work in the fields of economics, finance, banking and business studies, and also those who work in the field of education. This section will focus on what can be called professionalism in the culture of global marketisation.

Professionals in the culture of the sacred

The very idea of a 'profession' (as a 'calling' and not simply a job) and of 'professionalism' (as a process and a way of life) had its origins in religion (Durkheim, 1992). Specifically, in Europe, professionalism was formed in the religious culture and habitus established by the hegemony of the Catholic Church. Thus the first professions of priesthood, medicine and law were shaped by a social milieu, which invested the technical activities of the practitioners with a spiritual, moral, ethical and even, on occasions, political significance. While under the jurisdiction and command of the temporal authorities of the time, such professionals had another allegiance, to the service of God and to revealed Truth as taught by the Church. This was the concept of professional 'vocation'. The priesthood existed to administer the Sacraments and to witness to the Truth; the physicians were called to continue the work of the Great Physician and lawyers were called to administer the justice and mercy of God. To be a professional in its historical origins was, at its best, to have a command of esoteric knowledge and competences set within a moral framework of service to the common good, guided by the teachings of religious faith. The notion of a 'calling' gave to the early professions a relation to the sacred. Over time, professionals such as physicians and lawyers began to form associations and organisations that codified the moral principles that ought to regulate professional behaviour. At another level, that of various merchants and traders, Guilds were established to regulate economic activity.[2] The culture of the sacred, as mediated by the Catholic Church, shaped these forms of regulation involving concepts such as the sanctity of life, service for the common good, the just price, the just wage, etc.

As Nisbet (1965) has argued, the Enlightenment as a philosophical and cultural movement in eighteenth-century Europe, with its questioning of traditional doctrines and values and its emphasis upon individualism and the free use of reason, marked the beginning of the end of the culture of the sacred as the dominant habitus in Europe. This major transition from a culture of the sacred to a culture of the profane, in which religion and ideas of a 'conscience collective'[3] were marginalised, provided an intellectual challenge for the French sociologist, Emile Durkheim. What would be the basis for social solidarity in the future? What sources of moral education and moral regulation could be found in the future? In this situation of potential anomie, Durkheim saw professions and professionalism, in new forms, as essential to the social order and stability of secular societies. The text, *Professional ethics and civic morals*, is in fact a collection of Durkheim's lectures delivered at Bordeaux between 1890 and 1900, and the book first appeared in English in 1957. It is still regarded as a classic in its sociological/historical analysis of the development of professionalism.

Professionalism in the culture of the profane

In modern English discourse, the use of 'profane' is often taken to mean that which treats something sacred in a hostile and abusive way. Durkheim used 'profane' in a quite different way, i.e., in an objective and analytical sense that referred to a major cultural change observable in Europe and particularly in France. This cultural change involved the end of the hegemony of the Catholic Church, of its Christian teachings and dogma, of the culture of the sacred that it sustained and of its associated values and practices. In its place Durkheim observed, especially in France, the development of a profane culture in which the dominant principles were reason, individualism, enterprise and relative personal autonomy.

Religion had retreated from its central role as regulator of social, economic and political life to a minor role as guide to some believers in their private lives. This newly established profane culture challenged Durkheim to consider in what ways social solidarity, social order and forms of moral regulation of human behaviour could be guaranteed in the future. The problem was, as Durkheim expressed it:

> It is not possible for a social function to exist without moral discipline. Otherwise, nothing remains but individual appetites, and since they are by nature boundless and insatiable, if there is nothing to control them, they will not be able to control themselves.
>
> (1992, pp. 10–11)

Recognising that the Church could no longer be the regulator of social and economic activity, Durkheim came to the view that this role had passed to the secular State, which he accepted would have to be 'the organ of moral discipline' (1992, p. 72) in profane culture. However, an all-powerful State, like an all-powerful Church, might become an oppressive force in society. Other social institutions were required to achieve a situation of some balance of power, institutions that in some senses could monitor the activities of the State. For Durkheim, these other social institutions would be found in the secular professional associations with their relative autonomy and codes of ethics. As Turner (1992, p. xxiv) puts it, for Durkheim: 'The real dislocation of modern society was the absence of intervening social institutions between the individual and the State; occupational and professional associations were intended to fill this gap.'

In this sense, professions and professionals had a potentially crucial political significance in society – in place of the Church, which had, on occasions, resisted the power of kings.[4] Durkheim believed that professional associations could provide a source of restraint upon secular governments in the future. Professions, with their associated codes of ethics, would also provide, in a secular mode, a continuation of moral education and moral regulation in the new cultural context. As Durkheim argued: 'the professional group is by no means incapable of being in itself a moral sphere, since this was its character in the past' (1992, p. 23). This morality and this form of regulation would find its justification in secular ethical reasoning, rather than in the religious precepts of an earlier age.

But there remained a major problem to which Durkheim devoted the greater part of his analysis. This was the problem presented by the growth of capitalist enterprise in France and its associated financial and business practices. Whereas pre-capitalist enterprise and trading had been regulated by the Guilds and by the Church, these agencies were no longer a powerful element in modern society. Therefore in the realm of capitalist enterprise and business relations, Durkheim perceived a moral vacuum. *Professional ethics and civil morals* presents a powerful analysis and critique of this situation, which has obvious relevance to many of our contemporary situations and challenges. Of course, Durkheim's observations relate to the capitalist and business world of the nineteenth century, but the issues they raise challenge us to consider what has changed since his time. In this sense, he presents us with an agenda for contemporary research, analysis and discussion, with these statements:

- 'This lack of organisation in the business professions has one consequence of the greatest moment; which is, that in this whole sphere of social life, no professional ethics exist' (1992, p. 9).
- 'This amoral character of economic life amounts to a public danger' (1992, p. 12).
- 'Clearly, if there has been self-delusion to this degree among the classical economists it is because the economic functions were studied as if they were an end in themselves, without considering what further reaction they might have on the whole social order' (1992, p. 15).
- 'The more the markets expand, the greater the urgency of some regulation to put an end to this instability' (1992, p. 16).

Within the nineteenth and early twentieth century of the profane in Europe, Durkheim had great hopes that the established professions would provide a moral and ethical environment for society, which would compensate for the loss of the power of the sacred in social and economic life. As Professor of Education and Sociology at the Sorbonne he regarded the teaching profession as especially important in disseminating secular understandings of moral education in the schools of France. It could be said, that for Durkheim, teachers were seen as a form of secular priests of rational moral education who would replace the former role undertaken by Catholic priests. Nevertheless, it seems likely that he knew that the work of the schools alone would not compensate for the economic anomie and anarchy that characterised the sphere of capitalist enterprise growing ever stronger in France.

Professionals in the culture of global marketisation

If the great theorist of the transitions from the culture of the sacred to the culture of the profane (with its implications for the role of professionals) was Emile Durkheim, the leading contemporary theorist and empirical researcher of today's culture of global marketisation is Manuel Castells. In his massive three-volume studies of *The information age: Economy, society and culture* (1996, 1997, 1998), Castells has documented in detail the consequences of what he describes as 'The Rise of the Network Society'. This provides an authoritative analysis of the economic, social and cultural context of globalisation, the context in which professionals of every category are now working. It is necessary, in order to grasp the significance of this revolutionary change, to quote Castells at some length:

A new economy has emerged in the last two decades on a worldwide scale. I call it informational and global to identify its fundamental distinctive features. . . . It is informational because the productivity and competitiveness of units or agents in this economy (be it firms regions or nations) depend upon their capacity to generate, process and apply efficiently knowledge-based information. It is global because the core activities of production, consumption and circulation, as well as their components (capital, labor, raw materials, management, information, technology, markets) are organized on a global scale ... and competition is played out in a global network of interaction. It has emerged in the last quarter of the twentieth century because the Information Technology Revolution provides the indispensible material basis for such a new economy.

(1996, p. 66)

Castells goes on to argue that the cultural, social and political consequences of this economic revolution are far reaching. International competitiveness has emerged as a key dynamic in every society:

Together with the search for profitability as the driving motivation of the firm, the informational economy is also shaped by the vested interest of political institutions in fostering the competitiveness of those economies they are supposed to represent. ... The emphasis here is on the relative position of national economies vis-á-vis other countries as a major legitimizing force for governments. ... Practically all countries have to steer their economies in cooperation and in competition with others.

(1996, pp. 86–7)

What are the implications of all of this for professionals and professionalism in the culture of global marketisation? Although Castells does not address this specific question, it seems clear from his analysis that there are many implications. For those professionals who work in the fields of economics, finance, banking and business management, a preoccupation with profit yields and 'competitive edge' now becomes paramount over all other considerations. Durkheim in the nineteenth century had commented on the absence of professional ethics or of moral regulation in these spheres of activity.

In the intensified competitive conditions of global market capitalism, notions of professional ethics and moral regulation can now be categorised as outmoded impediments to business derived from a vanished age. The 'real world' of international business it will be said cannot be shackled by ideas of professional ethics or moral regulation that originated in a long-forgotten culture of the sacred or even a more recent culture of profane enlightenment and reason. This is the ideological claim of the 'free' market, i.e., to be free of state regulation or even moral regulation.

Writing from a Catholic perspective, Edward Hadas in a small publication, *The credit crunch: Making moral sense of the financial crisis* (2009) comments on the recent world financial problems[5]:

While only a few went so far as to endorse the slogan 'Greed is good', many economists argued for and obtained lighter regulation and greater reliance on 'market signals'. . . . One other factor may have played a role in the pre-crisis abdication of responsibility in finance. That is the refusal to take morality seriously in any economic discussions.

(p. 42)

But these implications are not confined to the world of business only. Established professions such as medicine, law and education (higher education and schools) are presented with ideological and political challenges to their professional ethics, values and commitments to common good service. What we are witnessing in contemporary society is an attempted market culture colonisation of all forms of social service in order to sharpen the overall efficiency and competitive edge of the total social formation and not simply the sphere of business activity. This is particularly apparent in the field of education.

In his studies of the economic success of the Asian 'tigers', Singapore, South Korea, Taiwan and Hong Kong, Castells (1998, pp. 256–82) argues that, among other things, strong state direction (by the 'developmental state') was apparent. This process of development involved transformations of educational systems to be more closely coupled to the needs of economic development. Educational institutions were 're-engineered' to become service agencies for increasing the competitive edge of the economy.

A similar development has been noted in the UK by Stephen Ball, Professor of the Sociology of Education at the University of London, Institute of Education. In his research-based book, *Education plc* (2007) Ball concludes: 'Within institutions – colleges, schools and universities, the means/end logic of education for economic competitiveness is transforming what were complex, interpersonal processes of teaching, learning and research into a set of standardised and measurable products' (p. 186).

Teachers both at school level and in higher education, who in previous decades have been regarded as professionals involved in the intellectual, cultural, social and moral development of children and young people, are now being reconstructed as agents to service the economic needs of the competitive state. Ball argues that, 'education is . . . spoken of within policy, in terms its economic value and its contribution to international market competitiveness', and a situation is developing in the UK in which there will be, 'a thorough subordination of moral obligations to economic ones' (p. 185). Knowledge itself is being reconstructed as a commodity in the market place that can be traded like any other commodity in the global economy.[6]

All of these arguments had been anticipated by Ball's predecessor at the Institute of Education, Professor Basil Bernstein. In a prescient section of his text, *Pedagogy, symbolic control and identity* (1996), Bernstein argued:

> There is a new principle guiding the latest transition of capitalism. The principles of the market and its managers are more and more the managers of the policy and practices of education. Market relevance is becoming the key orienting criterion for the selection of discourses. . . . This movement has profound implications from the primary school to the university. . . .

There is a new concept of knowledge . . . This new concept is a truly secular concept. Knowledge should flow like money to wherever it can create advantage and profit. Indeed knowledge is not like money, it *is* money. Knowledge is divorced from persons, their commitments, their personal dedications. These become impediments.

(p. 87)

In the culture of global marketisation, Bernstein was warning professionals working in schools and universities that their professional 'commitments' to the principles of a liberal and humane education were being devalued and that their 'personal dedications' in writing and research might be seen as 'impediments' to higher education plc or the university as a business corporation.[7]

If the work of all these analysts, Castells, Hadas, Ball and Bernstein, is taken together, it amounts to a major challenge to the future of professionalism. Will professions lose their relative autonomy in the face of the insatiable demands of the global market economy, a situation in which 'there is no alternative?' Will professions lose their political role as part of the balance of power relations in society? What will become of professional ethics and professional moral regulation of activity, if the very concepts of ethics and regulation are categorised as impediments to the maximisation of profit? The last section of this chapter will attempt to address some of these questions.

Professionals as critics and conscience of society[8]

Professionalism, at its best, has always attempted 'to speak truth to power.' At various historical periods, this 'truth' has been based upon the Truth of a revealed religion or a secular truth based upon reason, scholarship, evidence and research. Professionals have enjoyed a degree of relative autonomy from the demands of the State and the economy.[9] This autonomy, which always had to be fought for, was granted in respect of the powerful knowledge and competences that they possessed. At their best, such professions sought to operate with codes of professional ethics and notions of moral regulation and service to the common good. However, as Durkheim observed, the world of capitalist enterprise generally operated outside of the sphere of professional ethics and moral regulation. That sphere has grown larger since the time of Durkheim.

Under the hegemony of the contemporary culture of global marketisation all categories of professional and all forms of professionalism are faced with a radically changed environment. Global marketisation has generated versions of the Strong State,[10] of what Castells (1996) calls the 'developmental state', and Jessop (2002) calls 'the competition state'. The relative autonomy of professions is likely to be reduced by imperatives from the Strong State.[11] These forms of the Strong State will, at the same time, be working to increase the autonomy of the free market economy.

The second challenge arises from what I have called the 'attempted market colonisation of all forms of social service,' including education, health and social welfare systems. Market culture in these arenas will have a detrimental effect upon practices of professional ethics and moral considerations. They are, after all, impediments to 'progress.' Durkheim's hope that professions would be the necessary 'intervening social institutions' between the individual and the State will not be realised.

Current conditions present professionals and professions with a test of occupational integrity. Either they will accept the role of being simply technical experts and efficient producers or deliverers of State specified outcomes or they will find the moral courage to maintain a role (where necessary) of being also 'critics and conscience of society'.

Bernstein (1996) concluded his analysis of contemporary changes in education by saying 'what is at stake is the very concept of education itself' (p. 88). This chapter must conclude, in the light of the analysis presented here, that what is at stake is the very concept of a profession itself, as understood and practised historically. However, this raises a much larger question: does the present secular culture of global marketisation have the moral resources for the renewal of ethical professionalism? Alasdair MacIntyre (1985) is clear that it does not: 'the problems of modern moral theory emerge as the product of the failure of the Enlightenment project' (p. 62). Perhaps an answer to our present moral anomie may be found in revived forms of the culture of the sacred.

Conclusion: sources of ethical renewal for professionalism

Wilson (1999), in his analysis of the decline of religious faith in Europe, nevertheless concludes his influential book, *God's funeral*, with the observation that 'the immense strength of the Catholic idea played a demonstrable role in the collapse of the Soviet Communist system' (p. 354). If a great challenge to the culture of religion and of the sacred in the recent past, i.e., that of Communist atheism with imperialist intentions, has declined, it can be seen that a new challenge has emerged, that of global capitalist values. Soros (1999) has charted the nature of this new cultural and economic imperialism and has concluded that 'market values have assumed an importance at the present moment in history that is way beyond what is appropriate and sustainable' (p. 46).

Usher and Edwards (1994), in their study of the effects of globalisation on education, have argued that national objectives in education will soon be limited to 'fulfilling the requirements of the economy under conditions of global competition' (p. 175). However, what is remarkable about the growing literature on globalisation and education, is that the role of religion is generally ignored.[12]

While it is the case that the role of religion and of the culture of the sacred declined in influence in the profane culture of Europe from the eighteenth century to the twentieth, it is also the case, as argued by Karen Armstrong (2009), that there has been a resurgence of religions as a reaction to the hegemony of secularism.[13]

Analysts working within a secular intellectual paradigm appear to be relatively unaware of these developments. The fact that world–based religions such as Catholic Christianity and Islam are international power sources, which have missions other than those of economic globalisation, has been marginalised in globalisation analyses and debates.

One of the countervailing institutions against the hegemony of market materialism, individual competitiveness, commodity worship and the death of ethical professionalism is the Catholic Church and its various agencies throughout the world.[14]

In *Religion in the secular city* (1984), Harvey Cox made the profound observation: 'If freedom once required a secular critique of religion, it can also require a religious critique of the secular' (pp. 170–71).

A strong religious critique of the culture of global marketisation has recently been published by Pope Benedict XVI in his encyclical, *Caritas in Veritate: on integral human development in charity and truth* (2009). This statement is not addressed only to Catholics but to all 'persons of goodwill'.

The Pope presents an agenda of issues that should be debated and considered by all categories of professionals and by all agencies responsible for the education of professionals. Issues such as:

*   'Underdevelopment is the lack of brotherhood among individuals and peoples. As society becomes ever more globalised, it makes us neighbours but does not make us brothers. Reason can establish civic equalities but it cannot establish fraternity' (para. 19).
*   'The world's wealth is growing in absolute terms but inequalities are on the increase. The scandal of glaring inequalities continues' (para. 22).
*   'The conviction that the economy must be autonomous, that it must be shielded from the influences of a moral character, has led man to abuse the economic process in a thoroughly destructive way' (para. 34).
*   'Financiers must rediscover the ethical foundations of their activity so as not to abuse the sophisticated instruments which can serve to betray the interests of savers' (para. 65).

By statements such as this, the Pope is making a contribution to the renewal of ethical professionalism in the face of its demoralisation in contemporary world culture. The voice of the culture of the sacred has not been silenced in the culture of global marketisation.

It is fully recognised that Catholic Christianity is not the only source for the renewal of ethical practice in the professions. Ethical renewal can be empowered by the teaching of all Christian Churches, by those of other faiths such as, Islam, Judaism and Buddhism, and by secular humanists.

However, it is the conviction of this writer, that ethical and moral professionalism, which had its origins in the culture of the sacred, has its best hopes for renewal in a world culture in which reasoned forms of the culture of the sacred are again influential.[15] Such professionalism represents, at its best, the continuance of what MacIntyre (1985, p. 254) calls 'the tradition of the virtues' in contemporary conditions.[16]

Postscript

A 'critical friend' who read the first version of this paper suggested that I needed to add further reflections on the crucial question:

> What is the possibility of professions continuing to exist as relatively independent sources of 'speaking truth to power' and what resources can they find to maintain a moral and ethical culture and practice in the era of global marketisation?

This critic clearly believed that my conclusion, that ethical and moral professionalism had its best hopes for renewal in a world culture 'in which reasoned forms of the culture of the sacred are again influential', was too utopian and failed to engage with the contemporary conditions of moral and ethical pluralism, especially in the West.

For many modern professionals the beliefs, values and practices of the culture of the sacred are no longer relevant to the way that they lead their lives or perform their professional responsibilities. Theirs is a world in which secular, economic, humanistic and scientific values are dominant and in which precepts derived from Christian, Muslim or Jewish cultures of the sacred are either marginalised or completely rejected. My critic's point was that secular practitioners probably constituted the majority of professional workers, at least in the West, and that the future of professionalism was now in their hands. This raised a key question. In these new cultural conditions, how will the integrity of professional values be maintained in the future?

The answer would appear to lie in the initial and continuing formation of all those who claim the status of professionals, from the traditional categories of priests, lawyers, doctors, civil servants, academics and teachers to the many new categories generated by capitalist enterprise, scientific enterprise and mass media forms of communication and marketing.

If the concept of a professional is not to be reduced to that of *functional technical experts* (exempt from moral and ethical considerations) then the education of professionals (both initial and continuing) must include mandatory programmes that deal seriously with the political, social, moral and ethical issues related to various forms of professional practice.

In other words, the formation of professionals of all categories must always be a process of humane and inclusive education and not merely a process of narrow technical training.

The hope must be that the founding professions of priesthood, medicine and law will act as exemplars and role models for new and emergent professions to emulate in this crucial area of the larger responsibilities of the professional role. If the professions fail to resource and renew their social, moral and *ethical commitments*, then Durkheim's great project that professionals should be the necessary social intervening institutions between individuals and the State will not be realised. This will mean a future in which the Strong State and the Strong Multinational Corporation will possess an almost total hegemony.

Acknowledgements

I am grateful to Professor Johan Muller of Cape Town University for suggesting the need for this Postscript. I also thank Professor Alasdair MacIntyre of Notre Dame University, USA for encouraging comments on an early draft of the paper. Professor Michael Young, by inviting me to participate in the series of seminars that preceded this publication, has provided an invaluable stimulus to my thoughts in this chapter. I thank him for that opportunity.

Notes

1 See Ball (2008, pp. 50–72).
2 On the importance of Guilds, see Durkheim (1992, pp.17–27).
3 'Durkheim defines it as the totality of beliefs and sentiments common to the average members of the same society' (Bierstedt 1966, p. 44).
4 Examples from English history would include the resistance of Archbishop Thomas á Becket to the policies of King Henry II and of Sir Thomas More to the policies of King Henry VIII.
5 Unusually, among financial commentators, Hadas employs a discourse of morality. For Hadas on the role of Greed in the financial crisis, see Hadas (2009, pp. 34–43).
6 For a collection of chapters debating the place of education in the marketplace, see Bridges and McLaughlin (1994). For a critique of economics as applied to education, see Grace (1994, pp. 126–37).
7 For a critique of the corporatisation of higher education, see Conway (2011, pp. 158–69).
8 On the origins of this phrase, see Grace (2010, pp. 89–92).
9 The relative autonomy of professionals has, of course, varied in different historical periods and in different parts of the world depending upon the nature of the State and of the dominant ideology of the regime.
10 See Gamble (1998).
11 Michael Young argues that there is a crisis in the professions at this time:

> Professions assailed by state regulation in the case of teachers and medical practitioners, and by the encroachment of market relations in the case of law and accountancy. . . . The basis for the development and application of new specialist knowledge by professionals is weakened and their autonomy is reduced.
>
> (2008, p.97)

For a more developed statement, see Chapter 10, 'Professional knowledge and the question of identity.'
12 See Grace (2004, pp. 47–56).
13 While part of this resurgence has expressed itself in forms of religious fundamentalism (Christian, Jewish and Muslim), more moderate forms have concentrated on relating religious teaching to social justice projects in various parts of the world. Liberation Theology is one example of this new emphasis. See Gutierrez (1973).
14 The global system of Catholic educational institutions is particularly important in this respect. With 200,000 schools and colleges and over 1,000 universities, the Catholic

Church has at its disposal a powerful agency for the dissemination of its counter-cultural messages.

15 Those who disagree with this conclusion may want to consider the conclusion reached by Manuel Castells after his three-volume study of *The information age: Economy, society and culture,* vol. III (1998, pp. 390–1):

> The dream that the Enlightenment, that reason and science would solve the problems of humankind is within reach. . . . There is no eternal evil in human nature. There is nothing that cannot be changed by conscious, purposive social action, provided with information. . . . If people are informed, active, and communicate throughout the world; if business assumes its social responsibility; if the media become the messengers rather than the message; if political actors react against cynicism, and restore belief in democracy; if culture is reconstructed from experience; if humankind feels the solidarity of the species throughout the globe; if we assert intergenerational solidarity by living in harmony with nature; if we depart for the exploration of our inner self, having made peace among ourselves. If all this is made possible by our informed, conscious, shared decision, while there is still time, maybe then we may, at last, be able to live and let live, love and be loved.

This is clearly a Humanist credo that seeks to replace earlier religious credos.

16 'It must have been clear from earlier parts of my argument that the tradition of the virtues is at variance with central features of the modern economic order and more especially its individualism, its acquisitiveness and its elevation of the values of the market to a central social place' (MacIntyre, p. 254).

References

Armstrong, K. (2009) *The case for God.* London: Bodley Head.

Ball, S. (2007) *Education plc.* London: Routledge.

Ball, S. (2008) 'Performativity, privatisation, professionals and the state', in B. Cunningham (ed.) *Exploring professionalism.* London: Institute of Education.

Bernstein, B. (1996) *Pedagogy, symbolic control and identity.* London: Taylor & Francis.

Bierstedt, R. (1966) *Emile Durkheim.* London: Weidenfeld & Nicolson.

Bridges, D. and McLaughlin, T. (eds) (1994) *Education and the market place.* Abingdon: Routledge Falmer.

Castells, M. (1996) *The rise of the network society* (vol. 1). Oxford: Blackwell.

Castells, M. (1997) *The power of identity* (vol. 2). Oxford: Blackwell.

Castells, M. (1998) *End of millennium* (vol. 3). Oxford: Blackwell.

Conway, E. (2011) 'The future of Catholic higher education in Ireland', *International Studies in Catholic Education,* 3(2): 158–69.

Cox, H. (1984) *Religion in the secular city: Towards a post modern theology.* New York: Simon & Schuster.

Durkheim, E. (1992) *Professional ethics and civic morals.* London: Routledge.

Gamble, A. (1998) *The free market and the strong state.* London: Macmillan.

Grace, G. (1994) 'Education is a public good: On the need to resist the domination of economic science,' in D. Bridges and T. McLaughlin (eds) *Education and the market place.* Abingdon: Routledge Falmer.

Grace, G. (2004) *Catholic schools: Mission, markets and morality.* London: Routledge.

Grace, G. (2010) 'Reflections on the university and the academic as "Critic and Conscience of Society"'. *New Zealand Journal of Education Studies,* 45(2): 89–92.

Gutierrez, G. (1973) *A theology of liberation*. London: SCM Press.

Hadas, E. (2009) *The credit crunch: Making moral sense of the financial crisis*. London: Catholic Truth Society.

Jessop, B. (2002) *The future of the capitalist state*. Cambridge: Polity Press.

MacIntyre, A. (1985) *After virtue: A study in moral theory* (2nd edn). London: Duckworth.

Nisbet, R. (1965) *Emile Durkheim: With selected essays*. Englewood Cliffs, NJ: Prentice Hall.

Soros, G. (1999) *The crisis of global capitalism: Open society endangered*. New York: Public Affairs.

Pope Benedict XVI (2009) *Caritas in veritate: Love in truth*. Dublin: Veritas Publications.

Turner, B. (1992) 'Introduction' in E. Durkheim (1992) *Professional ethics and civic morals*. London: Routledge.

Usher, R. and Edwards, R. (1994) *Post modernism and education*. London: Routledge.

Wilson, A. N. (1999) *God's funeral*. London: Abacus.

Young, M. (2008) *Bringing knowledge back in*. London: Routledge.

Part Two

Knowledge, judgment and expertise

Theoretical perspectives

3 Abstract rationality in education

From Vygotsky to Brandom

Jan Derry

This chapter takes a step back from the immediate issues confronting professional education to raise questions about the nature of knowledge, focusing on the issue of abstract rationality and situated knowing. A contrast is often made between knowledge that can be applied universally and knowledge that is associated with specific conditions. Debate about professional knowledge and education has tended to consider these two positions to be polar opposites and mutually exclusive. In looking to the work of the Russian thinker, Lev Vygotsky, this chapter explores the possibility of a third way that overcomes the limitations of the other two. The line of argument developed from Vygotsky fits well with the more historical and social conception of knowledge proposed by Muller and Young.

What follows is an illustration of what is at stake in common conceptions of formal knowledge viewed through a criticism of Vygotsky made by James Wertsch. Wertsch argues that taken as a whole 'Vygotsky's writings reflect a kind of ambivalence with regard to where he stood on the ideals of Enlightenment rationality' (Wertsch, 1996, p. 38). Wertsch sees these ideals as potentially negative and for him they represent the logical, the universal, the timeless and the general by contrast with the rhetorical, the particular, the local and the timely. Vygotsky, however, had a far more sophisticated appreciation of the nature and scope of reason and its significance for education than that found in contemporary characterisations of his view of rationality. The chapter will go on, therefore, in section two, to provide an account of Vygotsky that corrects this picture and explores, in particular, aspects of his account of the relations of concepts to the world. In doing so the chapter is compelled to consider, albeit briefly, the influence that Hegel exercised on Vygotsky's thinking, because it was under the influence of Hegel in particular that Vygotsky developed his ideas about rationality. In section three these lines of thought are taken further in the light of the work of Robert Brandom, who shares Vygotsky's inheritance of Hegel. The discussion of Hegel's presence in Brandom's work serves also to show the way that, after having been ignored or even been disparaged by Anglo-American philosophers, Hegel's work is now being recognised in leading circles in contemporary philosophy (Brandom, 2000; McDowell, 1996). What is particularly interesting is that Brandom's attraction to Hegel, for the importance that he (Hegel) attached to the social nature of thinking, is precisely the same as Vygotsky's. The conclusion this chapter points towards is that the philosophical underpinnings of Vygotsky's work provide a radically different idea of rationality and epistemology from that characterised as abstract rationality, and that the importance of this for studies in education has been badly neglected.

An appropriate point at which to start the argument is a brief account of salient aspects of Wertsch's reading of Vygotsky.

James Wertsch's Vygotsky and the idea of the Enlightenment project

Wertsch characterises 'decontextualised rationality' in terms of forms of representation of objects and events whose meaning are derived from their position in abstract theories:

> The defining characteristic of the voice of decontextualised rationality is that it represents objects and events . . . in terms of formal logical and if possible quantifiable categories. The categories used in this form of representation are decontextualised in the sense that their meaning can be derived from their position in abstract theories or systems that exist independently of particular speech types. . . . the meaning of *five* or *electron* . . . can be and often is established by definitions that are abstract (i.e. independent of particular use) and hence identical across contexts.
>
> (Wertsch, 1992, p. 120)

He goes on to emphasise that although decontextualised meanings are thought to have some kind of primordial existence that underlies our use of language they actually grew out of discourses associated with the rise of literacy (Wertsch, 1992, p. 120). A further example of this can be found in Wells, who emphasises that semiotic practices and artefacts have enabled the sociohistorical development of scientific rationality to emerge and states: 'The fact that "scientific rationality" has come to be highly valued in Western cultures does not therefore mean that it is superior, in some absolute sense, to other modes of thinking' (Wells, 1996).

For Wertsch and Wells abstract rationality conceived in this way is just one historically and socially developed way that meaning is made: it is one of a variety of ways by which individuals make sense of their world depending on the practices that they participate in. This questioning of the privileged status of abstract rationality has contributed to the shift of attention of those concerned with pedagogy to the forms of making meaning and to their situated dimension. Alongside this shift and to some extent connected with it has been a questioning of the status of what was previously considered knowledge and truth. Thus the impact of Constructivism in educational theory with its emphasis on the meaning-making of the individual learner has challenged the relevance and significance of any particular system of knowledge.

The concerns that have been expressed about Vygotsky's work are often couched in broad terms that take the Enlightenment project to be committed to a conception of the nature and power of reason that is now found wanting. This general line of argument is rehearsed to different degrees throughout a good deal of what is currently published in educational research. Many educational writings have ignored the tradition of philosophy that is not only fundamental to the work of Vygotsky but also provides a different route for considering current educational issues (and cannot be captured by the critical characterisation of the Enlightenment project). Criticisms of Vygotsky require a proper appreciation of the philosophical terrain on which his work developed.

Wertsch's work on Vygotsky is particularly helpful as a counterpoint, because it provides a worked-out critique of abstract rationality in relation to concrete educational concerns. Wertsch has written repeatedly on the difficulties Vygotsky faced due to his writing in an Enlightenment climate; in fact he claims it is this climate that accounts for an ambivalence in Vygotsky's work between an approach to meaning with an emphasis on locale and culture, on the one hand, and a hard scientific realism and a hierarchical form of reason, on the other.[1]

He shares a concern with other commentators on Vygotsky's work, that the scientific concepts Vygotsky favours reflect the influence of an eighteenth-century rationality now undermined by what is understood about the failures of the Enlightenment project. However, it is interesting to note that although the Enlightenment is often characterised as epitomising an abstract, universalist and logo-centric conception of reason, it was historically, among other things, a search for meaning that could no longer be found in the secure foundation of a divine absolute. Seen in this light the Enlightenment involved a rejection of authority rather than the positive assertion of it, which modern critics perceive.

In his characterisation of the Enlightenment, Wertsch adopts Toulmin's revised account of what he terms the 'received view of modernity'; this he argues has profound implications for understanding Vygotsky's writings. (Wertsch, 1996, p. 37) In his book, *Cosmopolis: The hidden agenda of modernity*, Toulmin (1992) writes of a struggle between Enlightenment rationality and Renaissance humanism. Wertsch finds many explicit statements in Vygotsky's writings that correspond to what Toulmin terms the 'received view'; 'Time and again he shows a strong tendency to value and focus on logic, the universal, the general, and the timeless' (Wertsch, 1996, p. 37). The assertion (also made by Gordon Wells 1999) that Vygotsky was influenced strongly by the abstract rationalist aspect of the Enlightenment due to the time and context in which he worked (the Soviet Union in the early part of the last century) ignores the criticism of eighteenth-century rationality made by Hegel and its influence on Vygotsky. A general point at issue here is that the blanket attack on Enlightenment thinking has not only led to a loss of valuable elements of this tradition but has also overlooked its developments. Of these the development made by Hegel has, through the work of Vygotsky, direct and important implications for education. The abandonment of the pursuit of truth and the definition of learners as 'producers of knowledge' who exhibit a multiplicity of ways of meaning-making have made themselves felt within the educational practice. They come about as a result of a general disenchantment with foundationalism, understood as the thesis that all knowledge rests ultimately on a foundation of non-inferential knowledge. This understanding of foundation has no place in either Hegel's or Vygotsky's thought, which, as I have argued elsewhere, can best be described as 'antifoundational foundationalism'.[2]

It is in the context of his characterisation of Enlightenment rationality that Wertsch, while justifiably concerned with the inadequacies of an education process that fails to engage with the variety of ways that learners make meaning, points to the problems of privileging decontextualised rationality as the dominant form of 'meaning making'. Wertsch is representative of a number of writers who are troubled by curricula based on 'decontexualised rationality'. He questions the value of this priority noting that 'the general tendency to privilege the voice of decontextualised rationality exists in spite of the fact that empirical evidence indicates that people who have mastered relevant abstract reasoning processes often do not use these processes, even when the situation clearly calls for them to do so' (Wertsch, 1992, p. 122). Wertsch views the 'privileging' of particular mediational means (ways of solving problems), found in traditional processes of education, as indicative of the extraordinary authority accorded to abstract rationality since the Middle Ages. He attempts to establish a direct link between his criticism of pedagogical practices that privilege abstract or decontextualised rationality and Toulmin's argument about the received view of Modernity. Toulmin refers to Descartes' teachings that the 'demands of rationality impose on philosophy a need to seek out abstract, general ideas and principles, by which particulars can be connected together' (Toulmin, 1992, p. 33) and Wertsch restates Toulmin's summary of the received view that *'abstract axioms were in, concrete diversity was out'* (Wertsch, 1998, p. 67). Wertsch argues that 'the received view is routinely appropriated by people in our sociocultural setting and . . . results in viewing certain utterances and arguments as convincing despite the many critiques of this tendency' (Wertsch, 1998, p. 67). His concern with this privileging of abstract rationality over alternative ways of 'meaning-making' is linked to his characterisation of Enlightenment rationality as an abstract universalism that involves a particular conception of scientific concepts. For Wertsch this characterisation leads onto his criticism of scientific concepts and their relation to the world.

Wertsch develops his critique of Vygotsky by considering the arguments in Chapters 5 and 6 of *Thinking and speech*.[3] He is concerned with what he takes to be Vygotsky's emphasis on the relationship between semiotic expressions, such as words and sentences, and the world of objects. This he sees as compelling evidence for 'a side of Vygotsky that was deeply committed to Enlightenment traditions of Abstract Rationality' (Wertsch, 2000, p. 22). He asserts that at certain points in his work, Vygotsky approached meaning in terms of ostentation, drawing on Charles Taylor to provide an explanation of what this entails. This is helpful in providing a clear characterisation of a common conception of meaning not just in philosophy but also one present in much pedagogical practice and curriculum development.

In respect to ostention Wertsch draws on Taylor's distinction between *designative* and *expressivist* approaches to meaning to identify two trends – Rationality and Romanticism. Commenting on the view of meaning that he finds in Vygotsky's work he writes that: 'This view of meaning is grounded on the assumption that language functions primarily to *represent* an independent reality' [italics added] and quotes Taylor to the effect that:

> [W]e could explain a sign or word having meaning by pointing to what it designates, in a broad sense, that is, what it can be used to refer to in the world, and what it can be used to say about that thing . . . we give the meaning of a sign or a word by pointing to the thing or relations that they can be used to talk about.
>
> (Taylor, cited in Wertsch, 2000, p. 26)

Wertsch argues that the relationship between word and object found in the designative approach is consistent with Vygotsky's account of meaning in scientific concepts, the argument being that Vygotsky had the same epistemological view of the relation of word to world. Central to Wertsch's argument that Vygotsky was an ambivalent rationalist is the claim that Vygotsky operates with 'an assumption that language and meaning are basically concerned with referential relationships between signs and objects' (Wertsch, 2000, p. 20). It is the epistemological assumption implied by this claim that has significance for professional education and for the neglect of the importance of theoretical knowledge.

Vygotsky, abstract rationality and the social formation of mind

Like his contemporary Piaget, Vygotsky understood the importance of the inextricable connection between the development of human thought and epistemology. However, in Vygotsky's enquiry into the nature of mind this connection is conceived in a different way from that of Piaget and involves a number of ideas, of which the educational significance is still being worked out. These ideas include the role of concepts, the nature of scientific concepts and the role of tools in the development of higher mental function.

Central to Vygotsky's work is the idea of the social formation of the mind, which can be most simply stated as the idea that while it has an individual dimension, thought cannot be properly understood as a solely individual activity. This social conception of mind is at odds with orthodox Anglo-American approaches where thought is 'analyzed in terms of an individual's mental states'.[4] When this idea, of a social conception of mind, is acted upon, philosophical enquiry cannot help but enter terrains of concern, normally reserved for educationalists; that is to say the examination of the human mind can no longer be detached from the conditions within which it develops.

The type of connection that his findings demonstrated between thought and language is not readily captured by the idea that a thought is articulated in speech. Rather in contrast to the conventional view that speech is the articulation of thought, Vygotsky claims that thinking and speech go together. It is not simply a matter of articulating what is already conceived, but articulation is part and parcel of the process of conceptualisation. The significance for education of the idea that thought or concepts are only completed through their expression implies a rejection of the commonly practised mode of teaching known as 'the transmission mode'.[5] As Vygotsky stresses; 'direct instruction in concepts is impossible. . . . The teacher who attempts to use the approach achieves nothing but a mindless learning of words . . .' (Vygotsky, 1987, p. 170). Once a concept has been learnt the development of its meaning for the learner has only just begun.

While Vygotsky's dialogic and developmental conception of concepts is widely appreciated, his account of scientific concepts and the weight given to them is viewed as problematic. Vygotsky distinguishes between different sorts of concepts; and in particular, between what he termed 'everyday' or 'spontaneous concepts' on the one hand and 'scientific concepts on the other'.[6] These two types of concepts acquire their meaning and are learnt through different practices: everyday concepts are those that are learnt spontaneously in daily life. Scientific concepts are those learnt through formal instruction. Scientific concepts take their meaning primarily from their systemic relation with one another rather than through any ad hoc relation to the world. The differences between these two concepts and the type of experience they depend upon are crucial for Vygotsky. As an illustration of the two concepts and the differences they entail, the following extract from Kozulin's *Psychological tools* provides a vivid example:

> Here is a problem: 'A rope is tied around the Earth's equator. Then a ten-meter-long piece is added to it and the rope is pulled evenly so that everywhere the distance between the Earth's rope and the surface is the same? The question is: Would this distance be sufficient for a cat to sneak under the rope?'
>
> (Kozulin, 1998, preface)

Kozulin recounts how he was given the problem by his son while driving and was unable to use a paper and pencil to utilise the symbolic tools of mathematics to calculate the answer. Instead he relied on imagining the additional length added in one place (a loop of about 5m high) and then being spread out to extend the full length of the rope, resulting in a minute gap too small for the cat to fit underneath. The use of scientific concepts of *pi* and radius would have yielded the correct but counterintuitive answer of a 1.6m gap.[7]

It is important to be clear about the distinctive contribution and character of scientific concepts as well as their origin to avoid misunderstandings of his work as favouring abstract rationality in terms of its characterisation as a form of reason independent of any context. For scientific concepts are no less concrete than everyday concepts, they depend just as much on experience as everyday concepts, the difference being, instead of being direct their dependence is indirect through many enquiries over many generations. Scientific concepts bear the characteristics of abstract, formal thinking and as such are crucial for any process of education.

The extensive interest in the work of Vygotsky is in a large part due to the original implications of his work. While these implications range over such diverse fields as professional education, educational technologies and schooling, the potential impact of the work is inextricably tied up with a fundamental understanding of the relation of human beings to the world (*Mind and world*) and of what it is to be human, i.e., what is distinctive about thinking beings. Our cognitive powers clearly distinguish us from animals and machines yet many accounts of our relation to the world fail to make the distinction, or if they do make it fail to develop it sufficiently. Indeed, as has been mentioned here, the social nature of the human mind has generally been approached in education studies in terms of a multiplicity of forms of thought tied to context and mediational means, rather than in terms of an examination of what is distinctively and universally human about its character.

Criticisms of Vygotsky's work rely on an implicit epistemological framework that fails to recognise that his work lies in different territory from what is generally associated with 'abstract rationality', and this has implications not just for debates about knowledge but also for professional education. Hence the argument here for not only the importance of achieving a fuller grasp of the philosophical background to Vygotsky's work but also of appreciating misconceptions of abstract knowledge as separated from professional practice.

As has been made clear, then, this chapter takes a radically different approach from that of Wertsch and other commentators, by adopting a positive position vis-à-vis the enlightenment tradition, which Wertsch finds so problematic. In support of this position it draws attention to the work of the contemporary philosophers already mentioned whose reading of Enlightenment thinkers has much in common with Vygotsky. The influence of Hegel's *Phenomenology* on John McDowell[8] and Robert Brandom has been crucial for rethinking problems that have come out of analytic philosophy, such as the relation of language to the world, and it is suggested here that it is also a fertile source, via the work of Vygotsky, for education. It is here that an internal development within philosophy concerning epistemology has significant implications for education.

It is worth noting in passing, that epistemology has received revived interest as new developments have opened up possibilities for a cross-fertilisation between social theory, psychology and philosophy. In particular the reading of Hegel being worked through by contemporary philosophers steeped in the analytical tradition already mentioned, whose approach at first sight seems wholly at odds with Hegel, is proving especially interesting. For example Rorty, referring to Pippin's work on Hegel, has said 'Had we listened to Hegel, Wittgenstein's private language argument would have seemed a reiteration of the obvious' (Rorty, 2005). It is appropriate now to turn our attention to the influence of Hegel not only in Vygotsky but also in Brandom, and to connections between their work.

Hegel's Enlightenment: from Vygotsky to Brandom

Hegel, who was particularly important for Vygotsky, believed that Enlightenment thought had not achieved the liberatory goal of reason. To this end he developed, particularly in his *Logic*, a system of thought that established its own foundations as part of its process. This Hegelian system meets the objections levelled against

Enlightenment thinking by many contemporary critiques.[9] But as far as Vygotsky is concerned it does not appear to have been fully taken into consideration.

The explanation of reference in Wertsch's reading of Vygotsky's discussion in Chapters 5 and 6 of *Thinking and speech* is at odds with Vygotsky's Hegelianism. However, the 'ambivalence' that Wertsch detects in Vygotsky's work can be interpreted from the standpoint of Vygotsky's approach as the different paradigm from which he operates (Hegelian and inferentialist), which allows for both a universalising form of knowledge and the continual constitutive development of local meaning-making. Brandom has termed the paradigm in which this chapter argues Wertsch is operating, 'representationalist' and counterposed it to an inferentialist approach to meaning. Unsurprisingly, given the influence of Hegel on the work of Brandom, this is quite in line with Vygotsky's approach in *Thinking and Speech*. In line with this it could be argued that some of the concerns of those who take issue with abstract rationality are misplaced to the extent those concerns arise in the first place from representationalism.

At numerous points in his work Vygotsky labours to take issue with a conception that sees thought as occupying a 'representational' or simple referential relation to the world. The point he stresses when he speaks below of 'a system of judgments' is that the idea of 'general representations' is inadequate to express what a concept is in thinking:

> [W]e must seek the psychological equivalent of the concept not in general representations, not in absolute perceptions and orthoscopic diagrams, not even in concrete verbal images that replace the general representations – we must seek it in a system of judgements in which the concept is disclosed.
> (Vygotsky, 1998, p. 55)

This makes clear just how far he was from embracing a simple representational view of the world.

In educational practice some of the extreme polarisations implicit in constructivist positions (such as the idea that there is no way of ruling between any one set of ideas or another as 'we come no closer to the truth' – Gergen, 1999, p. 239) can be viewed as an outcome of the problem of understanding what 'objective world' entails within a foundationalist[10] tradition of epistemology. Constructivism as well as Constructionism are often counterposed to realism (Parker, 1998; Gergen, 1999). Hence the realism evident in Vygotsky's use of the phrase 'scientific concepts' is seen as evidence of a lack of appreciation on his part of multiple avenues of meaning-making in favour of didactic methods.

The critique of 'the Enlightenment project' as a version of abstract reason applied to the world in an authoritarian way has been extremely influential in education research, leading many commentators to question knowledge *per se*. When he criticises formal logic Vygotsky himself recognises the possibility of rationality controlling and regulating at the expense of richness and diversity:

> It is completely clear that if the process of generalizing is considered as a direct result of abstraction of traits, then we will inevitably come to the

conclusion that thinking in concepts is removed from reality. . . . Others have said that concepts arise in the process of castrating reality. Concrete, diverse phenomena must lose their traits one after the other in order that a concept might be formed. Actually what arises is a dry and empty abstraction in which the diverse, full-blooded reality is impoverished by logical thought. This is the source of the celebrated words of Goethe: 'Gray is every theory and eternally green is the golden tree of life'.

(Vygotsky, 1998, p. 53)

However, as this commentary on the generalisations of formal logic shows, Vygotsky's view of rationality is quite different from the one that construes 'the development of meaning [as] a matter of increasing generalisation and abstraction' (Wertsch, 2000 p. 20). In contrast to the impoverished version of reason that is sometimes attributed to aspects of his work Vygotsky argues that:

A real concept is an image of an objective thing in all its complexity. Only when we recognise the thing in all its connections and relations, only when this diversity is synthesised in a word, in an integral image through a multitude of determinations do we develop a concept. According to the teaching of dialectical logic, a concept includes not only the general, but also the individual and particular.

In contrast to contemplation, to direct knowledge of an object, a concept is filled with definitions of the object; it is the result of rational processing of our existence and it is mediated knowledge of the object. To think of some object with the help of a concept means to include the given object in a complex system of mediating connection and relations disclosed in determinations of the concept.

(Vygotsky, 1998, p. 53)

Vygotsky's emphasis on the systemic character of concepts is taken by Wertsch to be an indication of the type of decontextualised and abstract rationality that he views as so problematic for education in the current period. However, what Vygotsky refers to is not the abstract system he depicts but rather, like Brandom, an approach that prioritises inference over reference. For Vygotsky, the relation of a concept to an object is one that is necessarily part of a system of judgements, which involve the 'mediating connection and relations disclosed in the determinations of the concept' (Vygotsky, 1998, p. 53). This is the basis of an epistemology quite different from the one implicit in Wertsch's critique. Following Hegel, it conceives the relation of a thinking being to the world as necessarily social, since our responsiveness to the world that develops as part of our second nature operates within what McDowell[11] (drawing on Wilfrid Sellars) has called 'the space of reasons' (i.e., our responses are necessarily normative).

The prioritisation of inference over reference entails, in terms of pedagogy, that the grasping of a concept (knowing) requires committing to the inferences implicit in its use in a social practice of giving and asking for reasons. Effective teaching involves providing the opportunity for students to operate with a concept in the space of reasons within which it falls and by which its meaning is constituted. Participation in such a space does not require an immediate and full grasp of the reasons constituting the concept but rather only the ability to inhabit the space in which reasons and the concept operate in the first place.[12]

The idea that a sign, word or concept might be understood primarily as a relation of representation to the world is precisely what Hegel takes issue with in the *Phenomenology*. As Brandom reminds us, Hegel's achievement was to build on what Kant had already begun:

> The subtlety and sophistication of Kant's concept of representation is due in large part to the way in which it is integrated into his account of the inferential relations among judgments. It remained for Hegel, however, to complete the inversion of the traditional order of semantic explanation by beginning with a concept of experience as inferential activity and discussing the making of judgments and the development of concepts entirely in terms of the role they play in inferential activity.
>
> (Brandom, 1994, p. 92)

Brandom formulates his Hegelianism as a prioritisation of inference over reference. Similarly, Vygotsky's Hegelianism rejects the position that takes the meaning of a concept primarily in terms of its representation of an object. Instead, what has priority is the system of inferences in which the object is disclosed.

For Brandom the distinguishing feature of a thinking being is its responsiveness to reasons rather than simply to causes. Responsiveness to causes is characteristic of a machine or a parrot capable of responding differentially to a stimulus, but not of thinking beings qua thinking beings. A mechanical alarm may be far more effective in *perceiving* the dangers of a fire and sounding the alert than any human being. But when a human being shouts 'fire!' he or she is always doing more than simply making a warning noise. When a child of five (as opposed to a much younger child whose uttered sounds are only just beginning to operate as language) shouts 'fire!' he or she knows its implications. He or she appreciates the consequences of the exclamation 'fire!' and what follows from such an utterance. Brandom uses this example to illustrate his claim that human beings act and communicate *inferentially*. His point is that what distinguishes the human form of knowing from the type of 'knowing' we might ascribe to a machine is the Sellarsian point that knowing, for a human being, consists not merely in expressing a response but in knowing what follows from it – knowing the implications, or what Brandom calls the 'giving and asking for reasons' (Brandom, 2000, p. 195). As he puts it 'even non-inferential reports must be inferentially articulated' and this point is crucial to any understanding of human intellect:

> One of the most important lessons we learn from Sellars's masterwork, 'Empiricism and Philosophy of Mind' (as from the 'Sense Certainty' section of Hegel's Phenomenology), is the inferentialist one that even noninferential reports must be inferentially articulated. Without that requirement we cannot

tell the difference between noninferential reporters and automatic machinery such as thermostats and photocells, which also have reliable dispositions to respond differentially to stimuli.

(Brandom, 2000, p. 48)

I have just mentioned an alarm *perceiving* a fire. This is already an anthropomorphism that Brandom takes care to avoid. He talks of machines 'responding differentially to stimulus' by which he means they respond mechanically to a stimulus. The use of the phrase 'responding differentially' in place of 'perceiving' or 'knowing' is of crucial importance for it introduces a distinction that is hidden by our anthropomorphic use of language. The stimulus in this case – the fire – is a cause of their response; in the case of the human being who sounds the alarm the fire is the reason for their response. *The human perceives the fire as fire; that is to say that unlike a machine it has a concept of fire as part of a system of concepts.* For Brandom making a *report* as a human being is not merely to 'respond differentially' it is inferring rather than merely representing, since 'even non inferential reports must be inferentially articulated' (Brandom, 2000, p. 47). This emphasis on inference is drawn from Hegel's analysis of what *Sense Certainty* entails and, in keeping with Hegel, Brandom argues that 'in order to master *any* concept, one must master *many* concepts' (Brandom, 2000, p. 49). For Brandom, the responses that humans make involve an understanding of significance that is only possible by already appreciating other concepts. Where this is not the case, i.e., in the response of a parrot or machine, even though the response still may be the same, i.e., 'fire', then the human is not behaving as human.

The emphasis on inference that Brandom credits to Hegel is not without important implications for professional education. It provides a basis for a conception of knowledge and the process of acquiring it whereby the use and understanding of a word cannot be conceived simply in terms of the designative approach to meaning that Wertsch finds in aspects of Vygotsky's work. On the contrary, following Brandom, and Hegel, in order to understand it is necessary to 'make explicit' the connections and determinations that constitute a concept. For Vygotsky, these connections and determinations are not due to 'abstract rationality' (even though they are objective) but to the cultural-historical activity of human beings in the world of which they are part. Brandom explains this in terms of social practices:

> I think one of the most important lessons we can learn from Kant concerns the normative character of concept use. Hegel, as I read him, transposed this insight into a pragmatist key, with his idea that normative statuses are always the product of social practices. I see Hegel, already in the Phenomenology of Spirit of 1807, wrestling with a core of issues that we only recovered access to recently, largely through the efforts of the later Wittgenstein. I have in mind issues concerning the possibility of understanding conceptual objectivity in the context of a social practice account of the norms implicit in concept use.
>
> (Brandom, 1999)

Here is a view of meaning and objectivity radically different from the one contained in Wertsch's claim that Vygotsky was ambivalent about Enlightenment Rationality. From the viewpoint of common sense and in cases of poor practice, words are understood solely to take their meaning from the things they represent, and it is taken as a given that it is through awareness of this connection that learning occurs. Knowing as opposed to awareness of association requires a different stance. However, in the absence of an appreciation that there is an alternative to this approach to meaning (one which incorporates designation but only as secondary to the inferences that are the historical genesis of its meaning) the attack on 'abstract rationality' can lead to a damaging relativism, where the weight given to discourse, speech types and the historical consitution of meaning-making has led to an agnosticism for truth. The absence of any consideration of the inferential character of concepts has fostered the idea that an individual learner left to his/her own devices in a rich environment will 'create' knowledge. However, the design of such an environment requires more careful attention to detail than is often realised. Indeed it is often the case that the idea that the learning environment requires design at all is ignored.[13] By contrast a Vygotskian approach doesn't depend simply on individuals being placed in the required environment where they discover meaning for themselves. The learning environment requires design and cannot rely on the spontaneous response to an environment that is not constructed according to, or involves, some clearly worked out conceptual framework. For Vygotsky, concepts depend for their meaning on the system of judgements (inferences) within which they are disclosed. Brandom's careful study of concept use argues that concepts by their nature are not isolated from one another:

> To have conceptual content is just for it [a concept] to play a role in the inferential game of making claims and giving and asking for reasons. To grasp or understand such a concept is to have practical mastery over the inferences it is involved in—to know, in the practical sense of being able to distinguish, what follows from the applicability of a concept, and what it follows from.
>
> (Brandom 1994, p. 48)

To underline: for the Vygotskian approach, the connections are not arbitrary (nor the outcome of the individual learners 'creativity') but inform the meaning of the concept in the first place (whether explicit or not). It is through proper appreciation of the philosophy informing Vygotsky's work that we can reconsider the attack on abstract rationhy made within the field of Vygotskian research and with it develop a more robust view of the question of knowledge in professional education. The route out of the dilemma of theoretical uninformed practices on the one side and disembodied abstract knowledge on the other must start with a reconsideration of the notion of concept as representation seen atomistically, rather than inferentially.

Notes

1 The expression 'hierarchical form of reason' is used to capture the belief in progress towards a universal form of rationality of which different cultural groups exhibit characteristics that place them higher or lower on an evolutionary scale.

2 Derry (2000) 'Foundationalism and anti-foundationalism: seeking enchantment in the rough ground' in V. Oittinen (ed.) *Evald Ilyenkov's philosophy revisited*, Kikimora Publications, Helsinki.

3 The first English language edition of an edited version of this work translated the title as *Thought and language* and this is the name by which Vygotsky's work is commonly known. The English edition of the *Collected works, volume 1* (1987) used the more correct translation of *Thinking and speech*.

4 '. . . the disinterest of mainstream philosophy of mind in matters of education results from an inherited Cartesianism, according to which . . . mental contents can and ought to be analyzed in terms of an individual's mental states' (Westphal, 2000).

5 This is not to deny that learning can be supported in a number of ways including didactic approaches, which involve practice and habituation.

6 In the original Russian of Vygotsky's text the term scientific here has a more general meaning and applies to academic concepts.

7 (C is circumference of the earth, r is radius of the earth; R is the new radius after 10 meters is added to the circumference) $C = 2\pi r$; $C+10$ metres $= 2\pi R$; $r + 10/2\pi = R$; $R - r = 1.6$ meters (i.e., the additional gap).

8 McDowell credits Brandom's writings and conversations with shaping his own thinking and singles out a seminar on Hegel's *Phenomenology of spirit* that he attended in 1990, relating that 'the effect is pervasive; so much so that I would like to conceive . . . [*Mind and world*] as a prolegomenon to a reading of the *Phenomenology* much as Brandom's forthcoming *Making it explicit: Reasoning, representing, and discursive commitment* is . . . a prolegomenon to his reading of that difficult text.' (McDowell, 1996, p. ix).

9 Brandom claims that Hegel was struggling with issues concerning conceptual objectivity that 'analytic philosophy has had laboriously to rediscover in this century, due to the efforts of such thinkers as Wittgenstein, Sellars, Quine, and Kuhn' (Brandom, 1999). For a clear account of Hegel's work that opens the way to an understanding of these issues see Stephen Houlgate's *Introduction to Hegel*.

10 By using the shorthand 'foundationalist tradition' here I mean to capture the tradition that Hegel criticises in the *Phenomenology* – both dualism and representationalism are elements in a foundational approach to knowledge.

11 David Bakhurst (1997) has brought to our attention the links between McDowell's work and the Vygotskian tradition through his work on the philosopher Ilyenkov.

12 Initiation into such a space opens the opportunity for the development of word meaning.

13 Design here entails far more than the formalities involved in the sort of lesson planning that details what resources and activities will be used at which point.

References

Bakhurst, D. (1997) 'Meaning, normativity and the life of the mind', *Language and Communication, 17*, 1: 33–51.

Brandom, R. (1994) *Making it explicit: Reasoning, representing, and discursive commitment.* Cambridge, MA: Harvard University Press.

Brandom, R. (1999) Interviewed by Carlo Penco. *Epistemologia XXII*, 1999: 143–50. Online. Available at: www.dif.unige.it/epi/hp/penco/pub/brandom_inter.pdf (accessed 11 June, 2013).

Brandom, R. (2000) *Articulating reasons: An introduction to inferentialism.* Cambridge, MA: Harvard University Press.

Derry (2000) 'Foundationalism and anti-foundationalism: seeking enchantment in the rough ground' in V. Oittinen (ed.) *Evald Ilyenkov's philosophy revisited*, Kikimora Publications, Helsinki.

Gergen, K.J. (1999) *An invitation to social construction*. London: Sage Publications.

Kozulin, A. (1998) *Psychological tools: A sociocultural approach to education*. Cambridge, MA: Harvard University Press.

McDowell, J. (1996) *Mind and world*. Cambridge, MA: Harvard University Press.

Parker, I. (ed.) (1998) *Social constructionism, discourse and realism*. London: Sage Publications.

Rorty, R. (2005) '*Review of Robert B. Pippin. The persistence of subjectivity: On the Kantian Aftermath*', Notre Dame Philosophical Reviews. Online. Available at: http://ndpr.nd.edu/review.cfm?id=4101 (accessed 11 June, 2013).

Toulmin, S. (1992) *Cosmopolis, the hidden agenda of modernity*. Chicago: University of Chicago Press.

Vygotsky, L.S. (1987) *The collected works of L.S. Vygotsky, Volume 1 Problems of General Psychology*, (including the volume, *Thinking and Speech*); trans Norris Minick, Reiber, R.W. and Carton, A.S. (eds), New York: Plenum Press.

Vygotsky, L.S. (1998) *The collected works of L.S. Vygotsky, Volume 5, Child psychology*. R.W. Reiber (ed.), prologue by C. Ratner, New York: Plenum Press.

Wells, G. (1996) 'Learning and teaching "Scientific Concepts": Vygotsky's ideas revisited'. Paper presented at the Conference, 'Vygotsky and the Human Sciences', Moscow, September, 1994. Available online at: http://people.ucsc.edu/*gwells/Files/Papers_Folder/ScientificConcepts.pdf (accessed on 1 January, 2005).

Wells, G. (1999) *Dialogic inquiry: Towards a sociocultural practice and theory of education*. Cambridge: Cambridge University Press.

Wertsch, J.V. (1992) 'The voice of rationality in a sociocultural approach to mind', in L.C. Moll (ed.) *Vygotsky and education: Instructional implications and applications of sociohistorical theory* (pp. 111–26). Cambridge: Cambridge University Press.

Wertsch, J. (1996) 'The role of abstract rationality in Vygotsky's image of mind', in A.Tryphon and J.N. Voneche (eds) *Piaget – Vygotsky The social genesis of thought* (pp.25–42). Psychology Press, an imprint of Erlbaum (UK) Taylor & Francis.

Wertsch, J.V. (1998) *Mind as action*. Oxford: Oxford University Press.

Wertsch, J.V. (2000) 'Vygotsky's two minds on the nature of meaning', in C.D. Lee and P. Smargorinsky (eds) *Vygotskian perspectives on literacy research* (pp. 19–31). Cambridge: Cambridge University Press.

Westphal, K.R. (2000) 'Integrating philosophies of mind and of education: Comments on Cunningham' *Philosophy of Education, 1999*, 147–52. (Urbana, IL.: Philosophy of Education Society, 1999). Online. Available at: http://ojs.ed.uiuc.edu/index.php/pes/article/view/2040 (accessed 11 June, 2013).

4 Know-how and knowledge in the professional curriculum

Christopher Winch

Introduction: the idea of epistemic ascent

The idea of *epistemic ascent* is applicable to both academic and professional/ vocational curricula. The underlying idea is that knowledge can be categorised and the relationship between different kinds of knowledge can be described from the point of view of supporting the progression of learners, rather than just as a logical structure. In doing so one gains clarity about what is and what is not possible in curricular progression from simpler and more elementary forms of knowledge to more complex and advanced ones. Such clarity is important because careful consideration of the different kinds of knowledge prompts consideration of their relationship and of their appropriate introduction into the curriculum. The idea of growing subject expertise is central to the design of an academic curriculum and also to a professional/vocational one. By 'subject' is here meant a body of knowledge organised around a more or less defined field of enquiry that adopts characteristic methods of validating existing knowledge and acquiring new propositions (Hamm, 1989). It is no part of my intention to be dogmatic about what subjects there are, nor about the boundaries of fields of enquiry. Even less do I wish to adjudicate on the (often contested) methods employed in subjects. It is worth insisting, though, that some of the traditional academic subjects constitute ways in which the powerful in our society, including the ruling elites, actually think about and discuss the world. Anyone who wishes to take part in such discussions needs the acquaintance with these subjects that will allow them to do so. As a corollary, exclusion from such 'powerful knowledge' contributes significantly to an exclusion of non-participants from such discussions.

What is professional knowledge?

Perhaps one of the surprising findings that arises from the consideration of Epistemic Ascent in relation to the professional curriculum is that an exclusive concern with propositional knowledge quickly leads one astray. 'Professional Knowledge' is not solely identified with sets of propositions. Consider the contrast between a 'standards' and a 'learning outcomes' approach to assessment. If a curriculum is 'prescribed content' (Barrow, 1976) then assessment of curriculum content will reflect that content. If we assume that a form of assessment 'fit for purpose' will involve testing those propositions that constitute the subject then it would seem to follow that the most appropriate way of doing so is through specification of the propositions to be known and an instrument for ascertaining which of them the student knows (Coles, 2007).

A little reflection, however, points to the difficulty of adopting such a procedure. If the learning outcomes of a curriculum involve knowing propositions p1 . . . pn, then it looks like testing recall of these will be sufficient. Ability to recall the propositions will constitute the 'learning outcomes' of the programme. But this will not do. The first objection arises from the fact that ability to recall a proposition does not constitute knowledge of that proposition, let alone, in the case of professional education, the ability to draw on that proposition to make professional judgments. It can of course be objected that at school, college or even university, we learn most of what we know through the mediation of an authority whose legitimacy as a dispenser of knowledge we may have limited justification in believing. There is a point in this objection and it deserves very serious consideration, which there is not the space to do justice to here. However, it is important that at least some of the elements of rationality are attributed to the possession of the knowledge that a student acquires during his/her studies. Not least among these conditions will be the following:

1   We have some understanding of the propositions that we are said to know.
2   We understand at least some of the connections between these propositions.

The first condition suggests that we need to understand not only the references that are made within such propositions but also the concepts that they express. We cannot say, for example, that a student knows that Napoleon was crowned Emperor of France in 1804 if he does not know to whom 'Napoleon' refers, nor what an emperor is. The second condition suggests that we can find our way around the relevant conceptual field of the knowledge with which we are dealing. Thus, if a student of French History of the period between 1789 and 1815 cannot understand that 'Napoleon was crowned Emperor of France in 1804' entails that 'France ceased to be a republic in 1804', we are entitled to deny that the student understands the first proposition in any meaningful sense and therefore cannot be said to believe it either, even though it is true. Thus condition 1 collapses into 2, since understanding entails appreciation of the relevant conceptual connections. This cannot be secured through recall of single propositions.

It follows from such considerations first that a purely 'learning outcomes' approach to the assessment of subject knowledge is unlikely to be adequate and approaches that explore at least some of the rational grounds for belief (such as adequate conceptual grasp) are more likely to do so. We can also conclude that there is an important sense in which subject knowledge, insofar as it involves such grasp, entails that the student of the subject possesses an important kind of practical knowledge, namely how to make inferences in the material mode

(Brandom, 2000) within the relevant conceptual field. It is important to realise that propositional knowledge, or 'Knowledge that' (KT) cannot be adequately understood in terms of grasp of singular propositions, but must also include adequate conceptual grasp of the relevant field and some kind of acquaintance, with the objects of study within that subject (KA or knowledge by acquaintance). Without losing site of the distinction between KT and KH ('Knowledge how') we can confidently state that good subject knowledge entails the ability to find one's way around the subject through material inference.

There are, of course, debates about the breadth and depth of underlying subject knowledge that should constitute any particular field of professional knowledge. We can be clear though that the ability to recognise lists of propositions within the relevant subject area is not professional knowledge, and would have no more than very limited professional use. Even for those, however, who do not intend to make contributions to the body of knowledge within the subject or do not intend to validate or test existing knowledge, there is another important requirement, namely the ability to understand *how* knowledge within the subject area is validated, tested and acquired. This necessitates familiarity, not just with the physical procedures through which this is done, but with the inferential procedures that underlie them, for example inductive inference, the hypothetico-deductive method, levels of significance and confidence in the case of subjects based on the experimental method (using that term in a broad sense, not just meaning Randomised Control Trials (RCTs)). It is usually essential within the academic subjects for this kind of procedural knowledge to be taught practically through replication of key experiments, fieldwork, observation, etc. This is another important sense in which academic knowledge has a significant practical component (see also Muller, 2012). So we need to add a third condition for subject understanding to the two above:

3   We understand how subject knowledge is tested, validated and acquired.

. . . in some practical sense. This condition is quite important as it should assuage some of the worries that quite naturally arise from so much of the disciplinary element of professional knowledge being based on the testimony of educational authorities. Some knowledge transmission by testimony is unavoidable and it is in many or even most cases rational to believe propositions on the basis of authoritative pronouncement, if the student has good reason to believe that the authority is a reliable one (cf. Everitt and Fisher, 2000). In this sense, one has a justification, albeit not a fully satisfactory one, for believing in the truth of the proposition. However, this cannot be entirely satisfactory and growing expertise and confidence in a subject requires that a more objective justification be available for belief. This is where practical knowledge of procedures becomes important in ensuring that students understand that there are means of determining truth or falsity and that these are not arbitrary but are based on attaining the degree of certainty that it is possible to attain in a given subject matter (Aristotle, 1925, Bk 1, p. 3) While authority cannot be completely dispensed with, since one relies on authorities as to what the procedures for validating knowledge are, justification for belief is substantially increased in these circumstances and, with it, the possibility of independent judgement of truth and falsity.

This applies to all kinds of 'propositional' knowledge, both everyday knowledge that is not systematically organised into subjects and systematically organised knowledge. It is necessary to say something about this distinction in relation to professional education. All workplaces have their own particular locales and procedures, individuals and customs, particular networks of suppliers and customers, materials and transport links. Knowledge of all these is essential to the proper conduct of work and part of the necessary knowledge of the profession as it is practised in some particular time and place. In addition to this there is also the 'Background', as Searle (1995) has called it; the assumptions, reactions, habits and propositions that constitute the basis of our commerce with the world and fellow human beings (see also Rhees, 2001; Moyal-Sharrock, 2007). The latter is hardly the matter of professional education, we expect all rational members of our community to partake of the 'Background'. This situation is obviously different, however, for the former case, the contingent knowledge associated with particular enterprises and workplaces.

More on systematic knowledge

Systematic knowledge (often referred to as 'theory') lying behind a particular occupation is another matter. It is typically, but by no means exclusively, associated with academic disciplines such as Physics or mathematics. When the competent practice of an occupation depends on the ability to apply such systematic knowledge from one or more disciplines to workplace judgment and action, the occupation may be characterised as either 'technical' or 'professional'. Such occupations will require subject knowledge in the academic sense, namely practitioners' ability not just to recognise propositions but to find their way inferentially around their subject. The requirement for the possession of occupation-related subject knowledge is a substantive one that needs further examination, particularly since, in the English context, that requirement is often subject to pressure for attenuation, so that, in extreme cases, it becomes little more than the ability to recognise certain propositions as true. As we observed above, having this ability does not constitute knowledge.

First, its reduction to propositional recall, through for example a 'learning outcomes' approach to assessment, should be vigorously resisted, since, as argued above, it results at best in a test for true belief rather than knowledge and even this may be disputed. Second, it should not be reduced to knowledge of procedures for how to apply the systematic knowledge to practice as this knowledge does not, of itself, entail practical knowledge of how to apply the subject knowledge to practice.

It is useful to distinguish between a technical professional such as a Chartered Engineer and an 'executive technician' who only carries out procedures without needing to understand their underlying rationale. The latter need not be acquainted with the underpinning subject knowledge relevant to the occupation while for the former such knowledge is an indispensable component of professional judgment.[1]

What, though, of the idea that a professional does not need direct acquaintance with the subject underlying their occupation? It might be thought that, from the point of view of occupational effectiveness, all that is needed is for the professional to be able to draw on such knowledge when necessary.

Clearly subject expertise demands that an individual should be able to 'know their way around the subject' – that is be able to make relevant inferences within it, both material and formal (and in relation to some subjects, mathematical) and to have a substantial understanding of its central concepts and propositions. In this sense, grasp of a subject is very much to be thought of along the lines of Hirst's (1965) acquaintance with a 'form of knowledge'. Hirst, however, quite rightly drew attention to rather more than this.

The practical understanding of a subject should also extend to the ability to be able to validate existing knowledge claims and to acquire new knowledge. For example, reasonable acquaintance with the subject matter in an experimental subject would imply the ability to understand, through replication, key experiments and to actually carry them out. This ability is not, of course, equivalent to the ability to acquire new knowledge through the experimental method. This, it can be argued, is another and more advanced level of expertise that requires insight into relevant research and the ability to manage a complex project, building on a deep understanding of the subject and its evolution (Winch, 2013a, op. cit.). However, although some of the replicative activity might be part of the repertoire of someone intending to be a member of a profession, one would not normally expect them to have the ability to contribute significant new knowledge in the field. However, the ability to make some contribution to the subject, for example, to qualify general theoretical conclusions in certain circumstances or to devise instruments and procedures based on the underlying principles of the subject, should not be excluded and may even be expected. For someone operating as an engineer rather than as an engineering technician such ability would be expected as a matter of routine and may indeed constitute the main body of the work undertaken in relation to the underlying subject. It is only of a *researcher*, normally qualified at doctoral level, that one would expect substantial contributions to the underlying theory of the subject.

Epistemic Ascent and workplace practice – technique, skill, transversal abilities, project management, occupational capacity

Within the Anglo Saxon countries it is almost a reflex to talk about occupational know-how in terms of skill, as if there were no other kind of practical ability worthy of consideration. This tendency has had deeply damaging effects on the ways in which professional and vocational curricula are thought about and a major task of this chapter is to persuade readers that this is a damaging way of thinking about the role of practical ability in the professional context. In particular, I will argue, it is necessary to distinguish between what are often referred to as practical abilities: technique, skill, transversal abilities, project management abilities and occupational capacity. Acquisition of all of these is necessary for preparation for work that involves both a high degree of professional autonomy and a deep understanding of one's occupation and its role in the wider economy and society. In what follows I will illustrate why this is so and what their relationships are with each other. In an important sense these forms of 'knowledge how' are 'nested' or related in such a way that possession of the first is necessitated by possession of the second and so on. I will adopt the order of exposition that corresponds to the order of necessitation. One should be aware that although the nesting relationship is an important one it does not apply in every case. There may be cases where a 'higher' form of 'knowledge how' does not necessarily imply possession of a lower one. We need also to be aware of the role of personal characteristics that do not fit readily into the nesting analogy.

It should also be noted that none of these forms of know-how in any way precludes the possibility that systematic, disciplinary(or subject) knowledge may be necessary to exercise them. It is too often assumed that 'skill' and 'knowledge' are incompatibles. It is to be hoped that what has been said above is sufficient to dispel that idea. Professional expertise depends crucially on the ability to use systematic knowledge to inform practical judgment and action.

Technique

When one performs a task or carries out a procedure there is invariably a way in which one does so. This way may be more or less fully describable by the performer or an observer. Thus there is a way of planing a piece of wood, of boiling an egg, plastering a wall, laying a line of bricks, no less than there is for auditing an account or diagnosing a patient's illness. Typically a central part of professional education involves training in the performance of a technique. Mastery of a technique is usually a necessary condition of performing a relevant task. Again this applies as much to teaching a class, undertaking a chemical analysis or laying a line of bricks. However, it is not sufficient for someone to have acquired a skill that they have mastered a technique. Training in techniques is thus very important, but a professional education that confines itself to techniques is sorely lacking. Why is this? To understand this we need to look at the closely related concept of *skill*.

Skill

To have acquired a skill in carrying out a type of task is to have acquired the ability to carry it out in *contextually relevant conditions* (one of Stanley and Williamson's (2001) criteria for the possession of know-how). The contextually relevant conditions in which a skill needs to be practised in professional situations will typically include factors such as the following: commercial, financial and temporal constraints; variable and sometimes difficult weather conditions; hazardous external circumstances (e.g., speed, heights); the need to work with colleagues and customers; the lack of opportunity to correct errors and the exigencies of health and safety and legal restrictions; and, last but not least, the need to produce an excellent product or service within these operational conditions. These constraints are hardly trivial and they often make considerable demands on the inner resources of the professional worker. It can easily be seen that the conditions of practising a skill in 'operational conditions' are considerable and much more demanding than the bare practice of a technique in, for example, a workshop in non-commercial conditions. This is not to say, of course, that learning to master a technique does not make demands on and develop the character of the individual, particularly if the technique is a very intricate and demanding one to learn, drawing on systematic knowledge for its exercise. However, it is arguable in the practice of a skill in commercial or work conditions that it is not merely the ability to *acquire* the skill (i.e., to practise the technique in operational conditions), but its *exercise* that draws on personal resources of character above and beyond those required for the acquisition and practice of a technique. It is thus not true to assert, as some authors have done, that skill (or for that matter, technique) does not involve the exercise of personal characteristics such as courage, persistence, diligence, concentration, conscientiousness and attention to detail (e.g., Gough, 2013).

Although the term 'skill' is very often promiscuously used to denote any kind of practical ability, there is a range of contexts in which its use is utterly appropriate. These include manual and co-ordinative abilities, as well as intellectual ones (the skill of mental calculation when one is a shopkeeper, for example). There is even some sense in talking of 'social skills', provided this phrase is confined to the exercise of social technique in relevant social situations: tactfulness, politeness and adherence to etiquette and other norms are all good examples. However, it is quite wrong to identify the totality of an individual's abilities to interact with other human beings as 'social' or 'soft' skills, as this suggests that such abilities are largely manipulative, involving the practising of techniques in order to get what one wants from other people. Our social abilities invariably involve exercise of the *virtues*, which are not a separate action category but aspects of the ways in which we treat other people when we are not considering them merely as instruments for the satisfaction of our own wishes. We now need to consider those abilities that are not skills, although they may presuppose the possession of skills.

Transversal abilities

Many things that we do are dependent on our practice of certain skills but are not to be identified with them. They are not reducible to the practice of skills, nor are the same skills necessarily exercised in each case. English does not have a ready word for these abilities, which is one reason why they tend to be lumped together with skills, although Gilbert Ryle identified them as a subspecies of what he called 'adverbial verbs' (Ryle, 1979). German is able to make the distinction between *Fertigkeiten* (skills) and *Fähigkeiten* (transversal abilities) and the distinction is central to the design of professional curricula in countries following the German tradition. The ones that are particularly relevant in a discussion of professional education are those employed in work contexts, typically such as the abilities to: plan, co-ordinate, control, communicate and evaluate among others. They should be distinguished from 'planning skills', 'communication skills', etc. Why? Because one can exercise a 'planning skill' (e.g., drawing a flowchart, making a diagram) without actually planning *per se*. One can exercise the 'planning skill' without actually being able to 'plan' and in many cases individuals can 'plan' without necessarily commanding the apparently necessary 'planning skill' that may be set out in a professional curriculum. Planning, considered as something over and above exercising a planning skill, involves a degree of care about the outcome and a degree of attention to ensure that the outcome is achieved and this requirement is not captured by the exercise of particular 'planning skills', such as drawing a flowchart. Naturally one may plan and fail to carry out the plan, but one can also exercise 'planning skills' and do no more than merely 'go through the motions' of planning. It is this care and attention to the success of a complex outcome that is one major factor distinguishing transversal abilities from skills (cf. Winch, 2013b for more on the relationship between skills and transversal abilities).

It is obvious that such abilities are absolutely central to a profession's claim to autonomy in the workplace, that is, the ability to act without instructions or supervision. If such abilities (rather than their associated skills) are not recognised within professional curricula then it is reasonable to conclude that such curricula are not concerned with the development of professional workers who are able to operate independently. They are also a prerequisite for the ability, not just to perform tasks but to manage projects.

Project management abilities

There is no neat separation between the concepts of a *task* and a *project*. Nevertheless, we can say that, along a continuum, there are significant differences between the challenges that we set for ourselves in terms of *duration, complexity* and *scope for judgement* and *decision-making*. At one end of this spectrum we find projects. The ability to carry out a project is fundamental to many occupations. Thus, one would expect a professional bricklayer to build a two-storey house (as with the French CAP Macon qualification (see official definition on www.cfbtp-lemans.com/product/certificat-aptitude-professionnelle-maconnerie/for example) rather than merely to be able to lay lines of bricks, for a nurse to heal a patient (as opposed to merely be able to dress a wound), and for a farmer to carry out a year's farming operations (rather than plant a field of turnips).

Ability to manage a project in this sense entails that one does not need to be managed by someone else in relation to the execution of the project. Not only does the ability entail personal independence and responsibility but it necessitates the involvement of transversal abilities as well as skills. Typically, the management of a project involves the articulation of a sequence (often with recursive sub-cycles) from planning, through execution (including the overcoming of unplanned difficulties) to evaluation of success. Project management ability thus presupposes the acquisition of relevant skills and transversal abilities.

Are any of these different degrees of practical ability *transferable* and should this possibility be reflected in the design of professional curricula? The answer is perhaps a little surprising. There is little difficulty in showing that some skills (and the exercise of relevant techniques) can be exercised in a variety of different contexts, some more so than others. The abilities to read and write are perhaps prime examples. But does the ability to plan in the context of, say, bricklaying, transfer to the writing of novels? This is not necessarily the case as not only is the type of planning involved likely to be very different in each case, but the skills involved in the activity and hence in understanding of the activity are also likely to be different. The *transversality* of an ability involving the mobilisation of different skills by no means implies its *transferability* between different activities; the ability to manage a project in one field of endeavour can often tell us little about an individual's ability to do so in another.

However, it would not be true either to say that the acquisition of project management ability (and associated transversal abilities) in one area had no bearing on one's ability to do so in another. The reason may be found in the personal characteristics that are often necessary prerequisites of the exercise of such complex abilities as project management. The ability to carry through a successful project management cycle with its appropriate planning, co-ordinating, communicating, controlling and evaluating abilities makes considerable demands on the character of an individual who is capable of doing so. Patience, consideration for others, persistence, reflectiveness, adaptability, self-discipline, etc., are all both developed and required in the management of a project. Possession of these does not automatically mean that one will display them in other contexts, but it does involve a certain resilience, which may well make it more likely for individuals who can manage a project in one field of endeavour to acquire the necessary abilities in another sphere of activity, the more so if that sphere is in some way cognate with the one in which the ability was first acquired.

Thus transferability may in such cases arise via the development of personal characteristics rather than through the acquisition of skills. The possibility should be borne in mind by professional curriculum designers, while they should not at the same time lose sight of the constraints imposed by the particularities of the sphere in which the project management ability is first developed. We now turn to what many would think the ultimate aim of a professional education, the development of a comprehensive ability to practise the occupation.

Occupational capacity

The ability to manage a project successfully is, in many countries, not just a precondition of becoming a practitioner of an occupation but potentially of others as well. However, whatever occupation one settles on, *occupational capacity* is important and presupposes the abilities discussed in the previous subsections. This is particularly the case in those societies that have well-developed and formally defined conceptions of an occupation such as the German *Beruf*, which entail a wide ranging, interlocking sphere of activity as well as an established place in the social order for individuals who acquire occupational capacity (*berufliche Handlungsfähigkeit*) and practice it (Greinert, 2007; Hanf, 2011).

What does a fully-formed occupational capacity look like? Self-evidently it encompasses the varieties of professional know-how already described, but there are other important attributes. The first of these concerns *knowledge*. Nothing said so far about the exercise of skills and transversal abilities excludes the application of knowledge (including systematic knowledge) to practice. Indeed, in societies with well-developed forms of occupation, this is more or less the norm. However, the development of occupational capacity brings new requirements for knowledge in the form of systematic underpinning knowledge required for the practice of the occupation as a whole, including crucially, knowledge of the principles underlying practice of the occupation, including those necessary to understand how it responds to social and technological change (an aspect of what the Germans call 'Methodenkompetenz'). As we have already seen, a great deal of underpinning systematic knowledge is best conceptualised as a combination of 'know that' and 'know-how', as well as acknowledging that reflection on elements of underpinning knowledge can be a prelude to judgement and action. In addition, however, occupational capacity in a fully developed form entails civic awareness and know-how that encompass an understanding of the impact of the occupation practised, not just on related occupations, but also on the wider society.

The wider point is that one cannot intelligibly consider occupational capacity *solely* in terms of considerations internal to the occupation. The ends of the occupation do not themselves make sense except in terms of the economic activities that they serve and, more broadly to the extent that they satisfy human wants and needs. So occupational capacity also has to involve consideration of occupational ends in relation to the rest of the society. Some of these are more 'inward looking' than others: those connected with excellence in the way in which the goods are produced or service undertaken are a case in point, although even here, to the extent that there are effects beyond the occupation, these do need to be taken account of by practitioners. Those occupational ends themselves do not usually exist just as ends in themselves without any further means. Occupations make sense within a society because of their role in the division of labour and their contribution to the society/culture as a whole.

While it is possible for educational and commercial purposes to focus on activities that do have a strong intra-occupational focus, a broader professional education needs to take account of the ways in which the aims of the occupation relate to sectoral and ultimately social, civic and political aims. This also goes for the *effects* as well as the *aims* of an occupation, for these often apply well beyond the occupation, both in the way that the productive activities of the occupation impact on the wider society, and in terms of the way in which the products and services associated with the occupation have such an impact.

Why should professional education concern itself with such issues? The issue of the ends of occupations is, in one sense, unproblematic. Those ends are specified by a description of the kind of activity that it is; so for example medicine by the various activities involved in curing and preventing sickness, farming by the production of foodstuffs, and so on. However, closer inspection suggests that, within such a broad framework, there is the potential for variation. Practitioners of medicine, and therefore the medical curriculum, should consider whether, for example, prevention or cure should be priorities, what the limits of medical intervention ought to be, or the extent to which they should draw attention to extra-medical influences on mortality and morbidity (Wilkinson, 2005). Likewise, agricultural education for future farmers should consider such issues as environmental sustainability, the ethics of animal care and the health implications of what they produce (Kerschensteiner, 1901).[2]

If it be said that the only business of people in business is to make money or to satisfy shareholders then that is a particular (if contestable) answer to issues of occupational *telos* and not a dismissal of the question, as might at first be thought. Recent events in the financial world have drawn attention to the lack of thought that has been given to the question of the *telos* of banking and other financial activities, to the side-effects of those activities and to the narrow range of professional education that bankers often have, including at the highest levels. The consequences of such neglect are, quite obviously, far from trivial for the rest of society.

To summarise the discussion, it is possible to distinguish between two related aspects of the capacities associated with professional occupations that need to be considered in the construction of a comprehensive professional curriculum:

OC1: The integration of skill, knowledge, transversal abilities, virtues and attitudes, project management ability, in an overall ability to pursue, develop and nurture an *occupational telos*, the internal aims of the occupation.

OC2: The civic dimension and awareness and commitment to the extra-occupational (external) goods and bads that practice of the occupation may engender (the occupation's civic dimension).

The range of practical knowledge that can be considered part of a professional education has been considered. Curriculum designers may wish to ignore one or more of these aspects and there are clear cultural differences in the ways in which know-how and occupations are considered, which have a profound impact on professional education in different countries. In this chapter a framework for thinking about such issues has been set out that it is hoped may clarify some of the issues that arise in the design of professional curriculum curricula. It is, however, hoped that this framework will be exploited in order to enhance the quality of what is currently offered in professional education.

Putting theory into practice: the concept of professional judgement

It is often asserted that the key claim of a professional to that status is the ability to put their specialised knowledge into effect in professional judgments in work situations (e.g., Eraut, 1994). All that has been argued for here is consonant with that view. It is worth adding, however, that the judgements made are not usually just technical ones but also involve ethical and political considerations to which one's personal and occupational values are highly relevant. There is nothing mysterious about the link between reasoning, judgment and action. One of the most important matters that the curriculum for professional education should be concerned with is the development of the ability to reason, judge and act in complex and unpredictable work situations, and this should be reflected in appropriate assessment arrangements linked to professional curricula.

The best way to assess someone's ability to make appropriate judgments and to act on them is to get them to make such judgments and to act on them. It is also highly likely that we would wish to explore with them *post hoc* why they made such judgments and not others. It is futile to try to observe and to assess the *act of judgment*, because, as Geach (1958) argued, although such judgments are undoubtedly *episodic* rather than *dispositional* they are not necessarily *clockable* in real time (Geach (1958); see also Ryle, 1949, Chapter 5). Although the ability to make such judgments is a practical ability (which has to be acquired), it is far from clear that it involves some kind of mental technique. It is better to see our judgmental abilities arising from our communicative abilities such as to assert, to reason and to justify. These are then developed into a form of soliloquy and ultimately internal dialogue or even unthinking action (a trait of professional expertise probably given too much emphasis in the writings of, for example, Dreyfus and Dreyfus, 1996). Many of the things that we are able to do are partly beyond our ability to describe them; this does not make such abilities any less real (Read and Hutchinson, 2011). It is sufficient to say that we can acquire the abilities to judge and to act on judgment as extensions of other abilities (which in the context of this chapter include both skills and transversal abilities, such as being able to communicate and evaluate) and that we can readily judge whether an individual has acquired such abilities and to what extent. It is indeed odd to say that someone 'knows how' to make a judgment as this implies the presence of a technique for doing so. While this may be the case in some circumstances or for some aspects of judgment it is not universally the case. It was pointed out earlier that there is not necessarily a technique available for the exercise of every ability involved in professional action. Often we learn how to make good judgments not by learning a technique for judgment but by having to make decisions in difficult circumstances and then (possibly) reflecting on those decisions. The possibilities for doing so in conditions of increasing complexity should be built into the professional curriculum.

Conclusion: creating a curriculum framework – choice points and the possibility of comparision

In this chapter an attempt has been made first to identify the main components of a professional curriculum and second to show how these are related to each other so as to create a process of 'epistemic ascent' from novice-hood to expertise. It has been deliberately general, although it includes nothing that does not figure somewhere in professional curricula found in European countries. Many policy-makers, employers and indeed employees in the Anglo-Saxon countries might be inclined to dismiss large parts of what I have discussed as 'nice to know but not necessary to know'. Persuading them otherwise is likely to be a long and arduous business. A necessary preliminary, however, is to show that even when one constructs a very restricted curriculum, one is making choices, namely choices that may devalue certain kinds of know that, know-how or personal characteristics. My contention is that curriculum designers should be aware of such choices and should account for those that they do make.

Notes

1 Contrary to what some seem to have supposed (e.g., Ryle, 1949) the ability to draw on systematic knowledge as a prelude to action does not entail commitment to metaphysical dualism (see discussion later in this chapter).
2 Cf. Kerschensteiner, G. [1901] for a discussion of these issues in relation to vocational education.

References

Aristotle (1925) *Nichomachean Ethics*. David Ross (ed.). London, Dent.
Barrow, R. (1976) *Commonsense and the curriculum*. Oxford: Routledge.
Brandom, R. (2000) *Articulating reasons: An introduction to inferentialism*. Cambridge, MA: Harvard University Press.
Coles, M. (2007) *Qualifications frameworks in Europe – Platforms for qualifications, integration and reform*. EU Education and Culture DG: Brussels.
Dreyfus, H.L. and Dreyfus, S.E. (1996) 'The relationship of theory and practice in the acquisition of skill', in P.Benner, C.A. Tanner and C.A.Chesla (1996) *Expertise in nursing practice*. New York: Springer.
Eraut, M. (1994) *Developing professional knowledge and competence*. Brighton: The Falmer Press.
Everitt, N. and Fisher, A. (2000) *Modern epistemology*. London: McGraw Hill.
Geach, P. (1958) *Mental acts*. London: Routledge.
Greinert, W.-D. (2007) 'The German system of vocational education', in L. Clarke and C. Winch (eds) (2007) *Vocational education: International approaches, developments and systems*. Oxford: Routledge (pp. 49–61).
Gough, M. (2013) *What is really wrong with 'skills talk' and why caring is not a virtue*. Philosophy of Education Society, 2013. Available online at: www.philosophy-of-education.org/uploads/2013%20Conference/Papers/Gough.pdf (accessed on 30 August, 2013).
Hamm, C. (1989) *Philosophical issues in education*. Brighton: Falmer.

Hanf, G. (2011). 'The changing relevance of the *beruf*', in M. Brockmann, L. Clarke, G. Hanf, P. Mehaut, A. Westerhuis, and C. Winch (eds), *Knowledge, skills and competence in the European labour market* (pp. 50–67). Oxford: Routledge.

Hirst, P.H. (1965) 'Liberal education and the nature of knowledge', in R. Archambault (ed.) *Philosophical analysis and education*. London: Routledge.

Kerschensteiner, G. [1901] *Staatsbürgerliche Erziehung für der deutschen Jugend* in *Ausgewählte Pädagogische Texte*, Band 1, Paderborn, Ferdinand Schöningh (1964).

Moyal-Sharrock, D. (2007) *Understanding Wittgenstein's 'on certainty'*. Basingstoke: Palgrave Macmillan.

Muller, J. (2012) 'Forms of knowledge and curriculum coherence', in H. Lauder, M. Young, H. Daniels, M. Balarin and J. Lowe (2012) *Education for the knowledge economy?: Critical perspectives*. Oxford: Routledge (pp. 114–38).

Phillips, D.Z. (2001) *Wittgenstein's 'on certainty'? There like our life*. Oxford: Routledge.

Read, R. and Hutchinson, P. (2011) 'De-mystifying tacit knowing and clues: A comment on Henry *et al.*' *Journal of Evaluation In Clinical Practice*, *17*: 944–47.

Ryle, G. (1949) *The concept of mind*. London: Hutchinson.

—— (1979) *On thinking*. London: Hutchinson.

Searle, J.R. (2005) *The construction of social reality*. New York: The Free Press.

Stanley, J. and Williamson, T. (2001) 'Knowing how', *Journal of Philosophy*, XCVIII.8: 411–44.

Wilkinson, R. (2005) *The impact of inequality: How to make sick societies healthier*. London: Routledge.

Winch, C. (2013a) 'Curriculum design and epistemic ascent', *Journal of Philosophy of Education*, 47, 1: 128–46.

—— (2013b) 'Three different conceptions of know-how and their relevance to professional and vocational education', *Journal of Philosophy of Education*, 47 (2): 281–98.

5 Differentiating forms of professional expertise

Ben Kotzee

Introduction: the concept of 'expertise' in professional education

One of the interesting features of what is called the 'knowledge economy' (Drucker, 1969) is the sheer variety of the professional work that people do. The Standard Occupational Classification (2010) in use in the United Kingdom, United States and many other countries around the world, for instance, lists 840 separate occupational types. Even though many different forms of professional expertise exist, most theories of expertise within the field of professional education cast expertise in the same light. According to what has become the dominant way of thinking about expertise in professional education, expertise is developed through long practice in a field and not through theoretical study. As Eraut holds:

> Although many areas of professional knowledge are dependent on some understanding of relevant public, codified knowledge found in books and journals, professional knowledge is constructed through experience and its nature depends on the cumulative acquisition, selection and interpretation of that experience.
>
> (1994: 20)

The view in question has deep roots and echoes Ryle's (1949) distinction between knowing how and knowing that and Polanyi's (1966) discussion of the importance of tacit knowledge. However, it is safe to hold that thinking about the nature of 'expertise' within education is dominated by two conceptions of how a person becomes expert at something: Donald Schön's (1983) 'reflective practice' model of expertise and Hubert and Stuart Dreyfus's (1986) 'stage' model of expertise.[1]

Winch (2010) characterises the Dreyfus and Schön accounts of expertise as 'fluency' accounts of expertise. These models question the importance of theoretical knowledge to expertise and construe expertise, instead, as the ability to perform at a high level fluently and effortlessly on the basis of long practice in the domain. Because, according to this way of thinking, highly developed forms of expertise are largely unconscious, professional educators have, for some time, down-played the importance of *academic* or *theoretical* education as part of professional education and have, instead, placed more importance on the acquisition and evaluation of professional *competencies* and *generic skills* (such as problem solving, teamwork, critical thinking, etc.) through practice.

In this chapter, I will make the case that, while the field of education conceives of expertise mainly in terms of what Winch calls the fluency account, the view from other academic fields is more nuanced. I will briefly sketch the dominant approaches to expertise in three adjacent fields: philosophy, sociology and psychology. I conclude that taking a 'fluency' approach to expertise ignores what I call the 'differentiatedness' of expertise – the fact that different forms of expertise differ from each other in significant ways. I will end by sketching an account of how one must differentiate different forms of expertise from one another in order properly to understand them.

Three approaches to expertise

The philosophy of expertise: Ryle and after

Ryle (1946, 1949) famously distinguished between knowing how and knowing that. In making the distinction, Ryle sought to undermine what he saw as a Cartesian view of the mind – the 'intellectualist' picture according to which acting intelligently is a matter of being guided by a set of mental rules for the performance of that action. Ryle's argument can be summarised as follows. If the intellectualist picture is right, then any action must be preceded by an act of thinking or contemplating how that action should be done. But any act of thinking or contemplation will *itself* be a doing – weighing up the options and deciding how to do something is, after all, a mental act. But how does one know how to perform this mental act of contemplating what one should do? Would it, too, have to be preceded by another mental act in which one contemplates and decides how to execute the mental act that was to precede the action we were trying to explain? If so, Ryle holds, this would lead to a regress (1949: 30).

Rather than holding that knowing how comes down to having an intellectual grasp of the procedures or techniques involved in doing things, Ryle holds that knowing how comes down to '. . . a capacity for or a disposition to a set of behaviors . . .' (Fantl, 2008: 455). Most interpret Ryle as holding that knowing how comes down to ability. The key to know-how is not that someone is able of theoretically describing how something should be done, but that they are actually able to do that thing. Ryle's anti-intellectualism has played a significant role in underpinning (what Winch calls) fluency accounts of expertise that stress practical ability over theoretical knowledge when it comes to knowing how.

While influential in education, Carr points out why one need not believe the 'ability' account (1981: 53–4). First, we are very well acquainted with people who know *how* to do something without actually being able to do it. Take, for instance, this fictional example:

Raymond Blanc, the world's greatest chef, knows how to make an excellent omelette. He loses his arms in a car accident and is no longer able to make omelettes. However, he retains his knowledge how to make omelettes . . .

(Snowdon, 2004: 8)

The example illustrates that ability is not necessary for knowledge how and neither does being able to do something suffice for knowing how. Take this example by Carr (1979: 407):

Suppose a famous dancer was to perform before an audience, an item from his repertoire to which he has himself given the following title:

A Performance of Improvisation No. 15.

To the astonishment of a member of the audience who just happens to be an expert on communications, the movements of the dancer turn out to resemble an accurate (movement perfect) semaphore version of Gray's 'Elegy', though the dancer is quite unaware of this fact.

In the example, the dancer is quite clearly *able* to signal Gray's Elegy in semaphore, however, the dancer clearly does not *know how to* signal Gray's Elegy in semaphore.

Even more skeptical about Ryle's anti-intellectualism than Carr are Stanley and Williamson. Stanley and Williamson (2001) hold that knowing how should really be understood as a form of knowing that. What one really knows when one knows how to do something, Stanley and Williamson hold, is an answer to a question of the form 'how does one do x?' Stanley and Williamson offer an intellectualist account of knowledge how – an account in terms of knowing the *procedure* by which one does something.[2]

That the philosophy of knowledge how today splits between those advocating an intellectualist and those advocating an anti-intellectualist position should give one pause in thinking that Ryle had settled the question once and for all in favour of the view that knowledge how is distinctly different from knowledge that (and that it can only be acquired through experience).[3] Furthermore, even among those who defend Ryle's anti-intellectualism regarding knowledge how, great scepticism exists regarding what is commonly taken to follow from this position, *viz.* that theoretical knowledge is largely unimportant to developed expertise. According to Winch (2009), Ryle himself was guilty of portraying vocational education in too narrow a light as mere skill. One assumes that this criticism also extends to Rylean views of professional education and, in general, a more capacious understanding of education for work is needed that includes both theoretical and practical knowledge. While such an account can be reconciled with anti-intellectualism regarding knowledge how, the received view regarding knowledge how in the field of professional education still trades very heavily on Ryle and needs to be updated in many respects.

Approaches in psychology

According to Chi (2006) the psychological study of expertise today tends to approach expertise in one of two broad ways: the 'absolute' and the 'relative' approaches:

Absolute expertise   Those who follow the absolute approach to the study of expertise work by identifying exceptional practitioners in some domain (e.g., science, sports, music, etc.) and asking what enables this exceptional performance. Pertinently, on this view, experts are exceptional practitioners and are identified in terms of some absolute criterion of how well someone performs a task.

Relative expertise   Those who follow the relative approach to expertise do not see expertise as a property of exceptional people alone, but view expertise as a continuum. Rather than some absolute point of proficiency where 'expertise' starts, on this view, anyone who takes part in an activity can be said to have expertise in that activity to a greater or lesser degree; the greater skilled are called the 'experts' and those lesser skilled the 'novices'. The aim of the approach is not to identify what enables exceptional performance, but to study what leads to *improvement* – how do the less skilled become more skilled.

In addition to distinguishing between absolute and relative approaches, Chi also holds that expertise may be studied from two further perspectives:

1   ways in which experts excel at what they do, and
2   ways in which experts fall short in what they do.

Both the first and the second of these may alert one to what is distinctive about expert cognition and problem solving in that expert judgement seems to present certain advantages over lay performance but also comes with some associated costs.

Psychologists have derived different theories regarding the nature of expertise. According to Ericsson, expertise may amount to:

- individual differences in people's mental capacities (primarily, but not limited to intelligence)
- extended experience in the domain of expertise
- a qualitatively different (and superior) organisation of knowledge of the domain
- elite achievement resulting from the experience of a superior learning environment
- superior performance on selective tasks.

(Ericsson, 2006: 10–4)

Like the philosophy of expertise, the psychology of expertise provides mixed support for the view – common in education – that expertise is largely intuitive

Table 5.1

Ways in which experts excel	Ways in which experts fall short
• Experts generate the best solution (and do so more quickly and accurately than non-experts).	• Expertise is domain limited – experts do not excel outside their domain.
• Experts can detect features of a situation that novices cannot.	• Experts can be overly confident.
• Experts spend much time presenting problem situations to themselves qualitatively, including the right domain-specific and general information.	• Experts are prone to glossing over surface details.
• Experts are good at monitoring their own understanding and performance.	• Experts are dependent on contextual clues presented in their domain.
• Experts are more successful at choosing problem-solving strategies than novices.	• Experts can be inflexible.
• Experts are capitalising on opportunistic resources and information.	• Experts can be inaccurate in predicting what novices will be able to do.
• Experts use their cognitive efforts economically – they can retrieve information easily, can act automatically and can exert cognitive control.	• Experts can be biased and fixated on their own special domain.

Source: adapted from Chi, 2006: 23–7.

and developed through practice more than theoretical study. Criticising the Dreyfus approach, Gobet and Chassy (2009) discuss evidence that, depending on the domain, the growth of expertise is not a simple process of decreasing abstract or theoretical thought leading to an increase of more intuitive concrete thought. They cite the example of expertise in the domain of academic physics where it is the experts – naturally! – who reason at a 'deep, abstract level' and the novices who reason at a 'superficial, concrete level'. This contradicts the Dreyfus view. Furthermore, Gobet and Chassy cast doubt on whether the novice developing towards expertise always necessarily passes through a stage-like route to expertise. As Dall'Alba and Sandberg (2006) also point out, learners may skip a stage or fall back; one may even be in one stage in some aspects of a task while being in an earlier stage in some other aspect of a task. Gobet and Chassy explain that a progression from rule-based to intuitive knowledge and action is in many expertises accompanied by a greater ability to deal with abstraction and theory. This does not square well with the Dreyfus theory, nor with the educational idea that theory is unimportant to well-developed expertise.

Expertise has been studied in many domains, not only chess, but also medicine and surgery, flying, driving, software design, writing, music, sport, mathematics, etc. Depending on the specific form of expertise, the Dreyfus model, again, looks out of place. In fields in which verbal skill are important (such as writing) there is, obviously, far less stress on tacit knowledge that is manifested in physical ability. For instance, writing expertise depends on highly domain-specific knowledge (Kellogg, 2006) and in a field like software design, long practice does not necessarily lead to better performance – experience does not translate straightforwardly to higher ability (Butterworth, 2006). Even for what one would see as a relatively intuitive, or bodily task – flying – authors such as Schanefeldt *et al.* (1985) and Stokes, Kemper and Kite (1997) report that differences of knowledge exist between novice and expert pilots and are important. Whereas novices and experts do not show vast differences in declarative knowledge, the knowledge of the experts was found to be better organised; furthermore, the experts were more able to apply their declarative knowledge to problem situations (Durso and Dattel, 2006: 366).

Approaches in sociology

According to Evetts, Mieg and Felt (2006: 105), the interest of sociology in the notion of expertise has to do with understanding the '. . . contextual conditions of the development of expertise and its functions in modern societies'. Sociological interest in expertise has always been tied up with the study of the professions – those social groups that, as Abbott has it, 'institutionalises expertise in people' (1988: 323). Early studies of expertise in sociology focussed on understanding what sets the professions apart from other occupations. Among the distinguishing features of professions that were proposed were:

- a higher form of education and training as a prerequisite for working in the field
- public service
- a professional body
- a professional code of conduct
- a special relationship of trust and confidentiality with a client
- etc.

(For discussion, see Evetts *et al.*, 2006: 108 and Saks, 2012)

However, the definitional project fell out of favour due to the fact that a list of characteristics that all professions share was hard to pin down and also because there were many occupations that would count as professions under some but not all definitions. Furthermore, the criticism was expressed that lists of characteristics of professions were manipulated to 'glorify' some of the dominant professions over the others and that they were really a product of the ideology of the dominant professions rather than objective description (Saks, 2012).

Since the 1950s, sociologists who take a perspective on the process by which professions form argued that the professions do not have all of the characteristics attributed to them automatically, but that the rights and privileges of professional status were acquired after a process of political and economic manoeuvring by professional bodies. Many of these analyses, for instance by Larson (1977), were sceptical about this process and saw professionalisation mainly as an attempt to secure a monopoly on providing a certain service and to control the suppliers and fees of those in the profession. Such analyses were given weight by, for instance, Abbott's (1988) description of how professions carve out and maintain a jurisdiction. However, authors such as Freidson (1994) are more sanguine and hold that the monopoly and power of professions are not as complete or as stable as the more sceptical accounts contend. Rather than a 'conspiracy against the laity', the professions may represent an important organisational form that provides complex or specialised services to the public (and in which professionals are rewarded for that effort with autonomy and a certain degree of privilege) that is essentially non-bureaucratic or outside direct state control.

In addition to the professions, sociology has long been interested in another form of social organisation structured around the idea of expertise: science. In the sociology of science, Collins and Evans's (2006, 2007) work on expertise is perhaps best known. In contrast with the sceptical approach of, for instance, Larson (and in contrast with the scepticism of figures like Barnes (1977) and Bloor (1976) regarding scientific experts) Collins suggests that the field of science studies should acknowledge that scientific experts exist and that it is proper that non-experts follow expert advice regarding technical matters of public policy. Collins and Evans hold that the task of science studies is to design a 'normative theory of expertise', that is a theory that seeks to understand when expert advice should be followed in public policy and asks: '. . . who should and who should not be contributing to decision-making in virtue of their expertise' (Collins and Evans, 2006: 53). Collins and Evans's key innovation is to point out that it is not necessarily and not only the usual credentialed scientists (who work in universities or large research organisations) that should be counted as experts. Collins and Evans, for instance, identify striking examples of lay people who can make contributions to expert debate.[4] They also identify novel forms of expertise such as 'interactional expertise' that may be held by those who are not credentialed scientists in a specific field themselves, but have come to have an insider's knowledge of the field through regular social contact (Collins, 2004; Giles, 2006). Be that as it may, Collins and Evans locate the reason *why* the general public should defer to experts (whether they are credentialed scientists or lay people with a particular expertise to contribute) in the realm of the specialised or esoteric knowledge that they possess. What is essential, Collins and Evans hold, is the communicative ability that experts have in being able to co-operate with each other while drawing on the same body of theories and concepts; as such Collins and Evans place what lends legitimacy to experts more in the realm of theoretical than practical knowledge.[5]

The importance of knowing vs. doing in different domains

Different authors bring us to the same point. Is expertise essentially propositional – does it ultimately come down to having theoretical, verbal knowledge – or does it come down to being able to perform an action? An important observation to make at this stage is that the debate is very often conducted in terms of competing examples of knowing how to do things and that different examples often pull our instincts in different directions.

One anti-intellectualist example that is very popular in education is Polanyi's example of how one cannot state how to ride a bicycle. Even though I know how to ride a bicycle, I am not capable of explaining fully how I do it, showing, it is thought, that knowing how to do something and having available an explanation of how one does it are not the same thing. The example is of course, picked to fit the point and the use of very physical examples like cycling has been criticised by, for instance, Collins (2007) and McDowell (2007a and 2007b). Reacting to Dreyfus's example regarding how performance at sports (in this case, baseball) declines as one over-intellectualises an action, McDowell points out that this does not mean that the sportsperson's knowledge is in principle ineffable; rather, in some situations it is psychologically advisable and in others not advisable to verbalise the rules of what one is doing to oneself as one is doing it.[6]

Against these physical examples, in fact, an intellectualist can put up her own examples. Take the one of mental calculation: while many different procedures exist for mental calculation, it is important that – at least within one calculation series – one sticks to the same procedure. In certain other domains I can imagine, saying how one does what one does can even be thought to be essential to being able to do that thing. Take book-keeping or arguing a case in a court of law. Knowing how to do both of these things involves knowing how to represent – in exhaustive detail – exactly what one does at the same time that one is doing it. In book-keeping, for instance, one not only keeps track of money in different accounts and under different items in different accounts; one represents the presence and flow of money very explicitly and in a format that another person can understand completely. Part of good book-keeping is that it is understandable and clearly done in accordance with rules (the accounting rules). So too with arguing a case in a court of law: what one argues has to be clear and justifiable to anyone. In book-keeping and making a legal case, one may say, it is an important part of the thought process of the professional that it is both rule-guided and verbally transparent to another. While there are probably decisions that accountants and lawyers take intuitively, much of the quality of their work *depends* on its being not only correct in terms of the rules, but transparently in terms of the rules.

The point in all the foregoing has been to argue that – whatever knowing how is – it appears more or less intellectualist based on the *example* of knowing how that one appeals to (or based on the knowledge domain from which the example is drawn). Simply put, some expertises appear more and others less tacit.

The differentiatedness of expertise

How can one distinguish between different forms of expertise?

Recently, Collins (2013) has proposed a new model that points the way. Collins holds that most theories of expertise in psychology and philosophy have only stressed one facet of expertise and that is the degree to which expert performance changes as the novice progresses (through the various stages) towards expertise. In addition, Collins also stresses two other facets:

- the degree to which an expertise is 'esoteric', that is, the degree to which the expertise is widely distributed or the degree to which it is confined to few people
- the degree to which an expertise requires tacit knowledge.

Thinking in terms of these three dimensions of expertise yields a three-dimensional view of expertise (see Figure 5.1).

For Collins, as the novice becomes more expert, she moves from the front towards the back along the depth or z-axis; for Collins, this movement is seen as a process whereby the novice gradually becomes accepted as a member of the expert group. However, as far as movement along the x and y-axes goes, the picture is more complex than that – greater expertise is not always accompanied by an increase in tacit knowledge or an increase in esotericity.[7]

First, the novice gradually becoming accepted into the group of experts does not always imply an equal degree of growth in tacit knowledge. Collins mentions the example of expert performance in arithmetic or memory tasks. Experts at these tasks have both a very esoteric skill (placing them high on the y-axis) and are accepted as experts (placing them high on the z-axis) without having much tacit knowledge (placing them low on the x-axis). Collins holds that we should also classify expertise at chess or expertise at (the computer programming involved

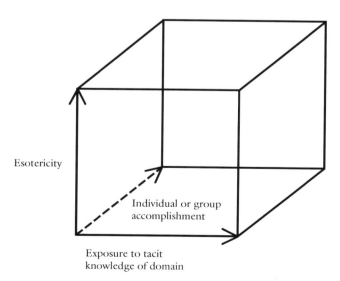

Figure 5.1 Collins's expertise space diagram (Collins, 2013: Figure 2).

in) artificial intelligence in the same way: seeing as these do not involve very much physical effort, but do involve much mental effort, it seems plausible to classify expert chess players as people who are both firmly embedded in some group of experts (high on z) and having a very esoteric ability (high on y), while demonstrating only moderate tacit knowledge (placing them low or in the middle on the x-axis).[8]

Second, Collins also considers the question whether growth in expertise, as well as gradual acceptance into a community of experts, always implies one's expertise becoming comparatively more rare or 'esoteric'. That this is so is not clear-cut. Take fairly widely distributed forms of expertise such as driving a car or speaking English. Both driving and speaking a language are very complex skills. While they can be seen as forms of expertise,[9] Collins holds, these forms of expertise are not esoteric, but are widely distributed. To put it in the language of the three-dimensional classification of forms of expertise, expertise at driving or speaking English involves socialisation in a group of experts (high on z) and much tacit knowledge (high on x) even though it does not involve much esotericity (low on y).

Expanding Collins's account for professional education

In taking seriously the differences between different forms of expertise, Collins's three-dimensional account of expertise is salutary. However, it also raises a number of questions:

1   The usefulness of the depth dimension. So far, we have been considering the usefulness of Collins's expertise space diagram in distinguishing different forms of expertise from each other. An important point to notice in this regard is that acquiring expertise *always* involves moving back along the z-axis, but does not always involve moving very far on the y-axis and x-axis. While it may be handy to keep in mind this movement along the z-axis, it seems that – in a sense – the z-axis is redundant when it comes to the interesting *differences* between various forms of expertise and that Collins could illustrate the differences in two dimensions rather than three. If the acquisition of *all* forms of expertise involves being accepted into a group of experts, then this factor does not play a role in distinguishing between different forms of expertise: for any given form of expertise, the novice will move further along the z-axis as they become more expert.

2   The status of the depth dimension. Given that the depth-dimension must refer to the degree to which a person is socialised as expert, there is a distinct difference between the depth-axis on the one hand and the vertical and horizontal axes on the other. What is involved in being accepted into the group of experts is different from acquiring esoteric and tacit knowledge in the sense that the first is a *social process* (a process of being accepted into or becoming part of a group) and the second is an individual or *cognitive* process (a matter of what an individual becomes capable of doing). Of course, part of what is interesting in Collins's sociology of expertise is the extent to which expertise is a matter of individual ability or is a matter of social recognition.[10] However, *for the field of professional education*, the question must be how the individual novice's knowledge and abilities change over time as she becomes more expert. The reason is that, without a perspective on the changing ability of the individual, the professional educator will not be in a position to answer questions such as whether the individual learner has learned anything, what they have learned and how well they have learned it. These matters of individual changing ability are simply essential to understand for the professional educator if they are ever to know whether a course of education is effective or not.

In putting matters this way, we are clearly confronted with questions regarding the *purpose* of the expertise space diagram and exactly what understanding of expertise it aids. As Collins puts it (2013: 267–8) sociology and psychology may differ as to whether they are interested in the depth dimension of the diagram or the front face and he himself puts the expertise space diagram to at least three uses:

- placing individuals in relation to how much socialisation as expert, esoteric knowledge and tacit knowledge they possess (e.g., Collins, 2013, Figures 7, 8 and 9)
- delineating groups of people (or entire domains of novices and experts) in terms of socialisation as expert, esoteric knowledge and tacit knowledge (e.g., Collins, 2013, Figures 3, 4, 5 and 6)
- describing educational trajectories that individuals take through expertise space (e.g., Collins, 2013, Figure 10).

It is not the purpose, here, to criticise these uses. Rather, I hope it would not do too much violence to the basic model to suggest a fourth use and that is the classification of different forms of professional expertise in different regions of expertise space to show how they differ. The fourth use also involves a (slight) amendment of the model.

As I tried to explain in the opening sections of this chapter, it is interesting that different *forms* of expertise make different demands of the individual. Some forms of expertise demand great explicit knowledge of the individual, others great tacit knowledge and some a combination. Taking the idea of *socialisation* seriously, one can also say something else about the *individual ability* needed by different professionals in different fields and this is the degree of *social skill or understanding* that different professionals need to bring to their work. An expert nurse, I would venture, needs to bring a great deal of social skill or understanding to his/her work, while an expert at computer coding need not necessarily display the same social skill. The point is not to hold that computer programmers can get by without social skill – everyone living in a society needs a great deal of social skill already simply to communicate and co-operate with others. Rather, the point is to say that, if one accepts a reasonable level of social skill as 'ubiquitous' among anyone living in a society, one can still distinguish developed forms of this skill that some may possess to a greater degree than others. Inasmuch as some professional expertise requires very highly developed social skill and others somewhat less, it appears very useful to bring this into the model and distinguish between forms of expertise on this basis. This yields a depiction of expertise as shown in Figure 5.2.

Within this space, different forms of expertise can then be classified much as Collins proposes (see Figure 5.3).

One may think of forms of expertise that are high on esotericity, but low on tacitness and social skill, ones that are high on tacitness but low on esotericity and social skill, ones that are high on social skill, but low on esotericity and tacit knowledge and so-on through the combinations to expertises that are high on all three. Nothing in particular hangs on the examples, but one may imagine that a computer programmer, say, who needs much esoteric knowledge that must be expressible in terms of whatever programming language she uses, but does not necessarily need that much tacit, physical knowledge or social skill is an example of (i), a manual factory worker performing some repetitive physical skills may be an example of (ii), an unskilled carer (iii)[11] and a surgeon, say, an example of (iv).

It must be stressed that nothing hangs on these particular examples; I am entirely open to the idea that computer programming, manual factory work or caring indeed requires much more social skill, esoteric knowledge or tacit knowledge than I give them credit for. Equally the implication in identifying surgery as an example of an expertise requiring all three dimensions is not that this form of expertise is superior to the others. The point is simply to say that there are differences between the cognitive demands that different forms of expertise make

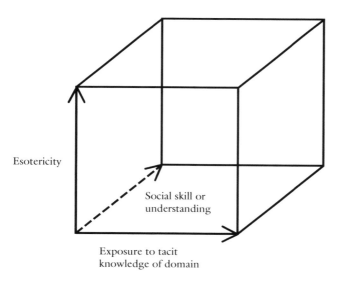

Figure 5.2 Adapted expertise space diagram.

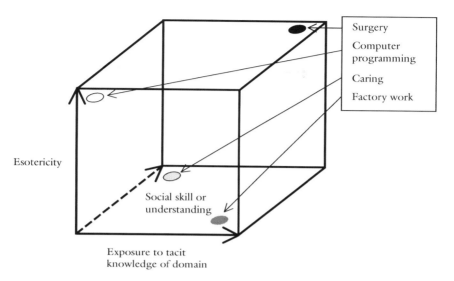

Figure 5.3 Differentiating forms of expertise.

on the expert and that one can illustrate the relevant differences between these forms of expertise by placing them side-by-side in one space.

Furthermore, classifying different forms of expertise in this way has a clear educational use (see Figure 5.4). Collins sketches a number of educational trajectories that novices can take through the expertise space. Thus, the journey of someone taking a very theoretical university degree – perhaps one that involves no practical work – could take the student from low on the x, y and z-axes to high on the y-axis, some way along the z-axis and low on the x-axis. Someone doing, say, a laboratory-based PhD in psychology, that involves theoretical and experimental work as well as great contact with people, would travel from a point low on the x, y and z axes to a point high on all three axes (seeing as this sort of educational programme involves the development of all three forms of capability).

The specific utility of this way of thinking for education is this: in understanding how a course of education relates to preparation for a certain form of expert professional practice, curriculum designers need to ensure that the educational trajectory represented in Figure 5.2 matches the demands of the *form* of expert professional practice that the novice is being prepared for. An educational qualification that delivers a novice through the right mix of processes of socialisation, acquisition of esoteric knowledge and acquisition of tacit knowledge to the right point in the expertise space can be said to be well-aligned. However, if a form of expert professional practice demands a certain 'mix' of socialisation, esoteric knowledge and tacit knowledge and a course of education delivers only *some* of these (or delivers them in the wrong proportions), the course of

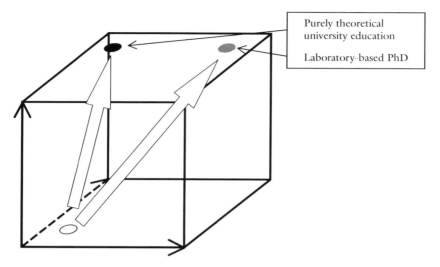

Figure 5.4 Two different educational trajectories (after Collins, 2013: Figure 10).

professional education can be said to be badly aligned. Examples of such badly aligned professional regimes may include, for instance, the overly theoretical medical education (focussing on factors such as mathematical and scientific knowledge – and knowledge of Latin) that used to predominate in the English-speaking world and is still found in some form in continental countries. It may also be found in courses of professional education that are too practice-focussed and neglect appropriate theoretical underpinning – such as when one attempts to train an electrical engineer only through practice and not also by imparting some theoretical knowledge regarding electricity. Last, one may imagine a course of professional formation that requires a certain degree of socialisation, but does not involve enough preparation in this regard – imagine, for instance, that one attempts to train a nurse wholly through distance learning and without becoming used to the practice of a group of real nurses. Such a course of education would also be badly aligned.

Conclusion

In this chapter, I investigated the relationship between professional knowledge and professional expertise. Contrary to the dominant 'fluency' accounts of expertise that are influential in education, the philosophy, psychology and sociology of expertise all suggest that professional knowledge plays a much more important role – alongside practice – than the education literature sometimes suggests. Key to understanding this role, I held, was that different expertises make different demands of experts. I outlined how Collins's model of an 'expertise space' can be adapted to make sense of these demands and can show how different expertises differ with regards to the demands they make of professionals in terms of social skill, esoteric knowledge and tacit knowledge.[12]

Notes

1 For discussions, see Kotzee, 2012a and Kotzee, 2012b.
2 Stanley and Williamson's account becomes more complicated when they hold that one must not only know the procedure verbally, but must know it in a 'practical mode of presentation'. Winch (2010: 25) criticises Stanley and Williamson for falling back on a form of ability account with this move.
3 See Fantl (2008) for a more complete depiction of the state of the knowledge how debate in contemporary philosophy.
4 Examples include the AIDS activists in 1980s San Francisco who made a contribution to the study of HIV and the Cumbrian sheep farmers who contributed to understand nuclear fall-out in Northern England after the Chernobil disaster of 1986. See Collins and Evans, 2006.
5 In a personal exchange, Collins disagrees that one should call this a matter of theoretical knowledge. He holds that the relevant knowledge is a form of linguistic knowledge: tacit knowledge of the relevant practice language.
6 See Dreyfus, 2005 and 2007 and McDowell, 2007a and 2007b.
7 In correspondence, Collins held that '[e]sotericity does not change for the individual, it is a property of the expertise and its epoch or location.' See, for instance, Collins, 2013, Figure 5 for how this plane is represented. My view is that allowing the individual's position on the esotericity axis to change will be helpful in classifying how an individual's expertise changes or develops over time and to demonstrate differences between expertises. This is a point of difference between Collins's position and mine.
8 Collins himself expresses uncertainty regarding exactly where to place expertise at chess in the expertise space (Collins, 2013: Figure 9). It is fair to say that the literature on expertise at chess contains hints in both directions – that tacit knowledge is and is not important in chess. See Gobet and Charness, 2006.
9 For the view that speaking is *not* a form of expertise, see Addis (2013).
10 In a personal exchange, Collins remarks that this is not merely a matter of social recognition, but the extent to which a person has become a genuine member of a group.
11 While some may doubt whether routine factory work or unskilled work count as 'expertise' at all, the point is that it is only by placing these forms of activities in one space that one can make sense of the differences between them.
12 I thank Harry Collins for his comments on a draft of this chapter. I have benefited greatly from discussing his three dimensional model with Collins; responsibility for any misinterpretations of the model is my own.

References

Abbot, A. (1988) *The system of professions: An essay on the division of expert labor.* Chicago, IL: Chicago University Press.
Addis, M. (2013) 'Linguistic competence and expertise'. *Phenomenology and the Cognitive Sciences, 12*(2), 327–36.
Barnes, B. (1977) *Interests and the growth of knowledge.* London: Routledge.
Bloor, D. (1976) *Knowledge and social imagery.* Chicago, IL: Chicago University Press.

Butterworth, B. (2006) 'Mathematical expertise'. In K.A. Ericsson, N. Charness, P. Feltovich and R. Hoffman (eds) *The Cambridge handbook of expertise and expert performance*. Cambridge: Cambridge University Press.

Carr, D. (1979) 'The logic of knowing how and ability', *Mind*, 88, 394–409.

Carr, D. (1981) 'Knowledge in practice', *American Philosophical Quarterly* 18, 53–61.

Chi, M. (2006) 'Two approaches to the study of experts' characteristics'. In K.A. Ericsson, N. Charness, P. Feltovich and R. Hoffman (eds) *The Cambridge handbook of expertise and expert performance*. Cambridge: Cambridge University Press.

Collins, H. (2004) 'Interactional expertise as a third kind of knowledge', *Phenomenology and the Cognitive Sciences*, 3(2), 125–43.

Collins, H. (2007) 'Bicycling on the moon'. *Organization Studies*, 28(2): 257–62.

Collins, H. (2013) 'Three dimensions of expertise', *Phenomenology and the Cognitive Sciences*, 12(2), 253–73.

Collins, H. and Evans, R. (2006) 'The third wave of science studies: Studies of expertise and experience'. Originally published 2002. Reprinted in E. Selinger and R. Crease (eds) *The philosophy of expertise*. New York: Columbia University Press.

Collins, H. and Evans, R. (2007) *Rethinking expertise*. Chicago, IL: University of Chicago Press.

Dall'Alba, G. and Sandberg, J. (2006) 'Unveiling professional development: A critical review of stage models', *Review of Educational Research*, 76(3), 383–412.

Dreyfus, H. (2005) 'Overcoming the myth of the mental: How philosophers can profit from the phenomenology of everyday expertise', *Proceedings of the American Philosophical Association*, 79(2), 47–65.

Dreyfus, H. (2007) 'The return of the myth of the mental', *Inquiry*, 50(4), 352–65.

Dreyfus, H. and Dreyfus, S. (1986) *Mind over machine*. New York: Free Press.

Drucker, P. (1969) *The age of discontinuity*. New York: Harper & Row.

Durso, F. and Dattel, A. (2006) 'Expertise and transportation'. In K.A. Ericsson, N. Charness, P. Feltovich and R. Hoffman (eds) *The Cambridge handbook of expertise and expert performance*. Cambridge: Cambridge University Press.

Eraut, M. (1994) *Developing professional knowledge and competence*. Brighton: Falmer.

Eraut, M. (2000) 'Non-formal learning and tacit knowledge in professional work'. *British Journal of Educational Psychology*, 70, 113–36.

Ericsson, K.A. (2006) 'An introduction to the Cambridge Handbook of Expertise and Expert Performance: Its development, organization, and content'. In K.A. Ericsson, N. Charness, P. Feltovich and R. Hoffman (eds) *The Cambridge handbook of expertise and expert performance*. Cambridge: Cambridge University Press.

Evetts, J., Mieg, H. and Felt, U. (2006) 'Professionalization, scientific expertise and elitism: A sociological perspective'. In K.A. Ericsson, N. Charness, P. Feltovich and R. Hoffman (eds) *The Cambridge handbook of expertise and expert performance*. Cambridge: Cambridge University Press.

Fantl, J. (2008) 'Knowing-how and knowing-that'. *Philosophy Compass*, 3(3), 451–70.

Freidson, E. (1994) *Professionalism reborn: Theory, prophecy and policy*. Chicago, IL: Chicago University Press.

Giles, J. (2006) 'Sociologist fools physics judges', *Nature*, 442, 8.

Gobet, F. and Charness, N. (2006) 'Expertise in chess'. In K.A. Ericsson, N. Charness, P. Feltovich and R. Hoffman (eds) *The Cambridge handbook of expertise and expert performance*. Cambridge: Cambridge University Press.

Gobet, F. and Chassy, P. (2009) 'Expertise and intuition: A tale of three theories'. *Minds and Machines*, 19(2), 151–80.

Kellogg, R. (2006) 'Professional writing expertise'. In K.A. Ericsson, N. Charness, P. Feltovich and R. Hoffman (eds) *The Cambridge handbook of expertise and expert performance*. Cambridge: Cambridge University Press.

Kotzee, B. (2012a) 'Private practice: Exploring the missing social dimension in "reflective practice"', *Studies in Continuing Education*, 34(1), 5–16.

Kotzee, B. (2012b) 'Expertise, fluency and social realism about professional knowledge', *Journal of Education and Work*. DOI 10.1080/13639080.2012.738291

Larson, M. (1977) *The rise of professionalism*. Berkeley, CA: University of California Press.

McDowell, J. (2007a) 'What myth?', *Inquiry*, 50(4), 338–51.

McDowell, J. (2007b) 'Response to Dreyfus'. *Inquiry*, 50(4), 366–70.

Polanyi, M. (1966) *The tacit dimension*. London: Routledge.

Ryle, G. (1946) 'Knowing how and knowing that'. In *Collected Papers* (Volume 2), New York: Barnes and Noble (pp. 212–25).

Ryle, G. (1949) *The concept of mind*. Chicago: University of Chicago Press.

Saks, M. (2012) 'Defining a profession', *Professions and Professionalism*, 2(1), 1–10.

Schanefeldt, R., Durso, F., Goldsmith, T., Breen, T., Cooke, N., Tucker, R. and DeMaio, J. (1985) 'Measuring the structure of expertise', *The International Journal of Man-Machine Studies*, 23, 699–28.

Schön, D.A. (1983) *The reflective practitioner: How professionals think in action*. London: Temple Smith.

Snowdon, P. (2004) 'Knowing how and knowing that: A distinction reconsidered', *Proceedings of the Aristotelian Society*, 104(1), 1–29.

Standard Occupational Classification (2010) London: Office for National Statistics. www.ons.gov.uk/ons/guide-method/classifications/current-standard-classifications/soc2010/index.html (accessed on 6 January, 2014).

Stanley, J. and Williamson, T. (2001) 'Knowing how', *Journal of Philosophy*, 98(8): 411–44.

Stokes, A., Kemper, K. and Kite, K. (1997) 'Aeronautical decision making, cue recognition and expertise under time pressure'. In C. Zsambok and G. Klein (eds) *Naturalistic decision making*. Mahwah, NJ: Erlbaum (pp. 183–96).

Winch, C. (2009) 'Ryle on knowing how and the possibility of vocational education', *Journal of Applied Philosophy*, 26(1): 88–101.

Winch, C. (2010) *Dimensions of expertise*. London: Continuum.

6 Professional knowledge and professional practice as continuous recontextualisation

A social practice perspective

David Guile

Introduction

The aim of this chapter is to introduce a discussion of the theory–practice relationship in professional formation and, in the process, to identify the implications of this discussion to rethink the design and delivery of programmes of professional formation. The chapter does so by adopting a social practice perspective based on the concept of 'recontextualisation' (Guile 2010). It begins by explaining the origins of this concept in Cultural Historical Activity Theory and the three principles – the object of activity, the normative context of human action, and the relationship between inference and action – that underpin the concept. The chapter then distinguishes between four expressions of recontextualisation – content, pedagogy, workplace and learner – to analyse the way in which: (i) forms of knowledge are selected from disciplines and work practice for inclusion in professional curricula; (ii) lecturers and workplace supervisors' conceptions of learning and teaching influence aspiring professionals' understanding of the content of their curriculum and their capability to mediate between theory and practice; (iii) forms of knowledge are embedded in workplace practices and artifacts and used by aspiring professionals to address routine and novel problems they encounter; and, (iv) aspiring professionals develop different modes of reasoning to operate effectively in the contexts of education and work. The chapter concludes by (i) identifying the implications of the concept of recontextualisation for the future design and delivery of programmes of professional formation; and (ii) explaining why and how the concept of recontextualisation employed in the chapter differs from Bernstein's, an influence on many of the contributors to this edited volume, use of the same term.

The concept of recontextualisation: background

One of the key debates in contemporary Learning Theory initiated by Jean Lave in her book *Cognition in Practice* (1988) has a major bearing on the relationship between knowledge and the professions that frames this edited collection. In short,

Lave argued that all forms of education were predicated on the notion of 'transfer' and proceeded as though: (i) the human mind is an attribute of an individual in isolation from the world; (ii) learning involves the mastery of abstract representations taught in educational institutions in discipline-based curricula in the form of propositional statements; and, (iii) individuals transfer what they have learnt by applying propositions to practice. Moreover, Lave argued in a subsequent book, *Situated Learning*, which was co-written with Etienne Wenger (Lave and Wenger 1991), that the concept of transfer should be replaced by the concept of 'participation'. This concept captured, for Lave, the relationship between cognition, practice and context, thereby enabling her to reveal that people use different resources – conceptual, material and social – as a way to engage with and evolve forms of occupational practice, rather than merely replicating in a new situation what they had been taught elsewhere.

Over the intervening years, one recurring criticism of Lave and Wenger has been that, by building their argument about apprenticeship as a model of learning through a focus on traditional, rather than modern, apprenticeships, they downplay the contribution that educational institutions make to apprenticeship through teaching theoretical knowledge to apprentices (Gamble 2006; Wheelahan 2010; Young 2000). In contrast, writers whose starting point is the concept of learning, rather than knowledge, have engaged with Lave's critique of the idea of 'transfer'. Two responses can be identified: some researchers have suggested alternative ways of conceptualising transfer, such as, 'consequential transition' (Beach 1999) and 'boundary crossing' (see Akkerman and Bakker 2011, for a summary); and, other researchers have developed or supplemented Lave and Wenger's ideas about participation to reflect the complexity of participation in modern work environments (see for example Billet (2002); Edwards (2010); and Fuller and Unwin (2003)).

The problem with both responses is that the former writers have never addressed Lave's argument about the limitations of transfer in relation to their own argument about the role of knowledge in professional curricula, while the latter writers have, with the exception of Akkerman and Bakker (2012), not considered the constitutive role of knowledge in programmes of professional formation.

In fact, Lave (1996) did engage with the issue of 'knowledge' in a later article where she argued that 'teaching curricula' (her term for educational programmes) should be remodelled so that learners are taught to think and act like historians, mathematicians, philosophers, etc., rather than taught the knowledge associated with those disciplines in propositional form. Were this suggestion enacted, it would involve the radical reform and redesign of curricula in all phases of education in advanced industrial society. There is, however, an alternative conception of the 'teaching' curriculum based on the concept of recontextualisation, which respects Lave's argument that transfer is an inadequate way to understand the relationship between theoretical concepts and professional practice, but without implying the radical transformation of educational institutions or curricula. This chapter will show how the concept of recontextualisation also offers a more adequate way of approaching the knowledge/practice relationship.

The principles of recontextualisation

The concept of recontextualisation first surfaced in a discussion that van Oers (1998) initiated in Cultural Historical Activity Theory (CHAT) to counter the post-Lave critique in CHAT that Vygotsky was insufficiently sensitive to the influence of context on learning. Stated simply, the concept presupposes that every type of human activity is encountered and employed contextually. This does not mean, however, that forms of activity, or for that matter resources, are context-bound: human intentionality allows them to be used in different ways in different contexts. The concept recontextualisation has been subsequently developed (Guile 2010) as a way to analyse the relationship between forms of knowing, learning and acting in and between the contexts of education and work. To see why recontextualisation can be used in this way and why, as a result, it offers a new way to think about the relationship between theory and practice in professional education, it is necessary to understand the principles that underpin the concept.

The first principle is that the *purpose* of an activity has a significant bearing on the way in which the parties involved deploy resources – conceptual (i.e., forms of knowledge), material (i.e., technologies) and social (i.e., people) – to accomplish that activity. In the case of forms of knowledge, for example, theoretical, legal, workplace, the chapter assumes they are produced through different types of social practice and their associated technologies (i.e., methods and tools of investigation). Theoretical knowledge is produced through discipline-based identification and verification of relationships that exist between phenomena. In contrast, workplace knowledge arises as a result of classifying phenomena according to similar features, distinctive usages, etc. This means that although I accept that theoretical and practical forms of knowledge can be distinguished analytically as separate, I also maintain that they have a 'mediated relationship' with one another (Guile 2010).

The way that I have illustrated the basis of this claim in other work (Guile 2010) is to borrow McDowell's evocative phrase (1996: 26), 'the unboundedness of the conceptual'. By this McDowell means human activity results in the conceptual permeating the natural and social worlds in ways that we take for granted or fail to appreciate. For example, the way in which we, in the case of the former, transform the natural landscape by building roads, bridges, etc. and, in the case of the latter, use scientific and social scientific concepts as a resource so they become, respectively, an embedded part of artefacts (i.e., buildings, computers) or social practices (i.e., organisation of work or curricula). In McDowell's phrase the unboundedness of the conceptual enables us to appreciate why we inhabit a mediated environment where we engage in intellectual or political debates, social events or work processes that are, in many instances, characterised by the commingling of the theoretical and everyday, rather than moving between separate conceptual and practical spheres.

The second principle is that all forms of human activity (theoretical and practical) occur in a *normative context* where conceptual and empirical claims are both judged. The term normative is very value laden. All too often, it is assumed to refer to an ideal existence or way of proceeding. My usage of normative is, however, rather different. Influenced by McDowell (1996: xiv) I argue that when we characterise an episode or a state as that of knowing we are not giving a logical description of that episode or state; instead we are placing it in the logical 'space of reasons' of justifying and being able to justify what one says.

The process of reasoning and justifying a claim can be a relatively straight-forward matter when a claim is being judged in purely theoretical or practical terms, for example, whether engineering is, in Bernstein's (2000) terms, treated as a 'singular' or a 'region' or whether taking a new job is wise or foolish. This is because we have recourse to, in the case of the former, the theoretical reasons that underpin the definition of singulars and regions, and in the case of the latter, someone's reasons for their actions. This is not to say that people automatically accept the conclusions that follow from considering those reasons, rather that a compelling case can be mounted as to why they should. The act of judging in the space of reasons becomes more complex, however, when the theoretical and everyday or practical are commingled in, for example, professional or vocational practice.

This claim can be illustrated through reference to Jonsen and Toulmin's (1988) discussion of the theory–practice relationship in medicine. The classic distinction between theoretical and practical reasoning, as Jonsen and Toulmin (1988: 23) observe, normally defines the former as proceeds from theoretical 'axioms' (i.e., we deduce what is the case from universal rules) and the latter from 'maxims' (i.e., we infer from practical cases what might be the case). Initially, this suggests that there is little, if any, relationship between the two modes of reasoning. Such a conclusion overlooks, as Jonsen and Toulmin (1988: 36) further observe, that what doctors actually do is to 'combine', or in my terms commingle, theory and practice in a distinctive way to diagnose a patient's condition. The diagnostic process is an interplay between the biomedical science doctors have gained from study, which positions them to perceive the human body differently from lay people, and to use that knowledge as intellectual background to clinical decisions, and their accumulating expertise in using particular procedures of clinical practice to recognise a patient's particular problems and determine how best to treat those conditions. My preferred way of expressing this process is to say that doctors are making conceptually-structured professional (i.e., practical) judgements in context-specific circumstances, rather than applying their theoretical knowledge practically or taking practical decisions that lack any conceptual content. Moreover, these judgements are all too often implicit or tacit in nature: they occur in the flux of working in a hospital or in general practice without explicit verbalisation. This does not mean, however, that a doctor is unable if pressed to articulate reasons for their diagnosis and subsequent course of action.

The issue of judgement leads us to the third principle of recontextualisation. This principle is that theoretical and practical (from now on, professional) reasoning presupposes *inferring* what follows from different types of concepts or actions and responding accordingly in specific situations. In making this argument, I follow Brandom (2000) and maintain that we grasp the meaning of any type of concept as we understand the inferences that can be made from and to it, and are able to articulate those inferences intelligibly in written or oral form (Guile 2010). From this perspective, human judgement is the primary unit of knowledge. Stated another way, claims need to be justified, the process of justification needs recourse to reasons, reasons are assessed in a normative context, and that context is the space of reasons. Of course, the space of reasons is differentiated. In the case of a professional curriculum the theoretical reasons associated with disciplines sit alongside the practical reasons associated with professional perception and action. This differentiation presents different, but ultimately related challenges for aspiring professionals.

In the case of the disciplinary content of a professional curriculum, the aspiring professionals' challenge is to 'get to grips with the content of a concept and conditions of its applications' (Bakker and Derry, 2011: 10). To do so, they have to develop the capability to manifest their understanding to others. I also follow Brandom and maintain that we develop the capability to do so as we learn to participate in the social practice of giving and asking for reasons (Guile 2010: 135–9), in other words, by asking why a concept emerged, what it enables us to understand, and what follows from that understanding. From this perspective, theoretical reasoning involves, at a minimum, the ability to: (a) understand the conceptual structure of a discipline; (b) to locate a concept in its sub-field within the discipline; and, (c) infer relationship from that concept to other concepts. In the case of professional practice the challenge for aspiring professionals is to develop the capability to use disciplinary knowledge, in conjunction with professional experience, as a resource in a specific context to pick out the salient features of that situation or event, and to then infer what follows and how to act. Moreover, it is this mediated relationship between theoretical understanding and professional experience that constitutes the basis of professional reasoning.

Implications of recontextualisation for professional curricula and practice

The aim of this section is to show how the concept of recontextualisation can be used to shed new light on the theory–practice relationship in professional education. The section does so by using the principles described in the previous section, in conjunction with the four expressions – content, pedagogic, workplace and learner – of recontextualisation mentioned earlier, in relation to Pharmacy. This subject has been chosen because it is an interdisciplinary subject that is offered in higher education systems worldwide to support professional formation, which is characterised by the features of a classic profession – an epistemological foundation, periods of work experience, and a license to practice.

Purpose of the professional curriculum

The principle is that the purpose of an activity influences the way in which any resource can be used to alert us to the first challenge associated with the creation of a professional curriculum. That challenge is *content* recontextualisation, in other words, determining which concepts from different forms of knowledge (i.e., theoretical, legal, workplace, etc.) are selected for inclusion in a professional curriculum. Clearly, this can be a consensual or a contested process depending upon the extent to which the parties (i.e., universities, professional associations, regulatory bodies, etc.) have full or partial jurisdiction (Guile 2010) or are free to use their personal preferences to influence the selection (Muller 2012) of content.

In the case of a professional curriculum, once agreement has been reached as regards which areas of knowledge and, by extension, which concepts, are to be included in a curriculum, they take on a new purpose in a professional curriculum. This is because the purpose of the curriculum is to support professional formation rather than immersion in a discipline. Typically, a Pharmacy curriculum will consist of, among other elements, areas from chemistry and biology, for example, organic chemistry (the study of structure, properties and reactions of organic compounds and materials in their pure form) and molecular biology (the study of the inter-actions between various systems of a cell). The primary purpose of organic chemistry and molecular biology in a Pharmacy degree is, in the case of the former, to support aspiring pharmacists to understand molecular biology, including pharmacology and, in the case of the latter, to prepare aspiring pharmacists for clinical practice where they will need to understand the way in which drugs affect biological systems if they are to treat patients safely. In the process of studying these areas, aspiring pharmacists may develop a good understanding of chemistry or biology but this would be an unintentional, rather than stated, outcome of their programme of study. This leads us to the issue of theory and practice and, as we are about to see, the second principle of recontextualisation helps us to do so.

Normative context of a professional curriculum and professional practice

The second principle of recontextualisation was that all forms of human activity, and in the case of professional education theoretical and practical activity, occur in a normative context (the space of reasons) where conceptual and empirical claims are both judged. What is distinctive about this context is that what counts as valid reasoning, adequate judgement, correct applications of concepts and an appro-priate professional response depends upon the norms being used in a particular practice.

The acknowledgement of the normativity of concept use provides a way to respect the difference and relation between theory and professional practice in a professional curriculum, and to consider how to assist aspiring professionals to do the same. For a professional curriculum to fulfill this goal, it helps if the parties (i.e., lecturers, visiting speakers, experienced pharmacists, mentors, etc.) contrib-uting to its delivery assist aspiring pharmacists to appreciate the norms that underpin their learning in both the contexts of education and work. This involves assisting aspiring pharmacists, in the case of the former, to: (a) grasp the reasons why different forms of knowledge have been selected to be taught in their Pharmacy degree; (b) develop their capability to reason theoretically with those forms of knowledge; and (c) understand the warrants they have to call upon to justify claims based on that reasoning; and, in the case of work, to appreciate how: (a) the forms of knowledge they encountered during their programme of studies are embedded artifacts (medicines), technologies (computer programmes containing data about medicines) and professional routines (dispensing medicines); (b) they develop their professional judgement by commingling the forms of knowledge they have learnt from their programme of studies with their profession-generated knowledge; and (c) the warrants they employ to justify their professional judgements arise from the aforementioned process of commingling.

The relationship between theory and practice is a demanding, but relatively more straightforward, challenge when the profession is based on a singular. A classic example would be the relation between the discipline of chemistry, the study of a PhD in chemistry, and the profession chemistry lecturer or research chemist. Here the codification, reasoning and warranting conventions are more or less coterminous for the discipline and the profession, and the development of expertise and identity is a process of the immersion in, and contributing to the development of, those conventions. This is, however, rarely the case for most professions and their relationship with their professional curricula and professional fields of practice. This is because most professions are interdisciplinary and therefore most professional curricula consist of forms of knowledge drawn from different disciplines, the professional field of practice, the technologies associated with the field, and the professional legislative and regulatory context. The challenge for lecturers and others involved with the delivery of interdisciplinary professional curricula is to assist aspiring professionals to appreciate that their process of professional formation contains a double challenge with a common root, and this common root is the basis of addressing the relation between theory and practice. The challenge is to: develop the capability to reason in theoretical and professional ways, albeit, the conceptually-structured professional ways discussed earlier; and, the common root is that both ways presuppose developing the capability to operate in the space of reasons by inferring what follows and acting accordingly, theoretically or professionally.

Professional curriculum, professional practice, inference and action

The third principle of recontextualisation – learning to infer what follows from a concept or action and to respond accordingly – provides us with the starting point for, as we saw earlier, supporting someone to reason in theoretical and professional ways. The gist of the earlier argument presented was three-fold: we grasp the meaning of any type of concept (i.e., theoretical, practical) by understanding the inferences that can be made from and to that concept; we develop the capability to articulate those inferences intelligibly in written or oral form through our participation in the social practice of giving and asking for reasons; and, we use our ability to do so to vary our mode of reasoning according to the norms of the practice (i.e., educational or professional) we are engaged in.

The concept of the giving and asking for reasons is predicated on the earlier argument that what is distinctive about, respectively, the 'space' in which humans live – underpinned by reasons – and human nature – we are susceptible to reasons and act in accordance with reasons. In relation to the argument presented in this chapter, I mean professionals develop the capability to form and revise their opinion about theoretical and professional matters based on an implicit or explicit process of reasoning, and then choose to act or not act in accordance with the conclusions they have drawn. The existence of different types of reasons and reasoning can sometimes appear to get lost when the concept of the space of reasons is invoked. One way to overcome this possibility is to follow Brandom (1994) and use the term the 'web' of reasons to distinguish between the reasons in play in a particular context, for example, education or work, and any relations that may pertain between them, compared with the wider space of reasons within which we all live. The advantage of the notion of web is that it is a common term that can be used to: (a) respect the difference that exists between theoretical and professional reasoning; and (b) capture the commingling of theoretical understanding and professional experience associated with professional reasoning. To see why this is the case, it is helpful to consider the processes of *pedagogic* and *workplace* recontextualisation.

The parties, for example, lecturers, visiting speakers, etc., involved in delivering a professional curriculum have the relative autonomy to determine their approach to learning and teaching. The pedagogic decision they make will, however, influence the extent to which aspiring professionals are positioned to grasp the relationship between theory and practice or to perceive it as a divide they oscillate between. The argument presented in this chapter is that a pedagogic approach based on the principles of inference positions aspiring professionals to grasp the aforementioned relationship. This is because the inferential emphasis on identifying relationships between concepts or between concepts and professional practice encourages aspiring professionals to think about the relationship between theory and practice, rather than to treat theory and practice as separate domains.

What is deceptive about this argument is that lecturers who use an inferential perspective explicitly or implicitly still tend to use lecturers, seminars and workshops, etc. as learning and teaching strategies. The critical issue is lecturers' pedagogic purpose rather than lecturers' choice of pedagogic techniques. An inferential approach to learning and teaching presuppose supporting aspiring professionals to grasp the relationship between the forms of knowledge contained in their curriculum and those forms of knowledge and professional practice, rather than to assimilate those forms of knowledge purely in their disciplinary terms.

This issue can be clarified by returning to the earlier discussion of the role of organic chemistry and molecular biology in a pharmacy degree. The reason for their inclusion is to assist aspiring pharmacists to understand all aspects of pharmacology. To fulfill this aim, lecturers face a number of pedagogic challenges.

One challenge is to explain the origins, premises and insights that flow from studying organic chemistry and molecular biology concepts, and to provide opportunities in the educational contexts for aspiring pharmacists to infer the way in which their study of those concepts enables them to understand pharmacology – for example, the way in which a drug may or may not affect a patient's biological system based on her/his case history.

To address these challenges, lecturers have two priorities. One is to sequence, for example, organic chemistry, molecular biology and pharmacology, so that aspiring pharmacists can appreciate the role of these disciplines in the pharmacy curriculum and in their transition to becoming pharmacists. The other is to avoid the following pedagogic and curriculum problems. The former is to teach organic chemistry or molecular biology as though students are being prepared to become experts in chemistry or biology. The latter is to sequence work placements for aspiring pharmacists at the end of their programme of study. The former is likely to result in the well-known problem of 'inert' knowledge (Bereiter and Scardamalia 1993), in other words, aspiring pharmacists will struggle to use concepts they have learnt in one context to reason theoretically and/or practically in another context. The latter is likely to compound the inertness of much of the knowledge aspiring pharmacists have learnt from formal study because, their engagement with the theory–practice relationship in their field of practice is being postponed until late on in their programme of study, rather than interspersed throughout to enable aspiring pharmacists to begin to develop their capability to reason and act professionally (Guile and Ahamed 2010). Both problems are more likely to happen if lecturers explicitly or implicitly draw on a transmission conception of learning and teaching. This conception is predicated, as Bakker and Derry (ibid.) remark, on the 'atomistic' assumption that 'simple terms must be learned prior to those that are more complex or prior to the combination of such terms in judgements before one can reason with those terms'. This emphasis on the gradual accumulation of knowledge is inclined to predispose lecturers to encourage aspiring professionals to follow the inner direction of a discipline, rather than helping them to grasp how to use disciplinary concepts as resources to address the dilemmas that arise in their professional practice.

Having discussed the process of pedagogic recontextualisation, it is now helpful to consider how aspiring pharmacists' experience of the workplace simultaneously continues and reverses the process of recontextualisation. To do so, we return to the field of pharmacy and the area of pharmacology.

Pharmacology consists of a number of sub-areas. One area is 'systemic pharmacology', that is, the action of drugs on physiological systems. Aspiring pharmacists are taught systemic pharmacology to assist them to understand the pharmacological basis of medicines and the way in which drugs affect biological systems, so they can when in professional practice assess the benefits that arise from one drug compared with another one, as well as anticipate Adverse Drug Reactions (ADRs) or idiosyncratic reactions that may occur. Translated into language introduced earlier, systemic pharmacology is, in some form or another, an embedded feature of most medicines available in a high street pharmacy, and that pharmacy is a conceptualised environment, for example, pharmacists' practices, such as dispensing medicines, are influenced by pharmacological concepts and legal stipulations. When undertaking work placements as part of their pharmacy degree, aspiring pharmacists, supported by experienced pharmacists and mentors, draw on their growing pharmacological understanding and experience of dealing with patients, to ascertain the likely effect of the medicine they recommend on a patient. Thus, they are engaged in a process of *workplace* recontextualisation of knowledge and experience.

The outcome of this process is the development of aspiring pharmacists' professional judgement. This judgement, as we can see from the description above, involves a commingling of their theoretical understanding of pharmacology, their professional experience and a patient's description of their particular condition. In many instances, for example, when dispensing prescriptions issued by doctors or responding to patients who have straightforward conditions, pharmaceutical judgement is a fairly routine and eventually habituated process. When faced with more challenging cases that fall outside the limits of normal practice (i.e., not dispensing doctor's prescriptions), aspiring pharmacists have to engage in a more deliberate and nuanced process of recontextualisation to ensure they recommend the most suitable medicine and even a supplementary medicine to address any side effects that may arise from the main medicine. This process would be easier, however, if pharmacists in general had access to patient's medical history. The professional division of labour between doctors and pharmacists proscribes this from happening. It is beyond the scope of this chapter to explore why this is the case. Nevertheless, it is important to note that this division of labour, and its ensuing jurisdictional responsibilities, circumscribe to some extent the sources of information pharmacists can use to recontextualise their accumulating theoretical and professional understanding of identical or similar conditions in relation to the patient they are treating.

The unifying thread that runs through the three forms of recontextualisation – content, pedagogy and workplace – described so far is the formation of aspiring pharmacists' expertise and identity. To accomplish this goal, aspiring pharmacists have to simultaneously engage with the opportunities to learn provided by the different processes of recontextualisation as well as exercise their agency to develop the ability to reason in theoretical and conceptually-structured professional ways. The existence of two different modes of assessment to express their understanding, on the one hand in written and oral forms in accordance with academic conventions and warrants (i.e., theoretical reasoning); and, on the other hand, in oral forms in accordance with professional conventions and warrants (i.e., professional reasoning) perpetuates the idea that these are separate and different modes of reasoning. Viewed from the argument presented in this chapter about the mediated relationship between theory and practice, which arises as a result of the way in which the conceptual is embedded in professional routines and practices, we can see that theoretical and professional reasoning are different, but related, processes of thinking and acting.

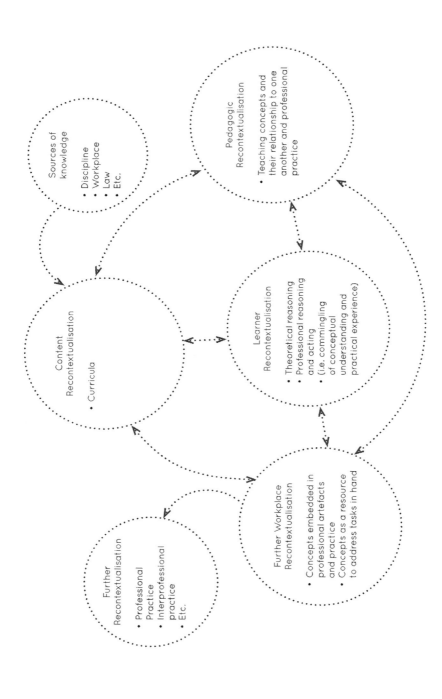

Figure 6.1 The continuous recontextualisation of knowledge and professional practice.

This conception of theoretical and professional reasoning therefore offers a rather different angle on the well-known distinction between 'knowing that' (i.e., propositional knowledge) and 'knowing how' (i.e., practical knowledge and skill), which is frequently invoked to demonstrate the difference between theoretical and practical (in my terms professional) reasoning. The debate in philosophy veers between maintaining the latter is 'reducible' to the former or that there is an 'intimate relationship' between knowing that and knowing how (Winch 2012, p. 2). I follow the latter position and maintain that the basis of the relationship between theoretical and professional reasoning is as follows. The former presupposes the capability to express understanding, ideas and arguments in accordance with disciplinary conventions, whereas the latter presupposes commingling theoretical knowledge and professional experiences to make conceptually-structured professional judgements in context-specific circumstances.

Conclusion

This chapter had two aims: to use the concept of recontextualisation to reconsider the relationship between theoretical and professional knowledge, and to highlight the implications of this process of rethinking for professional formation. In the case of the former, the chapter has shown that the theory–practice issue manifests itself in four ways in the: (i) construction of professional curricula (content recontextualisation); (ii) approach to learning and teaching (pedagogic recontextualisation); (iii) organisation of and the engagement with work (workplace recontextualisation); and (iv) development of theoretical and professional reasoning (learner recontextualisation). Furthermore, the chapter has argued that the concept of inference opens up new ways to think about the mediated relationship between learning and teaching in the contexts of education and work and, by extension, the way in which aspiring professionals develop their ability to reason theoretically and professionally. In doing so, the chapter has shown that the assumed divide between theoretical knowledge and professional practice is the product of binary thinking in some areas of the human and social sciences, rather than the existence of an absolute separation between theory and practice.

In the case of the latter, parties involved with the design and delivery of programmes of professional formation could use the concept of recontextualisation to reappraise those programmes in the following way. They could convert the expressions of recontextualisation into criteria to consider the extent to which programmes assist aspiring professionals to: (i) develop their theoretical and professional reasoning or leave them unclear about this relationship; and, (ii) offer some preparation for interprofessional work or leave them to discover how to work interprofessionally when they are employed (see Guile and Ahamed for a practical illustration of the conceptually framed examples below). Treated as criteria, the notion of:

- *context recontextualisation* could be used to ask questions about whether the sequencing of modules facilitates immersion in the knowledge base of

the profession or the discipline, and if the latter how to overcome the problem of inert knowledge;
- *pedagogic recontextualisation* could be used to ask questions about whether lecturers and workplace supervisors are supporting aspiring professionals to infer the relationship between theoretical knowledge and professional practice, and if not how to assist programme teams to develop their conceptions of pedagogy to achieve that goal;
- *workplace recontextualisation* could be used to ask questions about whether aspiring professionals are being supported in the workplace to commingle theoretical knowledge and experience to develop their professional reasoning and acting and, if not, how assist people with a managing, developing or coaching role in the workplace to develop their pedagogic approach to achieve that goal;
- *learner recontextualisation* could be used to ask questions about the extent to which aspiring professionals are developing the identity and expertise to operate effectively in the contexts of education and work and, if not, to ascertain which aspect of the process of recontextualisation is inhibiting the development of identity and expertise.

In addition, parties involved with continuing professional formation could also use the expressions of recontextualisation to reappraise aspects of those programmes, for example, the notion of workplace recontextualisation could be used as a criterion to ask questions about the opportunities mid-career staff have to identify and work intra- or interprofessionally to solve problems.

Finally, it is important to conclude by acknowledging that the concept of recontextualisation developed in this chapter has some affinities, and some differences, to the way in which Bernstein has employed that term. Broadly speaking, my argument that the purpose of an activity influences the way in which theoretical knowledge is used and understood as different parties move it from one context to another is similar to Bernstein's (2000) discussion of the movement of knowledge from its disciplinary context to a curriculum context so it can become teachable.

The difference between Bernstein's and my use of the concept of recontextualisation emerge in the conceptual and substantive domains. In the case of the former, I interpret Bernstein as treating knowledge structures in fairly deterministic terms. He implies that the hierarchy of concepts in a subject should exercise a powerful influence on the way in which concepts are sequenced in a curriculum. In contrast, I argue that the purpose of an activity has to influence the way in which concepts associated with particular subjects are introduced to aspiring professionals and both, in turn, influence the type of professional identity that is developed, and used the example of pharmacy to demonstrate this claim. In the case of the latter, Bernstein, in nearly all his work, was concerned with schools and uses the concept of recontextualisation to explain how disciplines are transformed into curricula. He does not consider, therefore, the way in which other forms of knowledge, for example workplace knowledge and legal knowledge, which have always been a part of interdisciplinary professional curricula, are also included in such curricula, and therefore the part different forms of knowledge have always played in facilitating professional formation in the context of education and work.

In contrast, the argument presented in this chapter is that recontextualisation is a continuous, iterative and multifaceted process, that manifests itself in different ways and can, if attended to in the ways the chapter has identified, assist aspiring professionals to develop their theoretical and professional reasoning in initial professional formation, and to continue to refine these forms of reasoning during their ongoing professional formation. Hence the title of the chapter: Professional knowledge and professional practice as continuous recontextualisation.

Acknowledgement: I would like to thank Keith Wilson for his assistance in helping me to incorporate the examples from pharmacy into the chapter.

References

Akkerman, S. F. and Bakker, A. (2011) 'Boundary crossing and boundary objects'. *Review of Educational Research*, *81*(2): 132–69.

Akkerman, S. F. and Bakker, A. (2012) 'Crossing boundaries between school and work during apprenticeships'. *Vocations and Learning*, 5(2), 153–73.

Bakker, A. and Derry, J. (2011) 'Lessons from inferentialism for statistics education'. *Mathematical Thinking and Learning*, 13: 5–26.

Bereiter, C. and Scardamalia, M. (1993) *Surpassing ourselves: An inquiry into the nature and implications of expertise.* Chicago, IL: Open Court.

Bernstein, B. (2000) *Pedagogy, symbolic control and identity: Theory, research and critique* (revised edn). Lanham, MD: Rowman & Littlefield.

Beach, K. (1999) 'Consequential transitions: A sociocultural expedition beyond transfer in education'. *Review of Reseach in Education*, *24*(1): 104–39.

Billett, S. (2002) 'Workplace pedagogic practices: Co-participation and learning'. *British Journal of Educational Studies*, *50*(4): 457–81

Brandom, R. (1994) *Making it explicit: Reasoning, representing, and discursive commitment.* Cambridge, MA: Harvard University Press.

Brandom, R. (2000) *Articulating reasons: An introduction to inferentialism.* Cambridge, MA: Harvard University Press.

Edwards, A. (2010) *Being an expert professional practitioner: The relational turn in expertise.* Dordrecht: Springer.

Fuller, A. and Unwin, L. (2003) 'Learning as apprentices in the contemporary UK workplace: Creating and managing expansive and restrictive participation'. *Journal of Education and Work*, *16*(4): 407–26.

Gamble, J. (2006). 'Theory and practice in the vocational curriculum'. In Young, M. and Gamble, J. (eds) *Knowledge, curriculum and qualifications for South African further education.* Cape Town: HSRC Press.

Guile, D. (2010) *The learning challenge of the knowledge economy.* Rotterdam: Sense.

Guile, D. (forthcoming) 'Professional knowledge and professional practice as continuous recontextualisation: A social practice perspective'. In Fenwick, T. and Nerland, M. (eds) *Rethinking Professional Learning.* London: Routledge.

Guile, D. and Ahamed, F. (2010) *Modernising the undergraduate pharmacy curriculum.* LLAKES Research Paper 26. ESRC Research Centre Learning and Life Chances in Knowledge Economies and Societies, Institute of Education, University of London.

Jonsen, A. and Toulmin, S. (1988) 'Theory and practice'. In Jonsen, A. and Toulmin, S. *The abuse of casuistry: A history of moral reasoning.* Los Angeles: University of California Press.

Lave, J. (1996) 'Teaching as learning'. *Mind, Culture and Activity,* 3(3): 149–64.

Lave, J. (1988) *Cognition in practice.* Cambridge: Cambridge University Press.

Lave, J. and Wenger, E. (1991) *Situated learning.* Cambridge: Cambridge University Press.

McDowell, J. (1996) *Mind and world* (2nd edn). Harvard, MA: Harvard University Press.

Muller, J. (2012) 'Forms of knowledge and curriculum coherence'. In H. Lauder, M. Young, H. Daniels, M. Balarin and J. Lowe (eds) *Education for the knowledge economy? Critical Perspectives.* London: Routledge.

van Oers, B. (1998). 'The fallacy of decontextualization'. *Mind, Culture and Activity,* 5(2), 135–42.

Winch, C. (2012) *Dimensions of expertise: A conceptual exploration of vocational knowledge.* London, Continuum.

Wheelehan, L. (2010) *Why knowledge matters in curriculum.* London: Routledge.

Young, M. (2000) 'Bringing knowledge back in: A curriculum for lifelong learning'. In A. Hodgson (ed.) *Policies and the future of lifelong learning.* London: Kogan Page.

7 What binds professional judgment?

The case of teaching

Yael Shalem

Introduction

Judgements in teaching include both instructional (epistemic) and regulative (moral) aspects. Teachers have to exercise professional judgement when selecting emphasis for the content to be taught, designing a sequence of contents in a specific topic, choosing correct examples to demonstrate a concept, interpreting learners' errors, dealing with cultural differences among learners, and so forth. Some of these decisions are subtle, others are explicit. Some are made in situ and others pre or post facto. Broadly, there is an agreement that professional judgement in teaching derives from theoretical knowledge (educational theories and subject matter knowledge; this chapter will concentrate on educational theories), and from working knowledge (variety of contextually specific experiences). What is less clear is how theoretical knowledge, which is formal, systematic, ordered and context independent, informs teachers' professional judgement that is situated and context-dependent. Concepts developed to explain this relation such as 'reflection in action' (Schön 1983) and 'situated learning '(Lave and Wenger 1991), locate professional judgement in everyday professional practice, attempting to create finer distinctions within informal learning, but neglect the role of theoretical knowledge in the exercise of professional judgement. This is a serious neglect (Muller 2009; Young 2010; Young and Muller 2010; Winch 2010; Kotzee, 2012) that must be addressed, if teaching is to be considered a field of expertise; if a judgement made by teachers is to be distinguished from an ordinary judgement. Placing teachers' judgement primarily in experiential knowledge contributes to further de-professionalisation in teaching.

What is needed instead is a way of showing how judgement in teaching depends on theoretical knowledge, the type that binds judgement to specific situations. In perusing this, I begin with Luntley's idea of 'attentional states', a phenomenological account that Luntley develops in order to examine the moral awareness involved in making a judgement in general (Luntley 2005, 2009), and more specifically in teaching (Ainley and Luntley 2007) and in nursing (Luntley 2011). Although his account is important for pointing to the determination involved in professional judgement, I believe that it falls short on two counts. Luntley refuses to demarcate what discriminates professional from ordinary judgement, and he does not develop the conceptual background or what he calls the 'constraining conditions' of judgement. In this regard, the knowledge dimension of professional judgement is backgrounded in his account. To investigate the knowledge dimension of professional judgement I turn to Winch's notion of 'empirical theory of teaching' (2004, 2010) and Abbott's work on 'knowledge classifications' (1988). Following on from Winch's explanation of the importance of content specialization in inferential thinking and Abbott's distinction between generic and subject-matter-specialised classifications I turn, in the last part of the chapter, to discuss two studies that offer knowledge classifications in teachers' knowledge of school history and English, respectively. I believe that these two studies provide an interesting example of the kind of professional knowledge that can help teachers to classify knowledge in situ and to exercise judgement more broadly. Using the theoretical tools I gained in the analysis of the above, I show why the first study (Schleppegrell, Greer and Taylor 2008 as well Schleppegrell 2011) does not provide sufficient constraining conditions and thus its binding power is somewhat weaker than the second. With the second study (Christie and Macken-Horarik 2007, 2011) I demonstrate the knowledge development that is needed in the field of teacher education, one that offers teachers an ordering principle that binds their professional judgement.

Professional judgement is an act of attention

The foundation of teacher's expertise, Michael Luntley argues, is in judgement – the capacity to attend to the particular with normative compulsion (Luntley 2005: 286–7; Ainley and Luntley 2007: 5). When a Mathematics teacher pauses mid-sentence and says 'you don't put the equal sign here, it must go there', or when an English teacher says 'you can't discuss poetry *like that*' (my examples), they display, according to Luntley (2009: 361), 'object-dependent knowledge'. By commenting on a particular event – 'you can't discuss poetry *like that*', an English teacher is marking out an important situation. This teacher is 'committing [her] cognitive resources to working along a certain line of considerations' – she is 'anchoring' her cognition on 'particular points in the environment' (Luntley 2009: 288–9, my addition) that she believes are worthy of her attention for *that* educational situation. This teacher, Ainley and Luntley argue, displays conceptual knowledge. She might not have the conceptual name for the judgement that she is making but her ability to discriminate a moment worthy of attention, 'amidst the complexity of the classroom environment' (Ainley and Luntley 2007: 20), is proof that her engagement is conceptual.

Luntley concedes that a good judgement is constrained by good reasons and by abstract laws (2005: 286), but for him the constitutive conditions of good judgement in teaching consists of the ability to reason and the normative compulsion that is involved in choosing a moment to attend to, amidst the complexity of classroom life (ibid.: 289). The knowledge that informs the act of making a judgement (including of what type it is, how it is classified, and its strength to mark out situations as specific) is backgrounded in his account. 'Object-dependent knowledge' is not different from any other propositional knowledge. To understand the awareness a teacher displays in exercising professional judgement we need not look, he says, for some kind of distinct way of reasoning. Rather, we need to accept that human beings have the capacity for 'directedness in their thinking' (2005: 290), for locking into 'particular bits of the environment' (ibid.: 289). An ordinary person or an expert acts in a particular way, framing 'singular states which bind the rest of cognition to certain options' (ibid.: 290). There is nothing special about the epistemic standpoint of experts, he argues, 'that warrants the thought that experts deploy a different kind of knowledge subject to different forms of justification, warrant or rationality' (Luntley 2009: 364). Luntley wants 'a seamless integration of expert knowledge' (ibid.: 361), one that accepts that 'experts exhibit a highly nuanced inhabiting of the environment' but that 'such mode of inhabiting can be brought within the province of ordinary conceptual thought' (ibid.: 362). To understand professional judgement in teaching, he seems to imply, research need not bother itself with *what* teachers know but with *how* they know – that they have acquired attention skills. Luntley's account, I believe, locks teachers into the status of a craft worker.

A different account is provided by Winch. In his examination of occupational knowledge of teachers, Winch (2010) argues that seeing the core of teaching in practical wisdom will 'lead to a further removal of teaching from the established attributes of professional status, rather than bringing teachers nearer to them' (ibid.: 189). According to Winch, the teaching profession needs to develop an 'empirical theory of teaching', or a deductive knowledge account of the complex sequence of reasoning that typifies the practice of teaching a subject matter (ibid.: 110). With the term 'empirical theory of teaching', Winch combines a normative account (what teaching ought to be) with empirical analyses that guide actors on how to act:

> Most professions do not just rely on normative theory which sets out how they *should* act, they also have at their disposal a body of *empirical* theory concerning how the world is, which provides the *basis* for individual judgements as well as general prescriptions about how to act.
>
> (Winch 2004: 189, emphasis in the original)

This type of account is context-sensitive but its deductive set of propositions are applied to 'classes of cases' rather than to a particular situation (Clarke and Winch 2004: 515). It foregrounds the organised propositional knowledge that the teaching profession enjoys (with all its weaknesses). It emphasises the differences between this knowledge type and contingent and discrete propositional knowledge, and how important the former is for professional judgement if it is to be both accurate and appropriate for situations in teaching (Winch 2010: 103). Clarke and Winch (2004) want a particular form of theoretical development for the profession, one that will provide ordering principles for the practical wisdom of teaching. To become situationally aware, practitioners do not need to learn how to learn, which is implied in Luntley's generic account of attentional skills.

Rather, practitioners need conceptual content that can be shown, with sufficient empirical evidence, to apply to 'classes of cases'. To learn a theory, Clarke and Winch insist, 'is to learn a body of knowledge of general application within a recognised subject matter' (ibid.: 516).

In order to develop the idea of empirical theoretical knowledge, I turn in the next section to Andrew Abbot's analytical work (1988) on professional knowledge. Abbott's work helps me to further elaborate the type of conceptual knowledge that professionals draw on when they exercise professional judgement, but also on how they draw on it. His analysis shows that inferential thinking (knowledge how) in professional work relies on access to two types of knowledge classifications (knowledge that) – 'academic' and 'diagnostic'. Consistent with Winch, when these classifications are formal *and* sufficiently specialised in specific subject matter, their guiding power is stronger.

Diagnosis, treatment and inference

Professions enjoy two reservoirs of knowledge, argues Abbott – academic and diagnostic. Both are formal bodies of knowledge but each is organised differently and constrains professional judgement differently. Academic knowledge classifications pull together propositions, formally, along consistent rational dimensions, thus producing relations and boundaries between ideas. They are stronger when they refer to subject-matter specific concepts. Concepts such as 'particle interactions' or 'underwriting' provide stronger classifications because they can only be explained by a singular discipline (Physics and Actuarial Theory, respectively). In educational theory, concepts like 'zone of proximal development', 'epistemological access', 'the pedagogic device', and 'criteria of education' provide similar kinds of classifications. Having these kinds of distinctive concepts (Abbott refers to them as 'positive formalism', ibid.: 102) secures the jurisdiction of judgement within the profession. Jurisdiction does not mean that the meaning of the concepts is not debated. It does mean, however, that the concepts are exclusive to the professional knowledge of a specific profession. Degrees of specialisation of content are central resources for the exclusivity claimed by professionals. In Abbott's terms: 'No one tries to explain particle interactions without mastering the abstract knowledge of physics. More practically, no one offers insurance companies advice on underwriting without having mastered actuarial theory' (ibid.: 103). A radically different type of classification falls into what is commonly called generic classifications, which Abbott calls 'extreme abstraction' (ibid.: 103). These classifications are much weaker; they refer to many classes interchangeably. Their applicability is so wide that when recruited into practice, they work like a metaphor and not like a concept. They are not able to frame relations in a sequential form between concepts of a specific professional domain. In current educational argot concepts such as 'efficiency', 'authentic experience' or 'critical thinking' are examples of this kind of metaphorical language, used by economists or psychologists of education but also by columnists and parents to describe an educational phenomena. Arguably, 'attentional skills' falls into this type of extreme abstractions.

The second reservoir of professional knowledge is 'diagnostic classifications' (Abbott 1988: 53). These classifications form a far more direct resource for the working knowledge of professionals, yet do not lend themselves to a 'standard sequence of questions' (ibid.: 42). They are not tips, routine skills or direct commands.[1] Criterion reference assessment and taxonomies of learning attempt to provide such classifications to teachers. Abbott explains the way in which professionals draw on the two reservoirs of knowledge. First, they collect information about a particular case (be it a specific disease, legal case, a building design in architecture or learners' errors in an exam) and assemble it into a complex picture, according to certain epistemic rules and criteria specific to the subject matter. Second, the practitioner takes the complex picture and refers it to classifications that are already known to the profession (for example, a concept in the field of law, a formal theory in architecture or a set of conceptions in a particular area of science or mathematics), and deduces the type of the case in particular (ibid.: 42). In order for a practitioner to align a specific case with 'the dictionary of professionally legitimated problems' (that is, its diagnostic classifications, ibid.: 41), the practitioner needs to know 'what kinds of evidence are relevant and irrelevant, valid and invalid, as well as rules specifying the admissible level of ambiguity' (ibid.: 42). This evaluative process is regulated better when the practice is bounded by systematically organised knowledge (or 'knowledge that') and by procedures for acquiring and testing claims about that knowledge (or 'knowledge how') (Winch 2010: 106).

Abbott's work on classifications can be understood by reference to Vygotsky's (1987) 'scientific concepts'. Classifications impose new orders of meaning on existing concepts. They do this by pulling existing concepts into new relations of abstraction and generality. Like Bernstein's (2000) idea of vertical discourse, Abbott's work points to the vertical relation between propositions, whereby the more general concept frames the relations between the subordinate concepts. In different ways all of the above work comes to a similar conclusion – that the process of building a case from different information relies on having access to a reservoir of deductive propositions or theoretical concepts that directs the experts' attention to specific features of the particular. Access to this reservoir of knowledge enables attention in at least two ways. First, it enables the practitioner to 'diagnose away' (Abbott 1988: 41) what is *not* relevant for the case, although this is a complex matter, which is often subjected to a few trials. Second, a practitioner who understands the subject matter they deal with (its academic classifications) would know to distinguish between less or more reliable evidence. At a minimum they will be acquainted with what Winch calls 'subject-dependent warrants'. At best they will master 'the appropriate procedures for knowledge generation within the relevant subject' (Winch 2010: 110).

The constitutive condition of judgement is reversed here. For Luntley, professional judgement is constituted by the ability to attend to the particular with compulsion. For Abbott and Winch, professional judgement depends on having access to a reservoir of knowledge that is tested, trialed and classified. This is what distinguishes professional from ordinary judgement. Logical clarity,

Abbott argues, belies the muddle of practice (1988: 42). It sets boundaries – within a subject area, about what can be included and what must be excluded, and what counts as conflicting evidence. Put strongly, it is not only that knowledge classifications guide practice; they are a necessary condition for practice. In Winch's words, 'The possession of relevant systematically organized knowledge is not a by-product of the action, but a prerequisite' (Winch 2010: 104). When academic and diagnostic classifications are aligned, the practitioner's inferential ability is well constrained (to use Luntley's undeveloped term).

Two criticisms are possible here. The first and the most obvious one is that not all professions have access to this kind of knowledge. Abbott is the first to admit that no profession, even the stronger and more organised ones (such as medicine or law), has achieved/can achieve a completely air-tight classification of cases. His use of the notion *art* to describe professional judgement is apt. Diagnosis, says Abbott, is a form of art:

> The information available may be inevitably ambiguous or incomplete . . . There are, moreover, likely to be several plausible colligations. The art of diagnosis lies in finding which is the real one. This holds as much for a financial planner ascertaining a client's true financial picture as for a doctor divining a patient's illness.
>
> (ibid.: 42)

The teaching profession, in particular, cannot be said to have access to tight and accurate academic classifications, let alone to diagnostic ones. Teacher knowledge, in other words, is not case-based (Muller 2012: 15). Moreover, different bodies of knowledge, the largest ones being psychology, philosophy and sociology, claim some or other jurisdiction in the field of education – each brings its arsenal of concepts, and their contestations about the meanings of these concepts. Second, strict rules of relevance are not available to all professions. While a doctor can (in some cases more than in others) disregard what Abbott calls 'the client's extraneous qualities' (for example, emotional, financial, social), a teacher cannot.

Do these two problems suggest that academic and diagnostic classifications that are formal and sufficiently specialised in specific subject matter cannot be developed in teaching? Recent research on knowledge innovation in different sectors (Foray and Hargreaves 2002, Foray and Raffo 2009), shows that knowledge innovation in the educational sector is very slow and one of the main reasons for that is the low level of codified (that is, formal) knowledge held by teachers. Foray and Hargreaves attribute this problem to the organisational structure of teachers' work and to the knowledge management of research in education (ibid. 2002: 10) and much less so to the epistemic structure (humanistic and not scientific) of teacher knowledge. This is an important distinction, which suggests that the slow development of codified knowledge in the field of education is not intrinsic to the knowledge-base of teaching and therefore is improvable.[2] I would add that any position that accepts that teaching is not a craft but is based on professional knowledge, must also accept that coding of professional knowledge is necessary, albeit with varying degrees of realisation.[3] Knowledge classifications are necessary for binding of teachers' professional judgement. They are important for curriculum decisions (Shalem 2010) and for assessment (Shalem and Sapire 2012). The introduction of the idea of diagnosis into educational argot is also noteworthy.[4]

With the advent of performance-based accountability, the growth in standardised evaluation studies of learners' achievement in a variety of school subjects furnishes the profession with new research opportunities (Shalem, Sapire and Huntley 2013). Current large-scale evaluation studies tend to call on a variety of generic classifications, most of which are not content specific and are not sequenced in terms of their efficacy for the specific problem identified. The PIRLS' Reading for Literacy Purposes (PIRLS 2006), for example, is reported along four 'permanent benchmarks' ranging from a low benchmark (400 scale score) to an advanced international benchmark (625 scale score). Annual National Assessment's results (Department of Basic Education, 2011, 2012) are reported along seven 'performance levels' ranging from Not Achieved to Outstanding Achievement. [5] It is questionable whether the conclusion to the 2011 report that 'schools and the education departments have gained important experiences in better assessment and, through this, a better focus on what must improve' (Department of Basic Education 2011: 36) has any substance. It is also doubtful whether the expectation (Department of Basic Education 2012: 4) that statistical data of learners' achievement will help teachers 'to make informed decisions when planning a teaching program' will be realised. Analytical work that developed in response to these kinds of reports does not go much further. This is evident in broad claims such as 'learners in all three Grades (7, 8, 12) showed a lack of understanding of the mathematics and science questions as well as an inability to communicate their answers in instances where they did understand the questions. Learners performed particularly badly in questions requiring a written answer' (Howie 2004: 150). These generic classifications lack inferential rules that could take teachers 'to conclusions which are either actions or prescriptions for actions'(Winch 2009: 95).[6] In terms of professional jurisdiction, teachers are left with multiple possible inferences, ideologies and personal preferences but with very little specialised diagnosis of the problem. The above classifications of the problem open the door for 'numerous claimants' (Abbott 1988: 103) to dictate the treatment – from economists, management theorists, cultural studies theorists, to the bureaucracy.

However, there are other kinds of studies that do attempt to codify teachers' knowledge and provide diagnostic classifications for teachers. They may not rely on this expensive market of standardised achievement test data, but their analytical work is focused on providing inferential rules for practice teachers. Two of these studies are discussed below. The studies are different in the way they draw on academic classifications to create diagnostic knowledge for the profession (specialised to the subject matter or not), the sequence they order the classifications (formal and efficacy) and their jurisdictional power. They thus differ in terms of their inferential power for binding professional judgement. I argue that the second study is an example of codification that is formal, content rich and subject specific, and that its findings can apply to classes of cases.

The first study, based in the United States, develops knowledge classifications for teaching school History (Schleppegrell *et al.* 2008 and Schleppegrell 2011). This study responds to the problem of poor mastery by historically disadvantaged learners, defined as 'learners who have little opportunity to engage with academic language outside the classroom' (Schleppegrell *et al.* 2008: 176). Schleppegrell *et al.* argue that an analysis of different history curricula suggests that the proliferation of ideological preferences promoted by History textbook writers affects all learners but in particular historically disadvantaged ones. Each textbook writer, they explain, presents a different interpretive approach to what counts as important about a historical event, raises different questions, draws on different evidence and holds different values (Schleppegrell 2011: 200). This means that academic classifications about what history is and how to study it are contested and the curriculum specialists who select from the academic field do not send clear signals to teachers. In the absence of clear academic classifications, teachers' attentional skills, to use Luntley's language, vacillate between the ideological bias of the textbook (Marxist, post-modernist, feminist and so on), the common-sense of the learners (which varies depending on the social class-based experience a learner has access to) and their own personal preference. In this kind of curriculum environment, teachers struggle to transmit discipline-specific criteria of acquisition. History teachers have very few diagnostic classifications at their disposal.

Schleppegrell's work has been focusing on developing what she calls a meta-language for teaching school History. This is done to help teachers develop in their learners 'greater technicality, abstraction and precision' of interpretation of specialised knowledge texts (ibid. 2011: 198). What teachers need, she argues, is a deductive ordering principle that is free of any specific ideological perspective. In Winch's and in Abbott's respective terms, they need an analytical tool that is based on sufficient empirical evidence, can be applied to classes of cases, and its classificatory form is of positive formalism and not of extreme abstraction. This study offers teachers access to formal classifications, recontextualised from Systemic Functional Linguistics (SFL), to the goals of history education. The meta language that Schleppegrell borrows from SFL employs functional grammar strategies such as *participants*, *processes* and *circumstances*, use of references devices such as *pronouns* (complex noun group) and different modes of nominal-isation as well as logical connectors or conjunctions (Schleppegrell 2011). With this arsenal of linguistic resources – referred to as a register – teacher developers train teachers how to work with learners to identify:

- the agency in the text (how the author constructs some social actors as agentive and others as passive);
- the graphic of the text (how the author develops information about the central historical event of the text – how a cause is constructed, how difference of opinion is distilled from previous information and condensed into an abstraction); and,
- the author's perspective (what is the author's position about the event).

There are two problems with this mode of codification. First, the reading tools given to teachers are arranged formally (academic classifications) but not sequentially (diagnostic classification). In efficacy terms, this means that teachers need to use a great deal of guess work when selecting linguistic resources from the total reservoir, deciding on how to sequence them in the lesson, how much time to spend on each resource, how to adapt them for the cognitive age of the class, and, most importantly how to foreground the historical content of the lesson so that the identity of the subject matter is not over-determined by the register. Second, providing teachers with classification tools drawn from a subject matter they have not specialised in is risky. As history teachers, they have not been socialised into that subject matter and they are not privy to the recontextualisation of SFL concepts to diagnostic classifications in history. In sum, this study employs positive formalism, is based on empirical evidence, but the classifications it offers for binding teachers' judgements are not specialised to the subject matter they are trained in, which thus weakens the binding power of their inference.

The second study, based in Australia, intervenes in the endless debates on models of teaching school English (Christie's and Macken-Horarik's work 2007, 2011). Like the previous study, this study also responds to the problem of poor mastery (in this case, of English), but its classification of the problem and of the treatment are both specialised to the subject matter. The study is a response to the growing proliferation of models of teaching school English. Many of the models tend to foreground sociological and personalised approaches to text and background 'a principled linguistic method of analysis of text or system '(ibid. 2011: 182). Second, the pedagogy used by many teachers is not aligned with what they, in fact, value at the point of evaluation (ibid. 2007: 157). For example, in following one of the more popular models of teaching school English (Personal Growth), teachers tend to encourage children to write expressively, with very little guidance and support. The result is that 'the more successful students intuit the necessary registers and texts and hence the desired "gaze", while others struggle, unable to grasp what is required' (ibid. 2011: 185). As in the former study, English teachers have very little diagnostic classifications at their disposal – they are not able to classify learners' writing according to a preferred evaluation order:

> In the contemporary school curriculum, there are in fact many 'Englishes', even if the singular form is retained in the name of the subject. A review of its history . . . would suggest that it has been of the nature of the subject that it has proliferated many forms, or 'languages', each possessed of its own preoccupations, its own questions, its own value positions.
>
> (ibid. 2007:157)

This state of affairs, Christie and Macken-Horarik (2011) argue, affects learners of poor socio-economic background, in particular, for whom access to a range of 'semiotic practices'[7] is far less commonly available. Christie and Macken-Horarik looked for a way to construct a principled account of language acquisition. They turn to psychology of language acquisition, which offers them principles of child development (academic classifications) around which they build the disciplinarity of school English (ibid.: 176). With the use of the SFL model they identified constitutive units of English such as *knowledge of text and system*; *knowledge of culture and situation of subject English*; *knowledge of registers* and *different texts* (diagnostic classifications) and examined what it means to acquire them, developmentally, by years of schooling and chronological age (3–6; 6–8; 9–13 or 14; 14–15 or 16; 16–18), taking into account that a child's development is influenced by social class and family background (ibid.: 186).

This work enables a very interesting theoretical development. The six most prominent models of school English[8] become a reservoir of academic classifications and therefore resources for subject English that teachers can draw on, *albeit* in the appropriate developmental phase of language acquisition (diagnostic classifications sequenced in efficacy order), and therefore at different levels of complexity. This type of knowledge development, I argue, provides a much clearer ordering principle for teacher educators and ultimately for teachers. It binds trainers to attend first to the area of language to be acquired and the cognitive age of the learners and only then to one's ideological preference to one or other model of teaching school English. It also sends clearer curriculum signals to teachers. It offers teachers diagnostic classifications with which to identify the problem (what an acquirer of different social background needs at a specific age of language acquisition) and to organise the treatment (which model of teaching school English can best attend to the problem). This study shows what is entailed in privileging the logical structure of intellectual subject. Making the functional grammar of English visible makes it possible to show what knowledge counts in terms of the intellectual field, rather than in terms of one's own preference or ideological orientation.

Conclusion

Luntley is concerned that 'a teacher with good subject and pedagogic knowledge may be unable to put her subject and pedagogic knowledge into practice effectively in particular contexts' (Ainley and Luntley 2007: 19). His notion of 'attention', which signals a normative criterion, is his attempt to find the bind between the general and the particular. The problem, however, is that in claiming that there is nothing 'special about the epistemic standpoint of experts', Luntley devalues the role of theoretical knowledge in professional judgement. Reducing professional judgement to the ability to reason with moral compulsion will further contribute to the growing anti-intellectualism about professional knowledge (Winch 2010; Kotzee 2012). It is the argument of this chapter that if Luntley's idea of 'object-dependent knowledge' is to have purchase, the conceptual structure and complexity of the body of knowledge that underpins the inferential act involved in making a professional judgement must be unpacked and the distinctiveness of professional judgement, as distinct from ordinary ways of thinking, must be recognised. Without this, professional judgement remains context-bound and therefore mostly unreliable. Extreme abstractions cannot mitigate this. To this extent, many of the current evaluation studies of learner achievement fail to signal an inferential path to teachers. Codification of teacher knowledge goes a step towards what Winch calls for – the building of empirical theoretical knowledge.

The discussion in this chapter hopes to foreground three points about professional judgement in teaching. First, to explain why experts exhibit a highly nuanced judgement, research needs to demarcate the distinctive epistemic configuration of professional knowledge and not just the process of making a professional judgement. The knowledge that informs the decision to attend to the particular must be shown to be more extensive than what the specific situation entails. Classifications that are formal, content rich, domain specific, and contain externally verifiable evidence, bind judgement in specific situations. They provide the basis for the inferential act and keep the jurisdiction within the profession and protect its specialisation. Second, inferential ability is a crucial aspect of specialisation. Too little room for inference (for example in so-called 'scripted' teaching) belies specialisation; too much room for inference (generic classifications) makes professional judgement impossible to legitimate (Abbott 1988: 52). When the subject matter that teachers teach is contested by multiple academic classifications teachers struggle to develop useful attentional skills and their ability to bind themselves to an object weakens. Christie's and Macken-Horarik's work (2007 and 2011) shows a way in which psychology, which is a core discipline in education, can be utilised to signal optimal conditions for the acquisition of specific subject matter. Finally, an increase in professional agreement about academic classifications can only strengthen the jurisdiction and legitimacy of the teaching profession.

Notes

1   Abbott gives an example: to understand the dynamic of each type of psychological defense, academic knowledge of Psychiatry classifies different types of defenses (academic classifications), while the psychiatrist practitioner identifies a specific case (diagnostic classifications).

2   The irony is that the ICT sector is quick to jump on the bandwagon of codification by developing 'new methods of pedagogy and instruction technologies' (Foray and Raffo 2009: 14), a development that generates great anxiety among practitioners. Not only is teachers' tacit knowledge licensed by another jurisdiction, teachers, who have been using these pedagogical methods, may be found guilty for 'infringing patents' (ibid.:15).

3   See Taylor, in this book, on the importance of representing subject knowledge for teaching 'in a form which can be shared discursively and practically' and on attempts to codify it.

4   Media statement issued by the Department of Basic Education on the Annual National Assessments (Department of Basic Education): 4 February, 2011. www.education.gov. za/Newsroom/MediaReleases/tabid/347/ctl/Details/mid/1389/ItemID/3148/ Default.aspx (accessed on 7 June, 2011).

5   Department of Basic Education (2011) used four generic classifications.

6   For interesting error analysis studies see Dempster and Zuma (2010).

7   For example, accuracy of written expression, arrangement of clauses in texts and nominalisation, but also familiarity with the literary cannon and with different registers and text types.

8   The six models are: Basic Skills; Cultural Heritage; Personal Growth; Functional Language Studies; Cultural Analysis/Multiliteracies; and New Literacy Studies. The first model was developed in the nineteenth century and all the others developed as a response to it, and to the limitations identified in the subsequence models, leaving the field fragmented and under theorised.

References

Abbott, A. (1988) *The system of professions: An essay on the division of expert labour.* Chicago, IL: University of Chicago Press.

Ainley J. and Luntley, M. (2007) 'The role of attention in expert classroom practice', *Journal of Mathematics Teacher Education*, 10(1): 3–22.

Bernstein, B. (2000) *Pedagogy, symbolic control and identity: Theory, research, critique* (revised edn). London: Rowman & Littlefield.

Christie, F. and Macken-Horarik, M. (2007) 'Building verticality in the subject English' in F. Christie and J. R. Martin (eds) *Language knowledge and pedagogy: Functional linguistics and sociological perspectives.* London: Continuum.

Christie, F. and Macken-Horarik, M. (2011) 'Disciplinarily and school English' in F. Christie and K. Maton (eds) *Disciplinarity: Functional linguistics and sociological perspectives.* London: Continuum.

Clarke, L. and Winch, C. (2004) 'Apprenticeship and applied theoretical knowledge', *Educational Philosophy and Theory*, 36(5): 509–22.

Dempster, E. and Zuma, S. (2010) 'Reasoning used by isiZulu-speaking children when answering science questions in English', *Journal of Education*, 50: 35–59.

Department of Basic Education (DBE, 2011) Annual national assessment: Report on the annual national assessment 2011, Grades 1–6 & 9. Pretoria: Department of Basic Education.

Department of Basic Education (DBE, 2012) Annual national assessment: Report on the annual national assessment 2012, Grades 1–6 & 9. Pretoria: Department of Basic Education.

Foray, D. and Hargreaves, D. (2002) 'The production of knowledge in different sectors: A model and some hypotheses', *London Review of Education*, 1(1): 7–19. Available at: www.tandfonline.com/doi/pdf/10.1080/14748460306689 (accessed 1 August, 2012).

Foray, D. and Raffo, J. (2009) 'A small explosion: Patent in educational and instructional technologies and methods; what do they tell us', Available at: www.epip.eu/conferences/epip04/files/FORAY_Dominique.pdf (accessed 25 July, 2012).

Howie, S. (2004) 'A national assessment in mathematics within an international comparative assessment', *Perspectives in Education*, 2(2): 149–62.

Kotzee, B. (2012) 'Expertise, fluency and social realism about professional knowledge', *Journal of Education and Work*, 1–18, iFirst Article, Available at: http://dx.doi.org/10.1080/13639080.2012.738291 (accessed 20 March, 2013).

Lave, J. and Wenger, E. (1991) *Situated learning: Legitimate peripheral participation.* Cambridge: Cambridge University Press.

Luntley, M. (2005) 'The role of judgement', *Philosophical Explorations*, 8(3): 281–95.

Luntley, M. (2009) 'Understanding expertise', *Journal of Applied Philosophy*, 26(4): 356–70.

Luntley, M. (2011) 'What do nurses know?' *Nursing Philosophy*, 12: 22–33.

Muller, J. (2009) 'Forms of knowledge and curriculum coherence', *Journal of Education and Work*, 22(3): 206–26.

Muller, J. (2012) *The body of knowledge/le corps du savoir*. Mimeo: University of Cape Town.

PIRLS (2006) (Progress in International Reading Literacy Study) Technical Report. Michael O. Martin, Ina V.S. Mullis, and Ann M. Kennedy (eds). Chapter 12: 'Reporting Student Achievement in Reading', written by Ann M. Kennedy and Kathleen L. Trong. (International Association for the evaluation of Educational Achievement, Boston College). Available at http://pirls.bc.edu/PDF/p06_technical_report.pdf#page=175 (accessed 23 June, 2013).

Schleppegrell, M.J. (2011) 'Supporting disciplinary learning through language analysis: Developing historical literacy', in F. Christie and K. Maton (eds) *Disciplinarity: Functional linguistics and sociological perspectives*. London: Continuum.

Schleppegrell, M. J., Greer, S. and Taylor, S. (2008) 'Literacy in history: Language and meaning', *Australian Journal of Language and Literacy*, 3(2): 174–87.

Schön, D. A. (1983) *The reflective practitioner: How professionals think in action*. London: Temple Smith.

Shalem, Y. (2010) 'How does the form of curriculum affect systematic learning'? in Y. Shalem and S. Pendlebury (eds) *Retrieving teaching. Critical issues in curriculum, pedagogy and learning*. Cape Town: Juta & Co.

Shalem, Y. and Sapire, I. (2012) *Teachers' knowledge of error analysis*. Johannesburg: Saide.

Shalem, Y., Sapire, I. and Huntley, B. (2013) 'Mapping onto the mathematics curriculum – an opportunity for teachers to learn', *Pythagoras*, 34(1):11–20.

Vygotsky, L. S. (1987) *The collected works of L. S. Vygotsky. Volume 1: Problems of general psychology* (R.W. Rieberand and A.S. Carton, eds). New York: PlenumPress.

Winch, C. (2004) 'What do teachers need to know about teaching? A critical examination of occupational knowledge of teachers', *British Journal of Educational Studies*, 52(2): 180–96.

Winch, C. (2009) 'Ryle on knowing how and the possibility of vocational education', *Journal of Applied Philosophy*, 26(1): 88–101.

Winch, C. (2010) *Dimensions of expertise: A conceptual exploration of vocational knowledge*. London: Continuum.

Young, M. (2010) 'The future of education in a knowledge society: The radical case of a subject-based curriculum', *Journal of the Pacific Circle Consortium for Education*, 22(1): 21–32.

Young, M. and Muller, J. (2010) 'Three educational scenarios for the future: Lessons from the sociology of knowledge', *European Journal of Education*, 45(1): 11–27.

Part Three

Education and the professions

Case studies

8 The evolution of engineering knowledge

Hu Hanrahan

Introduction

This chapter addresses the question: 'What are the nature, organisation and scope of engineering knowledge?' The objective is to bring out the distinctive features of engineering knowledge as a component of engineering professional competence. By way of background other questions must first be addressed: 'What is engineering?'; 'What is engineering expertise?'; and 'Why is engineering knowledge an essential enabler of engineering professional expertise?'

Compact definitions of engineering, such as the application of science and technology for useful purposes do not do the field justice. A fuller statement such as that of the International Engineering Alliance is more informative (IEA 2013), incorporating the multiple dimensions of modern engineering: 'an activity that seeks to meet identified needs of people and societies by the purposeful application of engineering sciences, technology and techniques to achieve predicted solutions that use available resources efficiently, are economical, that manage risks.'

Engineering knowledge is one facet of professional competency, along with skills and attitudes. Engineering competency develops in stages and the mix of knowledge, skills and attitudes changes. Rugarcia *et al.* (2000) describe graduate competency in terms of interlocking components: 'Knowledge, the facts they know and concepts they understand; skills they use in managing and applying their knowledge and attitudes that dictate the goals toward which their skills and knowledge will be directed.' The key skill is the analysis of problems and synthesis of solutions based on engineering knowledge. An engineering degree in typical national systems is not intended to produce a fully-fledged professional; the graduate must typically undergo training and gain experience for at least three or four years before attaining the competence for independent practice. At this stage knowledge of both facts and concepts, and especially the context of engineering applications, will have expanded. Problem-solving skills will be enhanced to solve real-world problems in the face of constraints, risks and decision-making under uncertainty; this requires judgement based on experience. Attitudes must develop from the graduate's understanding the principles of responsible and ethical behavior to the professional's ability to act responsibly and ethically in real-world situations.

The range of engineering practice and of actual and possible applications is large; Auyang (2004) writes of engineering as 'an endless frontier'. Engineering knowledge is correspondingly large and complex and expands over time. Pitt's (2001) definition of engineering knowledge captures its essence: 'engineering knowledge concerns the design, construction, and operation of artifices for the purpose of manipulating the human environment' – provided that artifices and the human environment are not restricted to the physical world but also include processes and information. Because of its complexity defining a detailed scope of engineering knowledge is not feasible and we concentrate rather on its nature and organisation. As strategy for managing complexity we use a number of viewpoints on engineering knowledge in the remainder of this chapter. Each viewpoint abstracts a particular aspect of engineering knowledge. The set of viewpoints taken together provide an understanding of the nature and structure. This framework can be filled with detail in a particular area of practice, a task beyond the scope of this chapter.

The first viewpoint is *historical*. Engineering developed from millennia-old roots to be the key enabler of the modern world. This development can also be regarded as *evolutionary;* engineering is directed at useful purposes and engineering knowledge that is fit for purpose survives and is codified and added to the corpus.

A further classification of engineering knowledge arises by noting that engineering education, training and practice are broadly sub-divided into engineering *disciplines* and sub-disciplines. Numerous practice areas exist within or across disciplinary boundaries. The historical view shows how the main disciplines emerged.

We then classify engineering knowledge by type. Consistent with engineering being an essentially practical art that is enabled by a scientific base, we classify engineering knowledge according to being predominantly *conceptual* or predominantly *contextual*.

Focussing mainly on the conceptual body of knowledge, we classify knowledge further by identifying *layers* of knowledge where higher layers depend on and build on those below. The characteristic fundamental knowledge of the main disciplines is identified.

A cross-cutting classification emerges from the observation that typical engineering activity requires several *roles*, including those of the engineer, engineering technologist and engineering technician, recognised in many national systems. These roles are differentiated by the level of knowledge and skill required for their respective functions.

A history of engineering applications, knowledge and disciplines

The twenty-first-century body of knowledge in engineering is the product of development of both practice and knowledge over at least four millenia.

An early example of technical and organisational ingenuity is the building the Khufu (Cheops) pyramid in Egypt around 2500 BCE (Strandh 1982: 22). The master builders of Greece and Rome, for example Vitruvius (~75–15 BCE), were multiskilled, combining the functions of the modern architect, structural engineer, mechanical engineer, surveyor and construction manager while taking into account the legal and social environment (Auyang 2004: 14). Master builders practiced ingenuity, *ingenium* in Latin, both in the process and product of work. The title *ingeniator* for one who practices ingenium was used until the Renaissance and is the root of our modern word engineer. Many ingeniators practised military engineering, for example, Leonardo da Vinci (1452–1519) designed fortifications and machines for defense and attack for his political masters (Nicholl 2004: 180). Over time, the skills of the military engineer were applied to the wider good: the planning and construction of canals, aqueducts, roads and machines. From the sixteenth century, the ingeniator in the role of master builder concentrated on the technical aspects, leaving the architectural design to others. The notion of the civil engineer, in contrast to the military engineer, dates from the eighteenth century.

The scientific base of engineering developed over a long period, from Archimedes (287–212 BCE) through Leonardo da Vinci's inventions, Galileo Galilei (1564–1642) introducing theoretical predictions into the design of useful artifacts, Newton (1642–1727) launching calculus-based mechanics, Faraday's (1642–1727) work on electricity and Carnot's (1796–1832) pioneering work on steam engines, to give a few examples.

Engineering remained essentially an application-oriented art through the industrial revolution. Devising ever more ingenious and, in many cases, steam-driven machines led to the emergence of mechanical engineering. Winning of metal-bearing ores from the earth and the subsequent extraction of the metals were critical to progress. Mining engineering and metallurgy became more important as the importance of coal and iron increased.

By the mid-nineteenth century, physics and chemistry had become developed sciences with a substantial body of knowledge. The mathematical formalism required to express natural laws existed. Engineering could no longer develop using an exclusively practical approach. Practical engineering thus developed into science-based engineering.

Engineering is often described as a discipline but is so broad that its various branches are regarded as disciplines in their own right in the design of higher education programmes and in the organisation of work. The emergence of civil and mechanical engineering from military engineering has already been noted. Electrical engineering has its roots in key discoveries of the 1830s: Faraday's invention of the electric generator; Henry's practical motor and the telegraph of Cooke, Wheatstone and Morse. The latter nineteenth century saw the availability of electric power generation, transmission and utilisation, lighting and telephones.

New engineering disciplines emerged as the scope of engineering and its scientific base expanded. Large scale manufacture of chemicals requires processes at elevated pressures and temperatures, and the transfer of heat and movement of material. Chemical engineering therefore emerged as a discipline and field of study in the 1880s, branching mainly from mechanical engineering. The early-twentieth century saw the blossoming of industrial engineering to meet the need for specialist attention to manufacturing processes. Agricultural engineering emerged as an offshoot of mechanical engineering with the mechanisation of farming, irrigation and complex handling of produce from farm to market. Early in the twentieth century, the intensity of aircraft design, manufacture and operation became substantial and gave rise to aeronautical engineering as a focused form of mechanical engineering. Electronic engineering also dates from early in the century but came into its own during and after World War II, particularly with the invention of the transistor and integrated circuit. The even newer engineering disciplines of computer and software engineering date from the 1970s. The proliferation of products and systems such as copiers, automobile parts and assembly lines that contain mechanical, electrical and electronic components and are controlled by software has given rise to the hybrid field of mechatronics. The ancient discipline of military engineering has developed to now apply mechanical, civil and electrical engineering elements in military operations and civil disaster situations.

Engineering knowledge has expanded and areas of application have proliferated. Malpas (2000) proposed that the universe of engineering could be measured by the extent of applications and disciplines. His list of application sectors is informative rather than definitive: building and construction; energy; natural resources; engineered materials; agriculture and food production; defence and security; transport; healthcare; leisure and entertainment; and commerce, trade and finance. His list of engineering disciplines contains the main disciplines described above: civil (including structural engineering and building services); mechanical (including aerospace, marine and agricultural); chemical; mining; electrical and electronic (including computing, communications and control), as well as medical engineering. Tadmor (2006) identifies further offshoots from the main disciplines. Figure 8.1, developed from Tadmor's diagram, shows the branching that has taken place to yield new engineering disciplines. A noticeable feature of the tree is the way that new disciplines fall into groups related to the traditional disciplines: civil, mechanical, electrical, chemical, mining and materials. The reason for this grouping, namely common fundamentals, is addressed later in the chapter. Some modern disciplines arise from different bases, for example, environmental engineering has variants based in civil and chemical engineering respectively.

The large number of engineering disciplines reflects the great range of applications of engineering. They differ in the specialist knowledge required in application areas. For example, an expert in high voltage engineering has different specialist knowledge to one working in petroleum engineering.

Among engineering practitioners, the engineering discipline is a strong social force for association and pride. We show below that all engineering disciplines share common skill components of competency. Disciplines therefore have substantial commonality. Disciplinary boundaries are neither impermeable nor immutable

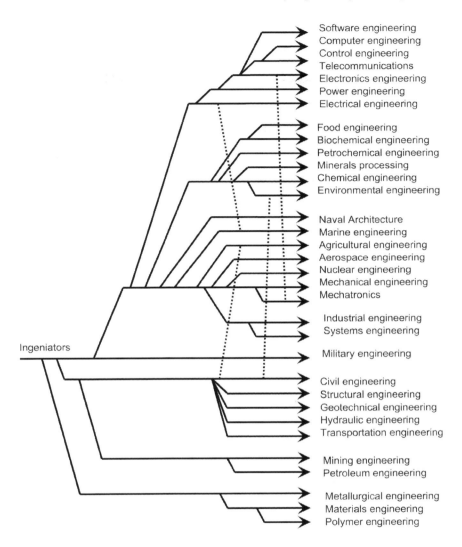

Figure 8.1 Development of engineering disciplines.

over time. Disciplines are effective units for promoting engineering practice and providing services such as continuing professional development. For regulating engineering practice, the entire profession is the effective unit.

Evolution of engineering roles

Two roles (apart from a large labour force) were essential to early military and civil projects: the ingeniator, who was responsible for devising how to meet the requirement and organising the work process, and the craftsman who provided the necessary hand skills. The increasing complexity of construction projects and the rise of machinery led to divisions of labour, for example between the architect and master builders already discussed.

As scientific and engineering knowledge developed, the engineer role changed from essentially practical to science-based. The engineer became the science-based problem solver, developer of new technology and pioneer of innovative applications. Figure 8.2 shows a number of splits that took place. During the Industrial Revolution a distinction arose between engineers who, while still essentially practical, were responsible for the conception and design of machinery and those skilled in their manufacture. The latter would become what today we call engineering technicians. Craftsmen and artisans had long been recognised for special demarcated manual skills and were also a source of the future technicians.

With the second industrial revolution, engineers became rooted in science, supporting innovation, creativity and change. At the same time many engineering technologies became established and served particular needs. From the 1960s the engineering technologist role became recognised: applying established technologies to address applications amenable to those technologies. Engineering technologists are educated in a narrower set of fundamentals and specialist areas than the engineer. They are expected to be master exponents of their technologies in solving problems.

The engineering technician role supports the engineer and engineering technologist roles in design, construction and operations by applying established methods. Engineering technicians have narrower knowledge bases and the way that they use the knowledge is consistent with their codified skills.

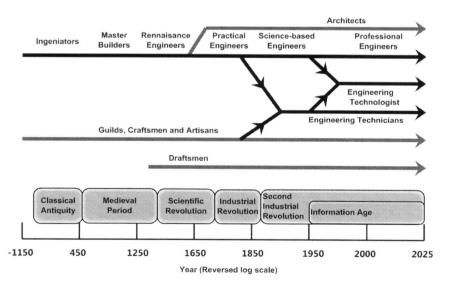

Figure 8.2 Evolution of engineering and related roles.

The above discussion suggests that the next step is to examine the knowledge required for a particular combination of discipline and role. As indicated in the introduction to this chapter, a direct attack on this problem is not tractable in view of the large number of such cases. Rather, we examine engineering competence to establish attributes that are common across disciplines and roles and their link to engineering knowledge.

Engineering competence

Competence consists of knowledge, skills and attitudes. The transferable skill and attitude components of engineering competence are common across engineering disciplines. The key competence is knowledge-based problem solving. Problems include planning, design, investigation, process and product improvement and may be technical or organisational. Problem solving depends in turn on the ability to analyse problems, to synthesise solutions and to evaluate the solutions and their consequences. Consequences include impacts on people, health and safety, the environment, sustainability, regulatory and ethical issues. Engineering practice requires communication with technical and wider audiences and managing processes to achieve engineering results. Practitioners in all roles and disciplines are affected to different extents by the impacts. All must have the generic skills listed here. The level of problem solving and the nature and manner of use of knowledge differentiates the required competence of the various engineering roles.

A significant consensus of the required competence for independent practice and at the graduate level has been developed by the members of the International Engineering Alliance (IEA 2013). The IEA graduate attributes (GA) provide exemplars of the outcome standard of programmes that provide the educational base for the professional engineer, engineering technologist and engineering technician roles. The professional competencies are outcome statements that are exemplars of the competence expected of engineers, engineering technologists and engineering technicians to qualify for independent practice.

Graduate attributes are formulated as outcome statements supported by range and level descriptors and a knowledge profile. We base the discussion of engineering knowledge on the IEA knowledge profile.

Classification of engineering knowledge: conceptual and contextual components

At an intuitive level engineers and engineering academics classify engineering knowledge into theoretical and practical parts along the lines of Pellegrini's (2011) description of the Swiss engineering education system at bachelors and masters levels adapted in Figure 8.3. This diagram is qualitative rather than quantitative. The more theoretically oriented engineers who proceed to the masters level at a Swiss technical university have a combination of theory and practice visualised in Figure 8.3. More application-oriented bachelors graduates of the universities of applied science have different combinations of theory and practice. This figure

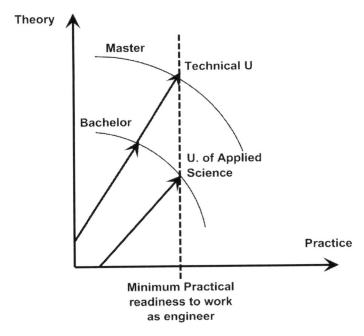

Figure 8.3 A model for engineering education in Switzerland. The vertical and horizontal scales and the loci are arbitrary (after Pellegrini 2011).

embodies two principles. First, at a particular level, say bachelors degree, different combinations of theoretical and practical knowledge are possible for different purposes. Second, to enter Swiss industry either after a bachelors degree (applied science/technologist route) or after a masters degree (engineer route), the graduate must have a minimum level of practical knowledge. This construction does not show the development after graduation to the level of competence for independent practice.

Pellegrini's theoretical and practical axes correspond respectively to the conceptual and contextual coherence of curricula described in Muller (2009). Conceptual aspects of a curriculum are related to the theoretical basis of the discipline and are highly codified, hierarchical, appropriately abstracted with a logical sequence of material to be learned. Contextual aspects are related to the practically oriented components in the curriculum. These are generally self-contained segments; sequence is of lesser importance except where a practical component depends explicitly or implicitly on particular theory. Conceptual and contextual components of the engineering curriculum are significant and are interdependent: the conceptual base underpins the practical techniques in many cases. Solving real engineering problems requires both components. Any aspect of engineering practice, for example the design of a structure or mechanism, has both theoretical and practical components. Classification of a particular piece of knowledge is not simply a trade-off between conceptual and conceptual emphasis; rather, we regard the conceptual and contextual components of a particular activity as co-ordinates that characterise the activity.

We examine the key characteristics of the conceptual and contextual components of engineering knowledge in the next sections using two established knowledge profiles as a starting point.

Knowledge profiles

The CDIO (Conceive-Design-Implement-Operate) Syllabus (Crawley *et al.* 2011) is a guide for engineering curriculum design to prepare graduates for the entire engineering product or system lifecycle. Under the heading of technical knowledge and reasoning, the CDIO Syllabus lists the underlying mathematics and science, core engineering fundamental knowledge and advanced engineering fundamental knowledge. As essential background to the conception, design, implementation and operation of systems, knowledge of the external, societal, environmental and business contexts is required.

The IEA graduate attributes knowledge profiles (IEA 2013) are defined for engineer, engineering technologist and engineering technician roles to support the outcomes defined for each role. The eight elements are shown here for the engineer role. The first four relate to conceptual knowledge:

- A systematic, theory-based understanding of the *natural sciences* applicable to the discipline.
- Conceptually-based *mathematics*, numerical analysis, statistics and formal aspects of computer and information science to support analysis and modelling applicable to the discipline.
- A systematic, theory-based formulation of *engineering fundamentals* required in the engineering discipline.
- *Engineering specialist knowledge* that provides theoretical frameworks and bodies of knowledge for the accepted practice areas in the engineering discipline; much is at the forefront of the discipline.

While specialist knowledge is strongly conceptual, is not usable without the contextual know-how and background. The next three descriptors are more contextual but relate to the application of conceptual knowledge:

- Knowledge that supports *engineering design* in a practice area.
- Knowledge of *engineering practice* (technology) in the practice areas in the engineering discipline.
- Comprehension of the *role of engineering in society* and issues in engineering practice in the discipline: ethics and the professional responsibility of an engineer to public safety; the impacts of engineering activity: economic, social, cultural, environmental and sustainability.

In addition an eighth statement (for engineers only) relates to ability to source knowledge from the *research literature* of the discipline; this knowledge will be both conceptual and contextual.

Knowledge profiles are differentiated across the roles. The engineer's and engineering technologist's knowledge of natural science, mathematics and engineering sciences is systematic and theory based but the technologist's knowledge base is narrower and the field of application more focused. The engineering technician's knowledge by contrast is more descriptive, formula-based and procedural.

The engineering technologist's contextual knowledge is focused on the role and impacts of the technologies used while the technician's method of dealing with impacts of activity is procedural.

The graduate attributes are generic statements that apply to education programmes in all disciplines. Most national standards do not have discipline-level content statements. Where programme-specific criteria are specified, high-level statements are used (Abet Inc. 2012). Contextualisation of the generic statements into disciplinary contexts is left to academics designing curricula and disciplinary peers in the quality assurance process. An encyclopaedic approach to defining engineering knowledge is not feasible. We therefore resort to more abstract viewpoints of engineering knowledge, first by examining the layering of engineering conceptual knowledge and then examining contextual knowledge.

Layered model for engineering conceptual knowledge

The IEA graduate attributes knowledge profile suggests that the conceptual base of engineering has four components: engineering specialisation, engineering fundamentals, natural science and mathematics. In general, engineering specialisations build on engineering fundamentals that in turn rely on natural sciences, while all rely to differing extents on a mathematical formalism. In this section, we examine the components and expose relationships that are key to understanding the nature and organisation of engineering knowledge.

Engineering today is a large and complex field because the body of knowledge supports a substantial and expanding range of applications. Expansion is driven by new applications, which are facilitated by new specialist knowledge, often emerging out of the research laboratory and by evolution of current practice to meet new needs. Expansion of knowledge occurs mainly at the engineering specialisation level. Engineering fundamentals, as identified below, are stable over time. Similarly, the natural science principles, for example classical physics, on which the engineering fundamentals are built, are stable. Advances in the natural sciences tend to feed into specialist applications, for example nanotechnology.

We illustrate engineering specialist knowledge in two disciplines: civil engineering, which is very broad, and food process engineering, which is a specialised offshoot of chemical engineering. Typical specialist subjects in university curricula in these disciplines are shown in Table 8.1. In the broad discipline, an undergraduate engineer typically studies at least three of the areas in depth. An engineering technology graduate may only have studied one area in depth, for example

Table 8.1 Specialist subjects in curricula of broad and focused disciplines

Civil Engineering	Food Process Engineering
Structural Engineering	Process Operations and Modelling
Geotechnical Engineering	Modelling and Simulation
Hydraulic Engineering	Process Control
Transportation Engineering	Food Process Design
Environmental Engineering	Food Engineering
Construction Engineering	Food technology

structural engineering. These areas have subdivisions that might be followed at masters level or in practice, for example structural engineering has main branches for reinforced concrete and steel structures.

In each of the examples, the specialist areas rely on sets of fundamental engineering sciences. Civil engineering fundamentals are engineering mechanics, analysis of structures, fluid mechanics, mechanics of solids and materials science. Food process engineering shares fundamentals with chemical engineering: chemical reaction kinetics, fluid mechanics, heat and mass transfer.

Both disciplines rely on a foundation of physics. Civil engineers must also be conversant with geology. Chemical engineering and its branches rely on chemistry as well, while food engineering has biological science underpinnings. Mathematics is used as a language, for analysis and as a basis for calculation and computation at all levels in both disciplines.

The two examples above illustrate the layering of engineering specialisations upon engineering fundamentals that in turn build on the natural sciences. Mathematics is as an essential facilitator at all layers: physical laws are expressed in formulas; engineering fundamentals are formulated through mathematics and at the specialist level; mathematics may be used in analysis and as the basis for computational aids for engineering functions.

A more important relationship between the three layers of knowledge arises from the need to deal with the complexity of engineering knowledge and its applications. In day-to-day engineering two approaches to managing complexity are used: a *systems approach*, which enables complex problems to be divided and solved and *abstraction*, which hides detail unnecessary for the purpose at hand. The systems approach involves dividing the problem into sections whose internal details are hidden (abstracted) and whose behavior is captured in a description of the interfaces between sections. For example, the design of a dam requires consideration of the water to be stored, the time-varying flow of the tributaries, the wall structure and the ground conditions, by hydraulic, structural and geotechnical engineers respectively. Each is an expert in the respective field and has an understanding of what each other knows and does. Specialists interact though mutually understood interfaces: the structure and the ground conditions; the structure and the static and dynamic water loading; the water body and the ground conditions; and the water body in relation to environmental and operational conditions.

The organisation of knowledge using layers provides abstraction as a means of dealing with complexity in practical situations. The natural sciences express their principles and laws to provide understanding of phenomena. This formulation is often at too fine a level of detail to be applied in engineering activity. Fundamental engineering sciences formulate and build on the underlying natural science principles in a way that supports their application. For example, while the consequences of the second law of thermodynamics are inescapable, it cannot be applied alone. Rather, models of recurring situations governed by that and other laws are developed, for example the cycles that occur in gas turbines and internal combustion engines while producing mechanical work (Crease 2008: 111).

Not all engineering science is rooted in specific physical phenomena such as mechanics, heat and electricity; systems and process-oriented subjects including system dynamics, control, communications, computation and discrete systems are equally fundamental and also form the basis for specialist topics (Auyang 2004). The fundamental engineering sciences are examined further in the next section.

Engineering fundamental knowledge in the disciplines

Over time, engineering knowledge and applications have proliferated, causing them to be partitioned by discipline. Proliferation is principally in the specialist areas; the number of fundamental engineering sciences is stable. Curricula designed for the engineer role have the widest range of fundamental engineering sciences relative to those for other roles. Examination of a wide range of engineer curricula across disciplines and countries indicates some sixteen fundamental engineering science areas, listed in Table 8.2.

Analysis of typical curricula reveals that individual disciplines rely on five to seven of the listed fundamental areas. The term area is used because education providers define modules or courses with different titles that package the total body of engineering fundamentals differently to make up a curriculum. For example, a popular module name is Applied Mechanics, which could contain elements of basic mechanics, mechanics of machines, or mechanics of structures.

The sixteen fundamental areas for engineer education programmes are depicted in Figure 8.4 for the main engineering disciplines. Engineering fundamentals do not stand alone but have affinities shown by linkages between the hexagons. For example, material science provides insight into the properties of materials that

Table 8.2 Fundamental engineering sciences

Engineering Mechanics	Transfer Processes
Materials Science	Electric Circuits
Mechanics of Solids	Electromagnetics
Mechanics of Structures	Electrical Machines and Systems
Mechanics of Machines	Electronics
Mechanics of Fluids	Computing and Software
Thermodynamics	Signals, System and Control
Chemical Reaction Kinetics	Discrete Systems Analysis

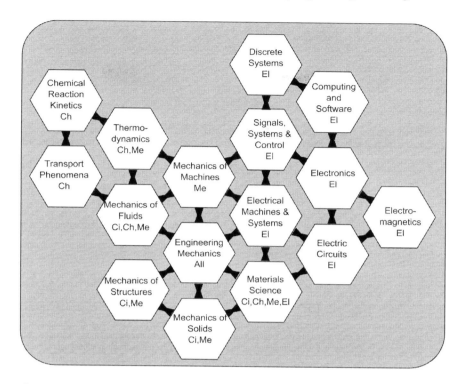

Figure 8.4 Fundamental engineering sciences and their affinities. Requirements in four main disciplines are shown thus: Ci = Civil; Ch = Chemical; Me = Mechanical; El = Electrical.

are important to the way they deform and break in mechanics of solids. Solid mechanics is important in structural analysis. Material science may have different emphases in different programmes: composite materials in civil engineering and electrical materials in electrical engineering.

All disciplines rely on engineering mechanics: the extension of basic mechanics to provide methods to support applications. Application of mechanics in other areas is formulated in the mechanics of solids, fluids, machines and structures. Mechanical, civil and chemical engineering have substantial commonality with differentiation coming in characteristic areas. Mechanical engineering relies on the mechanics of machines, that is assemblages of moving parts. Chemical engineering is concerned with large-scale chemical reactions and the physical processes in handling substantial volumes of material and energy.

Electrical engineering is a broad field with practitioners concentrating in fields such as electric power engineering, electronics or telecommunications. Power engineering, concerned with electrical machines and systems, has an affinity for areas of mechanical engineering.

The commonality and differences between the fundamental emphasis of disciplines is illustrated by an example. On face value, designing a building structure could not seem more different than designing a machine, for example a bulldozer. Fundamentals underlying structural engineering include the properties of materials and elements that bear load and endure stress and strain. The theory of structures provides the conceptual base for how the parts of a structure work together in resisting loads. In machines, some parts are structural while others move. Both types endure stress due to rapidly changing loading. Machine design also requires knowledge of the properties of materials and analyses of static and dynamic loads on elements. Mechanics of machines provides the conceptual foundation for the analysis and design of mechanisms. Structural analysis and the mechanics of machines are rooted in fundamental mechanics, which in turn relies on mathematical methods such as calculus and vectors.

The branching of engineering disciplines shown in Figure 8.1 preserves common threads of fundamental knowledge in the four main disciplines. Related branches share most, if not all, of the basic disciplines fundamentals. For example, agricultural engineering specialist areas rely on elements of civil and mechanical engineering. Depending on the emphasis of the programme, the fundamentals may be as for mechanical engineering but without thermodynamics. The engineering fundamentals of aeronautical engineering are identical to those of mechanical engineering; the difference comes at the specialisation level. Industrial engineering shares many fundamentals with mechanical engineering and in addition, discrete mathematical methods such as queueing theory and operations research. While military engineering may have been the predecessor of civil engineering, its modern form is a hybrid of civil and mechanical engineering, sharing the common fundamentals.

Contextual (or practical) components of engineering knowledge

Engineering activity is always directed at achieving a goal: the practical realisation of a product, service or process. At the professional level, this activity is mainly intellectual and brings together theory and practice. Contextual knowledge is essential to practice. As in the case of conceptual knowledge we, of necessity, restrict the discussion of contextual knowledge to its broad characteristics.

The blend of conceptual and contextual knowledge changes as the practitioner's career develops. At the graduate level, as reflected in the Pellegrini model in Figure 8.3, a theoretical base exists coupled with sufficient practical knowledge to start working with experienced engineers in industry. At the next level, the practitioner's competence is recognised by registration or, if engineering practice is unregulated, by supervising engineers as ready for independent practice. By this stage, practical training and experience has been gained at increasing levels of responsibility, together with conceptual knowledge. This is not the end of the development process. The practitioner then gains more experience in a responsible capacity that further enhances decision-making capacity. At some stage, the practitioner may be regarded as an expert in a practice area.

Experience of a range of applications and conditions is essential to the development of a professional's competence. The developing professional must experience the way that theory plays out in practical situations, where it has gaps, and how to proceed when the situation lies beyond the bounds of his or her knowledge. Experience is essential to develop an ability for decision making and exercising judgement in complex situations where factors to be taken into account are unknown or uncertain.

The IEA graduate attributes list identifies design knowledge, technological knowledge and knowledge of the engineer's duty to society as contextual knowledge. These are often captured in standards, codes of practice, methods and processes. Where this is not the case, the engineer must determine the process to be followed based on contextual knowledge. While engineering conceptual knowledge is hierarchical, contextual knowledge is generally segmented, often more dependent on aspects of conceptual knowledge than other contextual units.

The engineering design process involves cycles of analysis, synthesis and evaluation, supported by conceptual and contextual knowledge. Designers work at a level of abstraction appropriate to the task but are guided by and always subject to principles and laws of the natural sciences; in the words of aviation pioneer Glenn Martin: 'Structures and machines are unforgiving of the cheater and inevitably indict those who toy with the facts' (Augustine 2002). Engineering design knowledge is the store of reusable information on what is essential or effective and what is not: codes, standards, processes, empirical information, and knowledge reused from past designs. Each area of practice or design office has its own body of design knowledge that is developed and handed on by experience.

The essence of engineering technological knowledge is captured in the IEA definition of engineering technology: an established body of knowledge, with associated tools, techniques, materials, components, systems or processes that enable a family of practical applications and that relies for its development and effective application on engineering knowledge and competency (IEA 2011).

Engineering activity seeks to provide benefits for people, societies and economic activity. Activities typically involve potential negative or harmful effects that must be mitigated. Engineers therefore have broader responsibilities beyond their technical functions. Effective discharge of these responsibilities requires contextual knowledge in a number of areas: ethics, public health and safety, economic costs and benefits, impacts on people and communities, respect for cultural values, protection of the environment. Practitioners must ensure that solutions are sustainable. Engineering professionals must understand, recognise and mitigate risks associated with engineering activity and solutions.

Risks arise in a number of situations, such as the following:

- Engineering activity is a key enabler in exploiting natural resources, including mineral and bio-resources, which are accompanied by health and safety risks, environmental impacts and considerations of sustainability.
- Inherent in many activities is the need to work against or exploit forces of nature. Structures must be designed to support static and dynamic loads: their

own mass, their contents and external forces such as wind and seismicity. Other applications are protective against of natural forces and effects, including flood, tides, rain, hail and lightning.

- Much of engineering is concerned with sourcing or generating, transmitting, storing or utilising energy, for example electrical, natural gas or liquid fuel. Such processes have inherent hazards, which must be mitigated.
- The design and operation of industrial processes is essentially an engineering activity, involving hazards due to the use of machinery and equipment, use of materials and substances with possibly harmful physical or chemical properties and the processing of substances at high or low temperature, high pressure or vacuum or high velocity or momentum.
- Risks may arise because of the nature of the system or components. A system may undergo dynamical behavior, which must be kept within safe working limits by properly designed and operated controllers. System complexity may arise from the need to acquire, transfer, store or process critical information. Risks may arise simply because the systems or situations are complex or uncertain.

In summary, factors determining contextual knowledge required for a given task include: the extent of applicable standards, codes and regulation; the existence of procedures or the need to develop procedures for the task at hand; the need to use empirical or historical information; whether the process is repetitious or once-off; the risks and the difficulty of mitigating these; the process requires an understanding of and interactions with other parties; and the availability of technology matched to the goal.

The properties of conceptual and contextual knowledge in engineering are summarised in Table 8.3.

Conclusion

Engineering knowledge can be classified as primarily conceptual, that is belonging to a systematic, cumulative body of theory, or primarily contextual, that is, practical processes and knowledge about the environment in which the processes operate. Up to the mid-twentieth century, engineering was concerned with physical things: harnessing, exploiting or mitigating the forces of nature or exploiting natural resources. The need to organise work process had been long understood. From the 1950s, engineers became involved in the solution of problems of information and complex systems. Today we regard the basic materials of engineering as being both physical and informational.

Figure 8.5 shows a matrix framework for engineering conceptual knowledge using disciplines and roles as viewpoints. Each cell contains the knowledge profile for a combination of role and discipline. The layered model of engineering knowledge, supported by mathematics and contextual knowledge, is shown. Cells are porous and mathematical, natural science and engineering fundamentals are shared across cells, for example the fundamentals shown in Figure 8.4.

Table 8.3 Comparison of contextual and conceptual knowledge

Factor	Attributes of Conceptual Knowledge	Attributes of Contextual Knowledge
Constituents	Terminology, facts, concepts, principles, theories, models.	Areas of practice, tools, techniques, procedures, empirical knowledge, technologies.
Structure	Has an accepted structure in a discipline, cumulative, extending from fundamental to specialist, hierarchical, abstract.	Segmented by practice area; roles not cumulative.
Stability	Fundamentals tend to be stable, with specialities built on them.	Stability decreases with level, practice areas overtaken by developments.
Transferability	Generalisable and transferable.	Each methodology is relevant to a class of application.
Mode of Use	Analysis, synthesis, evaluation, of knowledge, to build models, . . .	Ranges from manual to intellectual.
Interaction	With other parts of conceptual domain and with practice area(s).	With other practice areas.
Risk	Linked to applying in practice area.	Arise in practice area and must be managed.
Regulation	Conceptual developments are regulated by academic, publishing and professional usage.	Activities involving risk tend to be regulated by qualification, regulation, codes of practice, codes of conduct.
Memory	Resides predominantly in the literature.	Resides predominantly in the practitioners.

Conceptual engineering knowledge has inherent layers. At the most fundamental level the natural sciences underpin the discipline – physics is the foundation of most. Mathematics supports all layers. The fundamental engineering sciences arise from a development of the laws and principles of the natural sciences into abstracted forms that efficiently support engineering specialist study and engineering analysis and design from fundamental principles. Engineering specialist knowledge is concentrated in but not confined to cells. Engineering specialist areas are built on the fundamental engineering sciences in a variety of ways ranging through deepening of the fundamentals, widening of the range of applications or addressing new classes of problem.

In a given discipline, the quantum of knowledge and the way it is used varies across the roles: engineers have a broad base and are competent to address complex, unfamiliar problems using a principles-based approach; engineering technologists have a narrower base but are masters of particular technologies and their application; and engineering technicians have a 'need to know' knowledge base and perform functions using established methods. The mathematical and natural

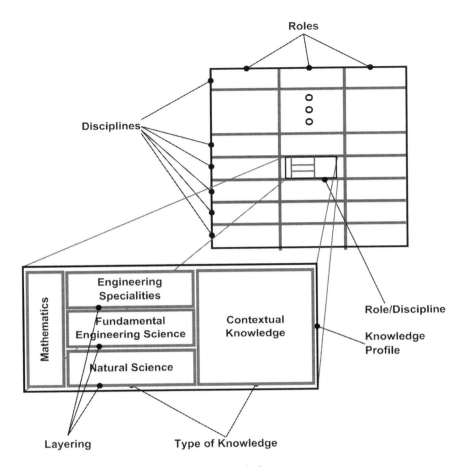

Figure 8.5 Viewpoints on engineering knowledge.

science elements are graded across the roles and recur with possible variation in different disciplines.

Engineering knowledge, coupled with a well-developed problem-solving ability, is the essential enabler of the solutions engineers provide in response to the needs of people, society, enterprise and the economy.

References

Abet Inc., (2012) Criteria for accrediting engineering programs: Effective for reviews during the 2013–2014 accreditation cycle. Online, available at: www.abet.org (accessed 26 August, 2013).

Augustine, N.R. (2002) 'Ethics and the second law of thermodynamics', *Bridge*, 32: 4–7.

Auyang, S.Y. (2004) *Engineering – an endless frontier*. Cambridge, MA: Harvard University Press.

Crawley, E.F., Malmqvist, J., Lucas W.A., and Brodeur, D.R., (2011) 'The CDIO Syllabus v2.0: An updated statement of goals for engineering education', Proceedings of the 7th International CDIO Conference, Technical University of Denmark, Copenhagen. Online, available at: www.cdio.org (accessed 28 August, 2013).

Crease, R.P. (2008) *The great equations*. New York: W.W. Norton.

International Engineering Alliance (IEA) (2011, Version 2), Glossary of terms. Online, available at: www.ieagreements.org (accessed 21 August, 2013).

International Engineering Alliance (IEA) (2013, Version 3), Graduate attributes and professional competencies. Online, available at: www.ieagreements.org (accessed 21 August, 2013).

Malpas, R. (2000) 'The universe of engineering', *The Royal Academy of Engineering*. Available at: www.engc.org.uk (accessed 27 August, 2013).

Muller, J. (2009) 'Forms of knowledge and curriculum coherence', *Journal of Education and Work*, 22: 205–26.

Nicholl, C. (2004) *Leonardo da Vinci: Flights of the mind*. New York: Viking.

Pellegrini, M. (2011) 'Education in engineering: Introduction', presentation at the World Engineers Convention, Geneva, September 2011.

Pitt, J.C. (2001) 'What engineers know', *Techné*, 5: 17–30.

Rugarcia, A., Felder, R.M., Woods, D.R., and Stice, J.E. (2000) 'The future of engineering education I. A vision for a new century', *Chemical Engineering Education*, 34: 16–25.

Strandh, S. (1982) *Machines: An illustrated history*. Gothenborg: Nordbok.

Tadmor, Z. (2006) 'Redefining engineering disciplines for the twenty-first century', *Bridge*, 36: 33–7.

9 On the cultivation of decorum

Development of the pedagogic discourse of architecture in France, 1671–1968

Francis Carter

The region of knowledge of architecture

Professional knowledge of architecture comprises a broad region that spreads from applied sciences and technologies to humanities and fine arts, integrating other regions of engineering, law and environmental studies. Courses in curricula for architects generally follow the epistemology of these singulars and sub-regions: architectural science and theory of structures, building services and environmental performance, building materials and construction, some implementation studies, design theory and its history, architectural design and drawing.

Design ('studiowork') is the big course, integrating these separated parts of knowledge in spatialized project work which, unlike professional curricula that first ease students through the underpinning singulars, begins with synthesis from day one. It combines careful analysis, leaps of creative imagination and precise technical execution – the conventions of architectural drawing providing the representational tools for visual thinking of this kind.

The breadth of this region makes it an interesting case study in the pedagogic structuring of professional knowledge. What recontextualizing rule gives coherence to such an expansive region? What is the pedagogic discourse which arises from such recontextualization?

Limits, method and theory

The chapter explores these two interlinked questions historically, with scope limited to the school of architecture at the *Ecole des Beaux Arts*, Paris (the School of Fine Arts, which included a separate school of painting and sculpture). This derived from an institutional model established by Italian Academies of Art in the sixteenth century, in turn following the printing of architectural treatises that codified and gave access to the design rules of Roman and Renaissance works. Though there are other influential pedagogic traditions in architecture (e.g., office-based 'pupillage' in Britain, or workshop-based 'design-build' learning in Germany), France's three-century long studio-based 'project competition' tradition had substantive influence on curricula for architects throughout the west and its colonies. Many Beaux-Arts pedagogic structuring principles and academic practices remain embedded in these courses today.

The method is a review of some seminal English literature on the history of French education for architects (principally Chafee 1977 and Egbert 1980, supplemented by the references listed). This literature is examined through the lens of Bernstein's pedagogic device using the analytical tools of fields of production, recontextualization (official and pedagogic) and reproduction, and corresponding rules (distributive, recontextualizing and evaluative), with some reference to classification, framing and coding (Bernstein 2000).

The historical evidence is divided into five periods from the mid-seventeenth century to the mid-twentieth century, summarized in Figure 9.1. However, the objective is analytical rather than historical: to identify principles for the pedagogic structuring of this professional knowledge.

The key issue in professional knowledge structures is the relation between practice and theory, which Bernstein correlates discursively as a discourse located in its 'original site of effectiveness' and de-located to pedagogic discourse. Pedagogic discourse in turn comprises two discourses: instructional, 'which creates specialized skills and their relation to each other', and regulative, 'the moral discourse which creates order, relations and identity' (the dominant discourse in which the instructional is embedded) (Bernstein 2000: 32). The potential discursive gap thus opened up between a material base and these de-located 'indirect meanings' is then the site 'for alternative realizations of the relation between the material and the immaterial' where imagination can play – in this case nurturing tremendous architectural creativity 'for alternative possibilities' and the 'yet to be thought' though, as this story will indicate, 'the distribution of power will try to regulate' (op. cit.: 30).

1650–1700: good taste in the service of the elite

Antecedents of the *Ecole des Beaux Arts* originate at this time, in the form of the *Académie Royale de Peinture et de Sculpture* and the *Académie Royale d'Architecture*, established by the French monarchy in 1648 and 1671 respectively. The academicians of architecture, the most knowledgeable practitioners of their day, were required to meet one day a week 'in order to confer and communicate to each other their knowledge [and to] teach publicly the best and most correct rules of architecture, in order to enable a seminary of young artists to be formed', with the professor appointed from among the academicians (Nicolas-Francois Blondel, the first professor, quoted in Léon 1925: 16). They were also required to take on pupils, selected from the students 'in the same way that the master formerly selected his apprentice' (op. cit.: 18).

At its inception there is a complete system in place at the Academy for the pedagogic structuring of knowledge: the eminent producers are the recontextualizers, and are also the teachers; the students in the teachers' lectures are also the pupils in the producers' workrooms. These articulations of the pedagogic device are as close as you can get them, directly connecting the production of knowledge and the recontextualizing field, with acquisition linking the field of reproduction back to the field of production. These fundamental arrangements, which link design practice and design theory, remain in place for the next three centuries, during which old practice trumps new theory – until irrevocable shifts in the field of production require that new practice trumps old theory.

The architect's encyclopaedic knowledge (op. cit.: 17) was recontextualized through aesthetic rules, with beauty understood to cohere in the proportions of classical architecture, as prescribed in the Roman and Renaissance texts:

> First of all, the Academy proclaims the existence of absolute beauty. Architecture is controlled by certain rules which are those of good taste [. . . It] devotes the majority of its meetings to comments on the sacred books of Vitruvius, either directly or through Italian exponents [. . .] it is the chief substance of its work.
>
> (op. cit.: 16–17)

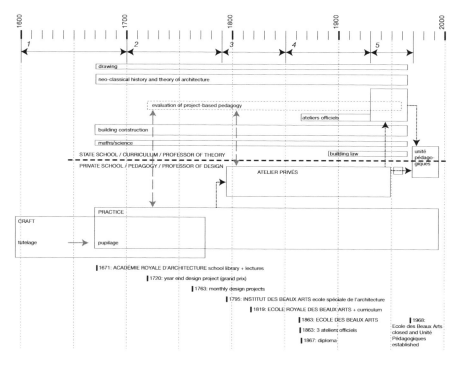

Figure 9.1 Development of curriculum and pedagogy for architects in France (data from Chafee 1977).

The Academy's school of architecture (hereafter called the School) provided lectures that by 1717 'had become a course lasting two or three years' (Chafee 1997: 61). Léon notes that despite the 'great the importance attached to the study of the ancient Orders, it is in the main a scientific education that is given to the pupils', with the first professors being members of both the Academy of Science and of Architecture (Léon 1925: 17). The recontextualizing rule of the historically and culturally determined aesthetic devices for coherent architectural composition, which is 'of good taste', does not exclude transmission of the technical requirements for architectural production.

Though the School offered lecture-based learning (the theory), the student learnt the art of design (the practice) vocationally as a pupil to an architect in the workplace. While knowledge of compositional skill and applied science are in balance in the curriculum, pedagogies of practice and theory have separated. Education of architects in France starts off with these two sides of pedagogic structure, and grows within that logic: over time the workplace design learning in the architect's office will become School-based learning in the design studio.

1700–90: the competition drawing

The didactic method of the competition drawing, previously established at Academies of Art, commenced as a year-end design project in 1720. Monthly projects started in 1763 as 'practice for the annual competition for the Grand Prix, as the end-of-the-year prize came to be called' (Chafee 1977: 65). This was the beginning of project-based pedagogy, the basis of most architectural education today. Rather than practicing design by assisting with the real work of the architect's office (or by doing exercises based on copying the master's work, perhaps with slight interpretation), the imaginary project now becomes the vehicle for learning to design. Though the design project is developed by the student while based in the workplace, inherent to the pedagogy of competition is evaluation outside of the office by the academicians in the case of the *Grand Prix*, and by the School in the case of the monthly competition projects. The professor (hereafter called a professor of theory) assumed a centralized role in setting the monthly projects and briefing the entrants.

The *Grand Prix* carried the award of three or more years' residence at the French Academy in Rome. From the 1780s winners were required to 'make a detailed study of an antique building that the Academy considered important, and to send the study to Paris for preservation in the Academy's library' (ibid.). The knowledge thus assembled is the measured and drawn record of the canonical built works – the basis for interpreting and understanding architectural aesthetics.

During the eighteenth century knowledge of compositional art and of building science were in a shifting balance – mediated by the 1762 appointment as professor of a second Blondel (Jacques-Francois), who had previously run a private architectural school, which combined theory of architecture with craft and engineering. Though French engineering knowledge developed in a different direction at this time, fusing theory and practice in 'a "horizontal" system of sciences in which each is connected to each by countless threads', mathematically and experimentally, Blondel retained 'the venerable distinction between the mechanical and the liberal arts', presupposing 'a certain distance between theory and practice', which required architectural students to continually move between the two (Picon 1992: 131–5). Picon makes the important point that 'Blondel maintained that critique and design were situated in the gap between [theory and practice]' (op. cit.: 135).

1790–1850: the private teaching studio

Despite suppression of the Royal Academies during the 1789 revolution, the School was continued informally by the teachers and was officially re-instated by the Convention – though not without tensions about assessment. An attempt to expand the jury for the *Grand Prix* failed, and the academicians retained their control over the high level aesthetic evaluation (Egbert 1980, 30–1). The divisions of knowledge of the Academies continued largely unchanged in the new *Institut de France*, which included a *Classe des Beaux Arts* (renamed *Académie* in 1816).

After the revolution the tutoring of competition project work no longer occurred in royal architects' production offices (*agence*), but in separate studios set up just for teaching (*atelier-privés*), of which the eminent architect was *patron* (officially titled *professeur d'architecture*). These were located close to the School, in cheap rented premises. The *patron* now moved between the *agence* and the *atelier-privés*, visiting about twice a week to review the work on the boards. Hereafter the *atelier-privés* will be called a private teaching studio, and the *professeur d'architecture* a professor of design.

Design teaching varied, based on each professor of design's approach. However, these were variations within the shared neo-classical canon of spatial organisation of the plan and character of the elevation. There was great competition between the private teaching studios for the award of the annual *Grand Prix*, and for students to enter a studio that had achieved many awards 'if only because those were the ateliers where the best students were exchanging ideas' (Chafee 1977: 89). It was this interaction between students (both *anciens* and *nouveaux*, old and new) that sustained the design learning – a 'studio culture'.

Although under the direction of the leading architects of the day, the private teaching studios were self-organising, set up and managed by the students, who selected the professor of design. However, this autonomy, with its potential to sponsor new ideas, was tempered by the academy's elderly members, the defenders of the nation's neo-classical orthodoxy, who awarded the *Grand Prix*.

In 1819 the syllabus was defined through a royal order, with pedagogic forms still divided between theory courses and project work. Lectures continued along four lines established from the start: theory of architecture and its history, underpinning knowledge of mathematics and science (assessed by written exam), descriptive geometry and perspective drawing, and construction.

The syllabus was organized in a four stage sequence: preparation for admission (for *aspirants*), the Second Class, the First Class, and the competition for the

Grand Prix. Design pedagogy was similar throughout. *Concours d'émulation*, the many competitive design projects, were of two types:

> Programmes were issued monthly, *esquisses* [sketches] alternating with *projets rendus* [rendered projects]. (The professor of theory wrote these programmes, and thus his was the most important chair in the Section d'Architecture.) Sketch *concours* required one drawing submitted after twelve hours of study; those for *projets rendus* usually required three larger drawings, submitted after two months.
>
> (op.cit.: 83)

The sketch design projects and first stage of the developed design projects (also a sketch of its essential form), were produced in the whole-day session, during which students were sequestered in cubicles (thus *en loge*). Thereafter, for the developed design projects, the student had to proceed with design in terms of the intent set out in the sketch. This work took place in the private teaching studio, with the guidance of the professor of design, who:

> [. . .] takes his pencil in hand to correct faults, he discusses possible solutions of the problem, and from this exchange of ideas in a common research the student, while keeping his own personality, impregnates his mind with advice based on experience. Thus the tradition of good proportions, beautiful forms, and ingenious planning is transmitted and perpetuated.
>
> (Defrasse 1925: 44)

Here design was an intense creative synthesis in terms of rules of composition, which had to be well understood and quickly interpreted, using the representational tools for making quick and complete architectural decisions in the uninterrupted workday. Design was conceptually driven, requiring upfront ordering of the essential ideas that relate the key parts to the overall whole, which then guided the development of the project. This ordered arrangement was known as the *parti* – meaning the 'abstract layout of the plan', or 'the conceptual disposition of parts decided by the designer at the outset' (Van Zanten 1977: 185). Development of the design project pursued the inherent spatial organisation of the compositional sketch *parti*, continuing the classical understanding of an inner (proportional and symmetrical) order to the form.

While there were written exercises and exams, mostly in the scientific subjects, drawn projects were also required in perspective and, in the Second Class, for construction: 'there were four construction *concours*, one for stone, one for iron, one for wood, and one for *construction générale*, each lasting about four months' (Chafee 1977: 83). Though the requirements for construction and building science were extensive and difficult to pass, evidence of this learning occurred outside of the design project in the Second Class and, it seems, not at all in the First Class. Design was evaluated in terms of compositional theory, but not necessarily buildability.

There is dual coding in this curriculum. The private teaching studio provides the pedagogy within which the practice of design is located – this 'practice-based' pedagogy extending through all stages of learning, unlike many other professional curricula, which contain a role playing or practice simulation module. The School classifies the parts of knowledge in the delivery of the lecture-based curriculum and the evaluation of knowledge learnt. The curriculum of coursework and evaluation is a collection, while design pedagogy provides integration of the collected parts of knowledge. This duality is spatialized: design work in cheap studios on the city streets, lectures and evaluation in the elaborate walled enclave of the School.

Transmission of design knowledge hovers as close as you can get to practice, with the professor of design (as prophet) providing a short circuit between design practice and design learning (acquired by laity in the worship room of the studio), which sidesteps the recontextualizing field (likely to peeve the professor of theory priests, who nevertheless are the interpreters of the 'sacred books of Vitruvius' and who control the higher altar of the assessment room) (Bernstein 2000: 37).

Other academicians (painters, sculptors, musicians) moderate the division between architectural professors in the adjudication of the *Grand Prix*, an evaluation which is the strong 'message system' that operates back through the pedagogy in the day-to-day teaching work of the studios.

Figure 9.1 indicates the late-eighteenth-century development of the private teaching studio, positioned outside of both the architect's office and the state School, and shown below the dotted line on the diagram that separates the public and private Schools, coursework curriculum from design pedagogy, and professors of theory from professors of design. This line represents a division between the recontextualizing field and the field of reproduction, cutting through the pedagogic recontextualizing field and separating the disciplinary knowledge into critical theory and creative practice, with technical parts of knowledge not structured into this dichotomy.

1850–1930: the industrial tension in aesthetics

During the second half of the nineteenth century the *Ecole des Beaux Arts* was hugely influential, among both French and foreign students:

> During those prosperous decades, buildings by architects from the Ecole were going up not only in France but throughout the French Empire, from Dakar to Saigon, and elsewhere around the world, from Glasgow to Rio de Janeiro, from Bucharest to Berkeley. In English speaking lands, a certain kind of architecture came to be called Beaux-Arts, and the name has stuck.
>
> (Chafee 1977: 106–07)

In the 1850s there were 37 private teaching studios, although most students were in eight or so large ones. By 1900 these had grown to about 80 students each, which 'were to endure for decades and some for more than a century' (op. cit.: 89–90). Others were short-lived: the controversial neo-Gothic theoretician Viollet-le-Duc's studio lasted only a few months in 1856 and he subsequently survived less than three months as professor of theory after student heckling in his lectures on function as the informant of form, and small riots in the streets thereafter (op. cit.: 100–03). He was also disappointed that his instigation of a move away from the competition system was rebuffed (Moore 1977: 150). In this skirmish the regulative discourse of studio culture prevents a shift in the instructional discourse of aesthetic criteria and assessment methods.

During this period there were two impacts of official recontextualization. In 1863 three Studios were set up in the School's own buildings (*ateliers officials*, official teaching studios). This was part of a reorganization of the School decreed by Napoleon III, 'intending to put the private ateliers out of business' – unsuccessfully as it turned out (Chafee 1977: 102). Despite the state's intention that these studios would emphasize contemporary issues of industrial construction and functional programme, they were quickly subsumed into the School's method of abstracted historicist composition (Moore 1977). However, the significant institutional shift was that the state School now included both lecture delivery and in-house design studios.

Government instituted a diploma at the end of the First Class in 1867, intended to be '[. . .] a sign of architectural proficiency and a culmination of studies less exclusive than the Grand Prix' (Chafee 1977: 105). Two shifts then occur, which generally endure in this tradition of education for architects:

- A major design project was introduced at the end of the First Class ('the thesis'), self-defined rather than a common competition project (ibid.).
- Buildability of the design project was now considered: comprehensively in the First Class thesis in relation to (but not at the expense of) style and composition; in the Second Class integrated in one building construction project rather than as separate technical parts (op. cit.: 83).

These shifts occur as the distribution changes from producing the one winner who would take a leading role in the high profile projects of the state to graduating the class of diplomates who would take on a diversity of design roles in both public and private sectors, in the context of the increasing industrial production of a diverse range of building types.

However, the pedagogy of design competition projects continued unchanged, and the *Grand Prix* competition continued on top of this exit diploma. Pioneering rationalists such as Labrouste and Perret, now recognized for pushing the boundaries of classicist design through the use of the new materials iron and reinforced concrete respectively, ran private teaching studios, which never won the *Grand Prix* (Egbert 1980: 63, 75).

By the end of this period tensions are increasingly evident in the field of production between these new construction materials and methods and the aesthetic rules of historical style. There were two divergent responses in the recontextualizing field to this design challenge: 'the rules of harmony are immutable [. . .] the sure guide to good taste', or 'form should simply result from calculations and scientific facts' (Defrasse 1925: 44).

However, rather than dislodging the recontextualizing rule of the aesthetic ordering of architectural composition, the problem is redefined within those terms as a question of 'new aesthetics which are derived from [new] materials' (Jaussely 1925: 62). So the increased horizontal span and reduced need for vertical support of new structural materials and systems simply result in a 'reversal of proportions' and 'contrast between vertical and horizontal lines', together with a 'simplification of articulation' (ibid.). However, framing does weaken, as a result of the need to allow students to explore this revision of aesthetic rules consequent on new structural systems (Defrasse 1925: 45).

Though the architect could 'no longer be simply an artist who [. . .] conceives merely the decoration', the artistic intent remains: 'he must himself imagine [the engineering] forms, on a completely logical and reasoned basis, construction and decoration being the product of one and the same brain'; in this way results could be secured 'in favour of the art of architecture' (Jaussely 1925: 62–3).

1930–70: from style to sociology

In the 1930s student numbers had outgrown the old private teaching studio premises, and rentals were becoming too expensive for these studios to be viable. The School started to build studios for them – 'they were becoming quasi-official' (Chafee 1977: 107). In the 1950s this problem of financial viability increased and the School gradually absorbed most of the large private teaching studios: 'One by one, their *patrons* were put on the payroll of the Ecole, each as a *professeur chef d'atelier*, and nearly all their students moved into the buildings of the Ecole, where the new *atelier officiels* were installed' (op. cit.: 108).

Massification also lead to the establishment of regional schools (totalling twelve by the mid-1960s), all implementing the centralized programme of instruction of the Paris School (International Union of Architects 1965: 105).

In this final form with the majority of design studios in-house the *Ecole des Beaux Arts* School of Architecture, though operating outside of the French university system, becomes a model for the twentieth-century university-based Schools then being established or consolidated in other western countries and colonies. Ironically, the model was beginning to fail in France. In the 1920s and 1930s the private teaching studios started to become so large that senior and new students worked together less, and much of the teaching was done by assistants rather than the master (Chafee 1977: 95). A victim of its nineteenth-century success, the school was unable to adapt to new twentieth-century design trends.

A report by the French section of the International Union of Architects submitted to its 1965 congress provides a sense of the difficulties faced by the School just before its collapse. Changes had occurred in the field of production, where the architect 'is no longer before a man like himself but under official departments, rules as variable as they are innumerable, committees which are by definition irresponsible' (International Union of Architects 1965: 109). However, these new conditions of practice do not change the view of what kind of professional consciousness was required: 'The sole possible arbitrator between the conflicting interests of financing bodies, technicians, clients and legal representatives the architect is none the less the creator who must eventually impose his own artistic, professional and moral requirements' (op. cit.: 110).

Changes had occurred in the official recontextualizing field, through increased state regulation of professional competencies, requiring compulsory qualification and registration (by law, since 1942). Preparation for examination was becoming more specified, with emphasis on educating the many ordinary professionals rather than the very talented few. However, the view expressed in this report is that:

> As art is not subject to a diploma and that only exact sciences are subject to a quota, the compulsory teaching of architecture leads today to examinations and therefore will lead in a short time and without remedy to the exaltation of techniques to the prejudice of the most exceptional talents.
>
> (op. cit.: 107)

So, 'never forget that what we examine is only a part of the architect's knowledge and that this part is not the essential one' (op. cit.: 108).

Changes had occurred in the recontextualizing field. Where previously a professor of theory was able to provide rules of analysis and compositional principles for all anticipated built work, the School was now working in conditions where 'architecture, its programmes and means have developed more in the last fifty years than during the preceding two thousand years', and where 'the concept of decorum which, for centuries, dominated public architecture is discarded on behalf of working and economic qualities' (op. cit.: 112, 113). So teachers 'have tried to renew the formula without succeeding in giving it the same permanent quality' (op. cit.: 112). However, the recontextualizing rule of the aesthetic ordering of form remains unshaken: 'if no harmony arises from the solution, architecture is not achieved but only construction', while 'technical education is only a minor point' (op. cit.: 107).

So, it seems, change in the pedagogic recontextualizing field would not be required. Although it was conceded that it was necessary 'to complete the existing teaching' to meet the increased specificity of official recontextualization, this response of pedagogic recontextualization was that 'we do not mean to destroy what is satisfactory' (op. cit.: 113). Evolution was preferred:

> In an endeavour to cure evident deficiencies and frequent excesses of plastic [artistic] skill to the detriment of the thoroughness of studies, we do not want to spoil the brilliant qualities of a more than centenary teaching which, on certain planes, remains remarkable.
>
> (ibid.)

Therefore, the evaluative rule remains intact: the *Grand Prix de Rome* is still advocated 'to bring into evidence students brilliant in composition', and it was suggested that other similar competitions would need to be created 'very rapidly [. . .] intended to emphasize new intellectual qualities', particularly for the design of town plans (ibid.). However, it was granted that the centralized system of education was 'too convergent', and would benefit from 'a liberalisation of pedagogic methods', with 'greater autonomy given to the regional branches' and with competition between 'several schools of a different spirit' (op. cit.: 111).

Unfortunately for them, the evolutionary recontextualizers were overtaken by revolutionary action in the field of reproduction, where students had been gaining increasing autonomy both within the society (through the strengthening of radical youth culture) and within the pedagogic structure (through the few external *ateliers libres* that still remained, and which became a force for change in the 1960s) (Pawley and Tschumi 1971: 538).

After the Second World War students had become increasingly disillusioned with the formulaic conventions of Beaux-Arts design and the competition system. In May 1968 this discontent overlapped with the leftist protests of University of Paris sociology students. The architecture students disrupted the *Grand Prix*, seized the premises, and prevented the School from opening for the new term. They demanded an end to 'the system of examinations and competitions', to 'conformist ideology' and 'the repetition of what the master does', and demanded a new focus on 'objective knowledge' and the 'real relations between the school and society' (Strike Committee 1968). The response of the decentralist De Gaulle government, whose sympathetic minister of cultural affairs had jurisdiction over fine arts education, was to close the *Ecole des Beaux Arts'* architectural section and end the *Grand Prix* competition (Egbert 1971).

The School was again split up into autonomous studio groupings, as *Unité Pédagogiques* – pedagogical units – distributed around Paris 'in buildings provided by the state [. . .] all, so to speak *officiels*':

> Each Unité Pédagogiques can teach architecture in the way it wants; each can establish its own curriculum [. . . one] continues to assume that architecture is a fine art [. . . one] considers structure to be the determinant of architectural form [. . . another aims] to reform society along Marxist lines.
> (Chafee 1977, 109)

Though the competition system and compositional virtuosity were rejected by most units in favour of collaborative work and social drivers of spatial organisation, complemented by attendance at university courses in sociology, the fragmentation into pedagogical units reasserted the autonomy of the late eighteenth-century private teaching studio as the social and regulative basis of the pedagogic structure. However, there is an instructional shift from visual aesthetics to social ethics, recontextualizing remaining in the domain of the liberal arts.

In Figure 9.1 this outline of mid-twentieth-century French pedagogy is indicated by the growth of *ateliers officials*, 'above' the division in the pedagogic recontextualizing field, at the expense of *atelier-privés*. However, rather like the seven eighths of an iceberg that is below the water line, underneath the institutionalized official teaching studio lurks the pedagogy of the private teaching studio. When the centralized institution fails in the late sixties, the entire pedagogy drops back into the field of production waters – partly *officials* but mostly *privés*!

Conclusion

In this case of the professional knowledge of architecture evident in the Beaux-Arts curriculum, how does integration of the expansive region work as pedagogic discourse? When the historical development is unravelled across the analytical framework of Bernstein's pedagogic device, it can be seen that there is a deep pedagogic structure of professional knowledge in operation here:

- The continuity of an aesthetic recontextualizing rule which brings the separated parts of knowledge into special relationship, compositionally.
- The continuity of tacit transmission of the art of good design judgement between expert practitioner and novice which, while incrementally separated from craft, mercantile and industrial production, remains the strong pedagogy (across the drawing board, creatively) – forming the dominant regulative discourse.
- The continuity of curriculum formation, which de-locates integrated knowledge of practice, through the epistemology of singulars and sub-regions, into scientific, technical, historical and graphic parts with theory of architecture, the explicit compositional rules for correct design skill, as the part of knowledge that controls evaluation (across the exhibited drawings, critically) – forming the main instructional discourse.
- The continuity of classical thought, evident in an internal ordering of the parts of the compositional whole and realized as generative conceptual idea organized geometrically, and which tends to de-link materiality and making from design thinking – informing the main evaluative rule (of development of the *parti*).

In this historical development both compositional design rules and vocational design pedagogy are de-located from the field of production, both processes driven by expert practitioners. The recontextualizing field of design theory and its history, derived from the record of good built works and combining aesthetic rules with cultural imperatives, is constituted first by means of the publication of summative texts. There follows the official recontextualizing field of institutional arrangements and distribution of awards for professional membership, and the pedagogic recontextualizing field of transmission. Teachers who combine expert practice with expert design tutoring are essential to sustain this pedagogic structure.

As the pedagogic recontextualizing field is populated staff identities and disciplinary territories divide. Professors of theory, institutionally appointed based on the academic scholarship evident in the quality of their published treatises, provide the theoretical tools of analytical skill in the lecture-based course and seed the evaluation of design in the project setup. Professors of design, socially appointed by the students based on their expert practice evident in the quality of their built works, hone the representational tools for visual thinking by working practically with(in) the students' drawings in the studio-based course.

Once the professional knowledge starts to be articulated on the basis of this deep structure it keeps going, with increasing formalisation and astonishing robustness for three centuries, right through the social disruptions of the French Revolution, the Industrial Revolution and Modernism – with traces continuing for the last half century through the Information Age. Though this process of structuring the professional knowledge has traction from the beginning it takes a long time to develop, combining slow increments that accrue over many decades with sharp moments of formalisation in response to societal crises.

The deep structure remains robust as distributive rules shift from a monarchical elite to the class of diplomates of an industrial republic to the mass of an emerging modernity, though the recontextualizing and evaluative rules do broaden as a consequence to include some astylistic logic alongside compositional artistry, some buildability alongside *parti*, with a concomitant adjustment of syllabus.

The combination of creative design pedagogy and critical design theory divides pedagogic recontextualization between types of teacher, pedagogy and pedagogic space. The tension can be held for as long as there is a common design discourse. As design practice in the field of production diverges between the past devices of neo-classical aesthetic control and the unfamiliar beauty of new industrial forms and materials first, and urban class consciousness second, this division shears: both pedagogic and official recontextualizing fields start to fragment.

The structural weakness is that technical design development and procurement knowledge, well integrated in what architects think and do in the field of production, and though comprehensively taught in the first case, are in limbo in the pedagogic structure. The realization of potential meaning restricts materialisation and implementation at the same time that it enhances composition. However, the structural strength is that, for as long as the tension between theory and practice can be held, critique and design (as Jacques-Francois Blondel maintained) are 'situated in the gap between them'. This observation resonates with Bernstein's theorisation of a potential discursive gap between a material base and indirect meanings. How do these two observations correspond?

The discursive gap opened up in this case of professional knowledge of architecture is a space between practice and theory, the located and the de-located, with dual internal structuring (see Figure 9.2). Here there are two sides to the material base: architects' practice where knowledge of the actual design of architecture resides, and architects' buildings where the actual architecture resides. Between these, to use Schön's term, is a 'reflective' link of reiterative practice where the architect develops an architectural approach from built project to built project.

The first material base is recontextualized as indirect design (studiowork), the second as indirect architecture (studio projects). Between these there is a reflective link of reiterative learning where the student develops an architectural imagination, from unbuilt project to unbuilt project. Between actual design work and indirect studiowork is a discursive gap of design thinking, based on doing design as the masters do it; between built architecture and imaginary studio projects is a discursive gap of evaluative critique, based on theory of design as evident in the canonical works. However, in theorizing that a discursive gap opens up a structure of pedagogic discourse, which is both instructional and regulative, Bernstein helps us to see that design and critique are themselves in an embedded relation.

As with all recontextualization, which derives from the field of production, here the recontextualizing field of compositional theory derives from the practice: the built works are the basis for formulating aesthetic rules and eminent practitioners are the recontextualizers who write the compositional text books that form the basis both of teaching design theory in the lecture room and assessing finished design work. I.e., this side of the pedagogic equation is instructional. However, a manual of aesthetic rules will not on its own add up to a pleasing composition that takes into account the circumstantial complexities of site or accommodation. That requires inventive and coherent design thinking, the creative work through which knowledge of doing design synthesis is gained. The commitment to achieving a designed work that is beautiful vests in the design course, with this value shared by design tutors and design students. I.e., this side of the pedagogic equation is regulative. As the last guardians of decorum proclaim, it is 'the creator who must eventually impose his own artistic, professional and moral requirements'.

The recontextualizing field of compositional theory survives for as long as the regulative discourse of the design studio considers it to be correct. If instructional theory gets too far ahead of regulative practice then design discourse runs such theory out of town (as befell the unfortunate proto-modernist Viollet-le-Duc). If instructional theory falls too far behind regulative practice then design discourse will at some point re-recontextualize (as befell neo-classical decorum).

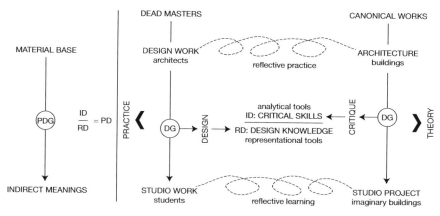

Figure 9.2 Pedagogic discourse of architecture, in the Beaux-Arts tradition (based on Bernstein 2000, 30–2).

In an inversion of the assumption that knowledge resides in the theory and skill in the practice, this review suggests that critical theory of design analysis provides the instructional discourse of skills (how you will know when the work is, or rather is not, good design – by problemetizing design error), whereas the practice of doing design work provides the dominant regulative discourse for knowledge of visual thinking (how you will know when you are doing design integration – by maximising the creative opportunity of conceptual ordering, what is valued here being good design judgement). This visual thinking, using the representational toolkit of architectural drawing rather than the theoretical toolkit of architectural analysis (though these two toolkits are in the same embedded relation), integrates parts of knowledge through the creative and technical performance of inventing and transposing the past inventions of architectural inhabitation, space, form and construction. Taken together, the pedagogic discourse of architecture is created. The apparent separation in the pedagogic recontextualizing field evident in this case study, stemming from a conventional division between the liberal and mechanical arts within the region, is connected in this way.

References

Bernstein, B. (2000) *Pedagogy, symbolic control and identity: Theory, research, critique.* Lanham, MA: Rowman & Littlefield.

Chafee, R. (1977) 'The teaching of architecture at the Ecole des Beaux-Arts', in A. Drexler (ed.) *The architecture of the Ecole des Beaux-Arts.* New York: Museum of Modern Art.

Defrasse, A. (1925) 'Architectural education in the present: France', in Royal Institute of British Architects (1925) International congress on architectural education, 28 July to 2 August 1924: Proceedings. London: RIBA.

Egbert, D. (1971) 'The rise of a new architectural education in France', *American Institute of Architects Journal*, October 1971: 44–7.

—— (1980) *The Beaux-arts tradition in French architecture illustrated by the Grands Prix de Rome.* Princeton, NJ: Princeton University Press.

International Union of Architects (1965) 'Reports by the eighth world congress of the International Union of Architects, Paris, 5th to 9th July 1965', unpublished report.

Jaussely, M. (1925) 'Architectural education in the future: France', in Royal Institute of British Architects (1925) International congress on architectural education, 28 July to 2 August 1924: Proceedings. London: RIBA.

Léon, P. (1925) 'Architectural education in the past: France' in Royal Institute of British Architects (1925) International congress on architectural education, 28 July to 2 August 1924: Proceedings. London: RIBA.

Moore, R. (1977) 'Academic "dessin" theory in France after the reorganization of 1863', *Journal of the Society of Architectural Historians*, 3(3): 145–74.

Pawley, M. and Tschumi, B. (1971) 'The Beaux-Arts since '68', *Architectural Design*, September 1971: 533–66.

Picon, A. (1992) *French architects and engineers in the age of the enlightenment.* Cambridge: Cambridge University Press.

Strike Committee (1968) 'Motion of May 15', reprinted in Ockman, J. (1993) *Architecture culture 1943–1968: A documentary anthology.* New York: Rizzoli.

Van Zanten, D. (1977) 'Architectural composition at the Ecole des Beaux-Arts from Charles Percier to Charles Garnier', in A. Drexler (ed.) *The architecture of the Ecole des Beaux-Arts.* New York: Museum of Modern Art.

10 Problematizing curriculum

Contemporary debates in engineering education[1]

Jennifer M. Case

> . . . the curriculum question has become a central concern in engineering education.
> (Ruprecht 2000: 360)

Curriculum is a hotly debated topic in education. Everyone has an opinion on what should be done to 'fix' the problem, be it literacy levels in the primary school, the ability of graduates to function in the workplace, or whatever. From the perspective of sociology of knowledge, this clamouring of voices is hardly surprising; given that curriculum is the key site in education where power operates. A crucial contribution of this field, in particular in the work of British sociologist Basil Bernstein, has been to provide detailed descriptions of the mechanisms whereby curriculum tends to operate to secure the interests of dominant groups in society (Bernstein 2000). Significantly, this work has started to deliver important insights into key aspects of curriculum that are essential for fostering the academic success of traditionally marginalized groups (Hoadley 2006). A striking finding has been that 'progressive' curricular arrangements, intended to deliver greater social justice and equality, in practice can actually serve to further disadvantage precisely those groups of students that they seek to empower (Muller 1998).

Work in the sociology of knowledge has tended largely to focus on schooling, but more recently there has been a growing interest in applying these theoretical tools to the context of curriculum in higher education. At the disciplinary level, this works involves explorations of: 1. How curriculum knowledge gets constructed, 2. The constraints that the knowledge structure of the discipline places on the curriculum, and 3. The range of identities that the curriculum makes available for students (Luckett 2010). Studies have been conducted so far in the disciplinary areas of history (Shay 2011), sociology (Luckett 2009) and design (Carvalho, Dong and Maton 2009). This chapter aims to contribute to this growing body of knowledge by a social realist exploration of curriculum as it plays out in the field of engineering education, signalling an approach that may also be productive when applied in other professional education contexts.

Engineering education is located at the heteronomous pole of the field of higher education, where external influences, particularly those from professional bodies and industrial concerns, play a significant role in determining what gets valued (Maton 2005; Kloot 2011). These external influences provide ongoing fuel to the curriculum debate in engineering education, largely focused on a concern about what graduates can actually 'do' when they enter the world of work, and generally issuing in curricular proposals that suggest a stronger focus on developing skills and engaging with 'real world' problems. A study of knowledge and curriculum in this field thus has potential value for other professional knowledge domains, disciplinary areas that also face outwards towards the world of practice, what Bernstein (2000) terms 'regions'.

Locating the curriculum debate in engineering education

Engineering curricula in most parts of the world are directly controlled by professional engineering bodies through regular audits. In South Africa, this body is the Engineering Council of South Africa, a statutory body that runs a delicate line between the interests of capital and those of the state. Moreover, in its interaction with the global professional community, it has an interest in ensuring that South African engineering graduates can get professional recognition in the key countries of the first world. Thus arose the most noticeable impact on engineering curricula in recent times, in the form of 'outcomes-based' accreditation, which was introduced initially in the revised US ABET criteria (Accreditation Board for Engineering and Technology (ABET) 2000), and thereafter in the accreditation bodies of partner bodies in the Washington Accord, a multinational agreement offering mutual recognition of engineering degrees, including the USA, UK, Australasia, Hong Kong and South Africa.

The shift to outcomes-based accreditation falls in line with much current popular thinking in higher education and in society in general, which asks questions about what graduates can 'do' rather than more traditional perspectives that centre on what graduates 'know'. This also matches the current demand from the cash-strapped industrial sector that has started to demand that graduates can deliver value from their first day in the workplace. The common refrain seems to be that the traditional engineering curriculum does not sufficiently prepare graduates for functioning in the workplace, as stridently expressed in the following quote:

> In recent years studies have been conducted in many countries to determine the technical and personal abilities required of engineers by today's industry. These studies have indicated some key concerns. Today's engineering graduates need to have strong communication and teamwork skills, but they don't. They need to have a broader perspective of the issues that concern their profession such as social, environmental and economic issues, but they haven't. Finally, they are graduating with good knowledge of fundamental engineering science and computer literacy, but they don't know how to apply that in practice.
>
> (Mills and Treagust 2003: 3)

The urgent tone noted above is reflected across much of the current discussion on curriculum in engineering education. In this climate of heightened urgency for change has arisen a substantial debate on what form the curriculum should take. Key positions on curriculum are outlined in the following section.

New curriculum models in engineering education

The traditional engineering curriculum involves an exclusive focus on basic science courses at the start of the programme, with the subsequent introduction of engineering science courses alongside more advanced science courses. Towards the final years of the degree, at the point where students have mostly grasped all of the advanced engineering science, there is the introduction of project work, focusing particularly on engineering design. One innovation that has been implemented in some places over the last few decades is the introduction of engineering science courses from the first year (see, for example, Reed and Sass 2000). In some cases these introductory engineering courses involve significant project work.

The current debate on curriculum in engineering education centres on what role project work should play across the whole curriculum, not just at the first year introductory level and in the capstone design courses. The most prominent labels for these new curriculum models are those under the banners of *problem-based* and *project-based* learning. Although there is further terminology, which provides variations on these themes (see, for example, Mills and Treagust 2003; Perrenet, Bouhuijs and Smits 2000; Lehmann *et al.* 2008), for the purposes of this chapter it will suffice to focus on the two key models. Problem-based learning (PBL) originated in medical education and in its pure form it rests on an assumption that students will learn best in 'authentic' learning contexts where they are tackling real-world problems and locating the necessary knowledge as they need it. Project-based learning typically refers to course modes where students are required to apply the knowledge that they have been taught; the focus here is on the application of new knowledge through the problem. This is of course the mode of teaching that has been long used in engineering education in the final year design project course, as mentioned above. Problem-based learning is a much more radical move where knowledge is only accessed as and when needed by the project.

Kirschner, Sweller and Clark (2006) use the label 'minimally guided approach' to describe problem-based learning together with related curriculum modes that have been fashionable across the twentieth century, particularly in school science, including inquiry learning, discovery learning and experiential learning. The most widespread application of PBL in engineering curriculum is most probably at Aalborg University in Denmark, a whole university where 75 per cent of the courses are offered in a project-based format. Lehmann and colleagues (2008) argue that the problem-oriented and project-based learning paradigm that they utilize in their engineering programmes is best placed for being able to incorporate problems around sustainable development across the curriculum.

The debate on curriculum in engineering education is thus largely centred around PBL and its variants. One of the strongest statements on the relevance of PBL to engineering education comes from Veldman and colleagues (2008) who, in the title of their recent article, state provocatively 'Can engineering education in South Africa afford to avoid problem-based learning as a didactic approach?'. With a departure point centred on outcomes-based education, they claim that PBL has the best chance of achieving curriculum alignment with the learning outcomes. They also claim that PBL is well placed to facilitate development of what they term 'non-subject-related skills'. Others are somewhat more guarded. Two recent review papers on the application of PBL to engineering education (Mills and Treagust 2003; Perrenet *et al.* 2000) suggest that it is not appropriate as a model for overall curriculum development, but is rather best applied in specific courses.

It would thus appear that most commentators are in agreement that project work should form a significant part of the engineering curriculum, and that this needs to run in a sustained manner throughout the curriculum rather than appearing only in final year as in the traditional capstone design course, or even additionally in first year as an introduction to engineering. The debate centres on what is more suitable: the highly publicized PBL model, which uses problems rather than traditional knowledge categorizations to structure the curriculum, or the more traditional project-based mode, which leaves the traditional organization of knowledge areas intact and couples these with projects to show applications of this knowledge.

Three exemplars of innovative curricula in chemical engineering

To provide some empirical illustration of the positions in this debate, three undergraduate chemical engineering curricula will be considered here: a well-established project-based curriculum at Imperial College in the UK (Perkins 2002), a recent curriculum innovation at University of Sydney in Australia that describes itself as problem-based (Gomes *et al.* 2006) and finally a curriculum renewal project at the University of Cape Town, which is in its early stages of implementation and uses a project-centred model (Case *et al.* 2013). All these universities are highly selective and take high-performing school leavers into their four year programmes. Imperial College and the University of Sydney take in students who have 13 years of schooling and offer a masters qualification in engineering, while the University of Cape Town takes in matriculants with 12 years of schooling and takes them through to an initial four year bachelors' qualification. All of these degrees are accredited under the Washington Accord.

At Imperial College the programme involves chemical engineering from the first year of study. There is an intensive use of project work running throughout the curriculum. The timetable reflects this structure, with lectures and tutorials in the mornings covering standard chemical engineering subjects (including mathematics and chemistry), as well as management and humanities, and design-oriented project work taking place on all except one 'free' afternoon. To progress to the following year, students need to pass with 40 per cent in both the (largely project-based) coursework and the final examinations. 'Mastery' assessment is a key part of the assessment, whereby students need to demonstrate 80 per cent proficiency in an integrative examination paper focusing on the essentials of chemical engineering. The last two years of the programme offer a range of different directions for students depending on the interests they have developed. Some opt for a year abroad, while others take elective directions based on particular specializations.

The University of Sydney recently undertook a complete rebuild of its undergraduate chemical engineering curriculum. The new curriculum is structured around a problem-based learning approach, emphasizing competency attainment, and aiming for strong horizontal (within a semester) and vertical (across semesters) integration. Courses were designed that fitted into the following categories, with each semester containing all these course types: (a) core principles (presenting fundamental chemical engineering concepts), (b) enabling technology (tools, often computer-based, needed to solve problems), (c) engineering practice (Core Practice courses) and (d) electives (either specialized or broadening).There are no dedicated mathematics courses after the first year; any mathematics needed is taught in the context of the relevant chemical engineering course. An important aspect of the delivery of the new curriculum is that each course is taught by a team of academics. There is a 'semester supervisor' in each year who focuses on obtaining the necessary horizontal integration across the courses. In years 2 and 3 of the programme, assessment of the core and enabling courses is via 'competency' assessment (similar to the 'mastery assessment' at Imperial College) and students are simply awarded pass/fail results. Assessment of competency is through a range of course assessments as well as the final examination. Because of the commitment to tight integration in the programme, student progression through the programme is largely 'plug flow' in nature, with only one uncompleted course being able to be carried into a subsequent year. Supplementary oral examinations are conducted with borderline candidates in order to keep as many students as possible in the planned curriculum.

The University of Cape Town has just rolled out a new first-year programme as the first stage in implementing a substantially reformed curriculum. A 'project-centred' curriculum design has been adopted where there is a strand of project work running throughout the curriculum alongside theory, with explicit reinforcement of the theory by the project work (see Crosthwaite *et al.* 2006). Mastery-type tests are used in both conceptual and skills-based aspects of the curriculum. The core chemical engineering part of the curriculum comprises one full year course per year for the first three years of the programme. In order to accommodate a broad range of student backgrounds and facilitate academic success, vacation 'boot camps' are introduced to allow for extra time on task for those who need it. Furthermore, sustainable development is introduced up front in the first year of the course.

What has been described here are three curriculum models that have sought to depart from the traditional engineering curriculum. In curricula at both

Imperial College and the University of Cape Town there is a retention of the traditional structure for the presentation of basic science and engineering science knowledge (through traditional subject structures and lecture/tutorial modes) with the inclusion of a strand of project work that runs alongside throughout the curriculum – the model at Cape Town possibly aims for more integration between project and theory (the project-centred model) than that at Imperial College (termed project-based). The revised curriculum at the University of Sydney demonstrates the problem-based curriculum model, where the traditional subject structure of the engineering curriculum is largely abandoned, and knowledge is marshalled as needed when tackling a set of carefully designed problems.

This chapter now turns to an explication of key tools from the sociology of knowledge in the context of engineering knowledge and curriculum, in order to build a base from which to interrogate these models of curriculum innovation in engineering education.

Using Bernstein's sociology of knowledge

Common-sense discussions of curriculum frequently conflate curriculum knowledge with disciplinary knowledge: these are seen to be one and the same thing. There is often also a further conflation of curriculum and pedagogy. Bernstein's 'pedagogic device' recognizes that these are distinct forms of knowledge each associated with a particular field of play: disciplinary knowledge functions in the field of production (in the arena of research and scholarship), curriculum knowledge functions in the field of recontextualization and is manifested in curriculum documents, etc., and pedagogy functions in the field of reproduction. In considering curriculum, a significant area for investigation is the process of 'recontextualization' where there is a selection and a reforming of disciplinary knowledge to transform it into curriculum. Importantly, as knowledge moves between one field and another, a 'discursive gap' exists where power interests are at play (Bernstein 2000).

Nonetheless, recognizing the emergent powers of knowledge it is clear that the underlying disciplinary knowledge structure will always place some limits on the form that the curriculum can take (Muller 2009). As Maton (2009: 55) writes, '. . . knowledge has its own causal powers and tendencies. That is, different structurings of knowledge possess different affordances – they lend themselves more to certain forms of pedagogy, evaluation, identity, change over time, and so forth, than others.' Thus a starting point for interrogating curriculum in a disciplinary area requires an examination of the discipline as represented in the field of production.

In Bernstein's terms, the disciplinary knowledge of professions can be described as a 'region', lying at 'the interface between the field of the production of knowledge and any field of practice' (Bernstein 2000: 9). The field of practice of engineering has a long-standing tradition of knowledge based on 'what works', the so-called 'heuristics' or 'rules of thumb'. For example, in chemical engineering it is known from practice that decreasing the temperature of a chiller by 10°C results in a doubling of the cost of the operation. For the purposes of this chapter we will call this 'engineering practice knowledge'. At the time that engineering disciplines established themselves as legitimate members of the academy (Noble 1977), there was a pulling away from the field of practice (on the shop floor) towards the field of production (in the academy) to establish the 'engineering sciences', which build on a set of recontextualized 'singulars'. Thus, for example, 'chemical engineering science' is a scientific field of its own that uses advanced mathematics, physics and chemistry. This field involves, for example, a complicated set of differential equations that describe the mass transfer of substances through a particular region in space.

In Bernstein's (2000) terms, engineering science knowledge (like other science knowledge) is a 'hierarchical knowledge structure', which 'attempts to create very general propositions and theories, which integrate knowledge at lower levels' (Bernstein 2000: 161). However, there are important although subtle differences in the logic of the structuring of engineering science knowledge compared to the natural sciences and early work by Smit (2012) is starting to trace these differences. Engineering science knowledge is of course the engineering knowledge that is valorised in the academy, compared to engineering practice knowledge, which some commentators suggest is more akin to an art than a science (Winkelman 2006), although Gamble's (2006) analysis of knowledge in the field of practice suggests that it too is underpinned by principled forms of knowledge.

In the recontextualizing process there is a contestation between these two different forms of engineering knowledge as to the prominence that they enjoy in the curriculum. Given that it was the engineering sciences that established themselves in the academy, at least in part in a move away from engineering practice knowledge, it is maybe not surprizing that the engineering sciences strongly dominate engineering curricula around the world. However, the professional voices, most notably through the mechanism of accreditation, have managed to retain an emphasis on practice through the inclusion of design courses, particularly at the final year level, which involve real-world problems where students are required to engage with contextual information and apply heuristics and other methods of approximation where appropriate. Recent work by Wolmarans and colleagues tracks the principled progression that underpins a sequence of engineering design courses (Wolmarans, Luckett and Case 2012), showing not only that these have their own inherent logic but also, crucially, that this logic is very different to that of the engineering science space in the curriculum.

The dominance of engineering science as the basis for engineering curriculum is currently under further contestation from another angle. There are those who argue that there are other knowledge areas, for example politics, economics and social science, which need to be incorporated into engineering for it to be able to fulfil its mission of responding to human needs. Bernstein has shown how the social sciences tend to have a 'horizontal' knowledge structure where parallel perspectives are set up against each other, rather than subsuming subordinate concepts into a higher structure. The incorporation of two different kinds of knowledge structures into one curriculum thus poses an interesting challenge to engineering educators.

An important contribution of Bernstein's framework for analysing curriculum is the analytical construct of 'classification', which refers to the boundaries between categories of knowledge. It is in the legitimation of these boundaries that power is exerted (Bernstein 2000). Traditional engineering curricula exhibit strong classification, especially at the lower levels involving exposure to a range of 'singulars', but the final year design project mentioned above involves a weakening of classification as students are expected to integrate engineering science knowledge from different areas, as well as incorporate engineering practice knowledge where appropriate. Alongside classification Bernstein identifies 'framing', referring to matters such as selection of content, sequencing and pacing, as the key means whereby control is exercised, socializing individuals into particular identity spaces. Kotta's (2011) study is a stark demonstration of the challenge that the weakening of both classification and framing in the design course presents to both educators and to students.

From this perspective one can see that traditional engineering curricula, which are largely prescribed and content-loaded, tend to be strongly framed. Bernstein conceptualises such a curriculum, involving strong classification and framing, as a 'collection code'. This concept is intended as an 'ideal type' but nonetheless versions of it can be recognized, for example in the early years of the traditional engineering curriculum. Both the project-based and problem-based models of curriculum outlined above tend to involve a weakening of both classification and framing across the curriculum, more radical and widespread in PBL. As seen in the curriculum from the University of Sydney, the organizing principles for the PBL-type curriculum are based on real-world contexts, not on the abstract conceptual organizers of the discipline. Selection of material tends to be less fixed, and depends on the particular problem at hand. Pacing of learning is more at the level of individual students and their needs. This form of curriculum relates to Bernstein's other ideal type, the 'integrated code'.

Bernstein's concepts of classification and framing have been more recently extended by Maton to apply not only to knowledge structures but also to what are termed 'knower' structures (Maton 2007). Knowledge structures speak to the relationship between the knowledge and the object of knowledge, while knower structures refer to that between the knower and the knowledge. Just as each curriculum will have an implicit (or explicit) knowledge structure, there is always a knower structure, i.e., a notion of what the ideal knower should be. However, knower structures can also be weakly or strongly framed and classified, just like knowledge structures. Maton suggests a further conceptualization of these as the strength or weakness of (1) the epistemic relation – classification and framing of the knowledge structure and (2) the social relation – classification and framing of the knower structure.

Traditional curricula in engineering, while certainly embodying an ideal 'engineer', tend to place relatively little emphasis on dispositions and attitudes of the student. Thus an increased focus on personal growth, implicit in most curriculum models that involve more project work, does, I argue here, imply a strengthening of what Maton terms the 'social relation' underlying the knowledge structure. This is not to mean that we necessarily return to the 'cultured gentleman' as the ideal knower of the traditional humanities curriculum, but this would nonetheless imply an increased exercise of power and control on the student's dispositions at the graduate outcome stage.

It is important to realise that Bernstein's theory does not immediately place a normative value on strong or weak classification or indeed on strong or weak framing. However, he suggests that if there are proposed changes in the modalities of classification or framing it will always be important to ask two key questions:

1   Which group is responsible for initiating the change? (dominant or dominated).
2   If values are weakening, what values remain strong?

(Bernstein 2000: 15)

With regard to the first question, Bernstein suggested that if a dominant group is requiring change this will be a rather different situation to if a dominated group is doing so. The former are likely to favour strategies that conserve the status quo, while the latter will favour subversive strategies. Considering calls for reform in engineering education, we need to examine whether the pressure for change is from within (autonomous) or without (heteronomous) the field. The curriculum debate outlined earlier is largely being conducted by engineering academics with an interest in teaching and learning. Slowly there is a growing interest in a scholarly engagement with these issues and a growing recognition of the value of education research, but these are early days and much of the debate proceeds with little reference to the education literature. Thus, Radcliffe and Jolly (2003) note the prevalence of the 'lone enthusiast' in engineering education, who is often able to infect at least a few other colleagues with their enthusiasm for a particular initiative. With regard to the current focus towards an inclusion of more project work, these resonate with the power interests external to the academy, notably, industry and professional bodies, who are increasingly focused on 'what graduates can do'. Furthermore, with the escalation of focus on teaching and learning in the academy, these calls for curriculum renewal are also in a favourable position with regard to internal power structures.

But whose interests do they ultimately serve? At this point we need to focus on those invisible people who generally move with quiet perseverance through our curriculum structures: the students. The traditional university set itself up to be able to work with an elite group of students from middle-class homes and high-quality schooling; the massified university of the post-war era is still struggling to come to terms with the fact that the students have changed. Traditional curriculum structures in engineering education have been shown to be insufficiently responsive to where students are coming from, but it is not automatically so that reformed curricula with different degrees of inclusion of project work will necessarily meet the goals that they have set for themselves in the context of the real and diverse student bodies that enter engineering studies in the twenty-first century.

Implication of new curriculum proposals

In discussing student learning Maton (2009) makes the distinction between 'cumulative learning', where new understandings are built on prior knowledge, or 'segmented learning', where new ideas get accumulated but not subsumed into existing understandings. This is of course a central concern in all of learning research and practice. It is fairly clear that curriculum design will play a crucial role in either constraining or enabling cumulative learning.

In an illustrative analysis of two curricula contexts that emphasize 'authentic learning', Maton (2009) shows that although these contexts had expectations that students develop abstract understandings of the knowledge areas, because of their teaching environment, which involved minimal guidance and only explanations of the task at hand, many students did not manage to fulfil these expectations: their new ideas remained rooted in the context of the problem. Maton argues that these contexts in fact 'set up many students to underachieve as it is the ability to generalize and abstract that is rewarded in such tasks' (p. 51). Furthermore, it is those students with less-advantaged backgrounds who are particularly disadvantaged by this kind of curricula arrangement, which requires one to utilize tacit knowledge – often of the sort that comes with a particular family background.

This is therefore the first caution for radical (PBL) curriculum reform in engineering: that in making less explicit the boundedness of the specialized knowledge that needs to be acquired, that one might particularly disadvantage those very students one is intending to help. A dangerous misconception of many progressive education agendas has been that the way to make academic knowledge more accessible is to dissolve the boundaries that exist in traditional curricula. At the heart of Bernstein's conceptualization of learning are the concepts of 'recognition' and 'realization' rules that focus directly on the central significance of recognizing and navigating boundaries. Rather than trying to blur boundaries, a truly progressive education aims to signal extremely clearly to students what these boundaries are and how they might navigate them. Above it was also noted that all of these innovative curricula involving a greater emphasis on project work might involve a strengthening of the social relation. This development could also have implications for student success and progression, especially those not from middle-class backgrounds with the kind of cultural capital that can predispose one to pick up these subtle demands. This will be a challenge to pedagogy and assessment, not to say that it should not be taken on, but it should not be taken on lightly.

Student identities and academic identities are closed tied together in a 'necessary' relation (Archer 1996) in that the very identity of 'academic' is only made possible by the presence of 'students' and vica versa. Thus, the possibilities for student agency are constrained by the practices of academics. Therefore, in interrogating new proposals for curriculum in engineering education, we also need to look at the potential impact that these could have on academics.

Kotta's (2011) investigation of student learning in the context of a relatively traditional curriculum points to the difficulty that engineering educators have in collaborating sufficiently to deliver just a portion of curriculum (senior design) that requires working in a more 'integrated code' manner. When the pedagogy failed, it was the students from more disadvantaged education backgrounds that suffered the most. Kotta traces the logic of the academic practices and identities to the values at play in the institution and provides a warning for engineer educators who think a shift to more project work will be easy to accomplish.

Bernstein points out that in a 'collection code' curriculum, because staff are differently specialized and linked together in a hierarchical system, very little collaboration is needed or is practised. An 'integrated code' system makes very different demands of staff: of necessity they need to collaborate since the organizational structure will require this. Bernstein issues a caution, noting that a model like this is 'highly vulnerable' because it will be open to a range of influences from the outside. Furthermore, the staff will need to form a strong social network if it is to be at all successful; simply 'no easy activity' (p. 11).

Muller (2009) also notes that because of the hierarchical knowledge structures in the 'hard' disciplines, there is little contention over what's in the undergraduate curriculum, and thus academics spend relatively little time on their undergraduate teaching (compared to those in the 'soft' disciplines). This continues into the postgraduate arena where again, relative to those in 'soft' disciplines, less time is spent on supervision, such that research output (and/or industry collaboration) can be prioritized. Thus it can be seen that the structuring of knowledge has a structuring effect on the social relations in the field.

Thus it is clear that a significant curriculum restructure towards a more integrated code has huge implications for academic identity and academic time. Importantly, if these relations remain unchanged, the integrated code curriculum will simply be a disaster. 'What matters' in the field of higher education will always be a matter for contestation, but one is unlikely to quickly see a radical shift of valuing.

Conclusion

This chapter set out to interrogate curriculum reform proposals that are currently on offer in engineering education, using tools from the sociology of knowledge. The debate in engineering education centres on concerns for what graduates can do when they enter the workplace. A key curriculum question is which of problem-based learning, with a reorganization of the curriculum around real-world problems, or project-based/project-centred learning, retaining a traditional organization of the curriculum, is more suitable. An analysis of these positions using Bernstein's tools of classification and framing together with Maton's elaboration thereof, shows that although both of these models involve a strengthening of the social relation (a greater exercise of control over legitimate student identities), the problem-based mode also involves a weakening of the epistemic relation (a blurring of knowledge boundaries).

For an analysis of any curriculum reform from a sociology of knowledge perspective it is important to analyse which groups are calling for the change.

Although, as noted above, there are significant external pressures on the engineering curriculum, it might also be noted that it is largely engineering educators with a passion for teaching and learning who are proposing particular curriculum models. The intentions are good. However, the analysis moves to a consideration of the likely implications of such curriculum modes for student learning, particularly in the context of a massified higher education system that has to cater beyond the needs of the elite. Preliminary research suggests that curricula with weakened boundaries, such as those represented by the more radical PBL versions, might indeed have outcomes quite contrary to those intended, with particular difficulties posed for students from weaker academic backgrounds. Furthermore, there is a serious likelihood that in the current situational logic in the academy, academics will lack the collaborative practices to properly 'pull off' such a curriculum move. This suggests a further detrimental effect on student learning.

At this point it is worth noting the important distinction between curriculum and pedagogy that comes with a social realist perspective (Young and Muller 2010). Good teaching in engineering has always involved pedagogies that help students make the link between engineering science knowledge and the real world 'out there'. However, this is not the same as making the real world the organizing principle for the curriculum, as is the case in the problem-based curriculum. In conclusion it is therefore suggested that what is needed is a curriculum that recognizes the boundedness of both engineering science and engineering practice knowledge, and which helps students to navigate between these terrains. In this light, it would appear that the more cautious project-based or project-centred models have a better chance of meeting the needs of all students, both in the realm of curriculum, but also, significantly, in pedagogy and assessment.

Note

1   This chapter is a revised and updated version of an earlier article published in the *Journal of Education*, Case, J. M. (2011) 'Knowledge matters: Interrogating the curriculum debate in engineering using the sociology of knowledge', *Journal of Education*, 51: 73–92. We are grateful to *JOE* for permission to do this.

References

Accreditation Board for Engineering and Technology (ABET) (1998) 'Engineering Criteria 2000', Baltimore, MD, available at: www.abet.org/accreditation-criteria-policies-documents (accessed on 13 January, 2014)

Archer, M. S. (1996) *Culture and agency: The place of culture in social theory.* Cambridge: Cambridge University Press.

Bernstein, B. (2000) *Pedagogy, symbolic control, and identity: Theory, research, critique.* Lanham, MA: Rowman & Littlefield Publishers.

Carvalho, L., Dong, A. and Maton, K. (2009) 'Legitimating design: A sociology of knowledge account of the field', *Design Studies*, 30: 483–502.

Case, J. M., Blottnitz, H. v., Fraser, D. M., Heydenrych, H. and Petersen, J. (2013) 'Thinking and practising curriculum: A new first year course in chemical engineering at

UCT", in B. I. Collier-Reed (ed.) 2nd Biannual Conference of the South African Society for Engineering Education (SASEE), Cape Town, pp. 29–38.

Crosthwaite, C., Cameron, I., Lant, P. and Litster, J. (2006) 'Balancing curriculum processes and content in a project centred curriculum in pursuit of graduate attributes', *Education for Chemical Engineers*, 1: 39–48.

Gamble, J. (2006) 'Theory and practice in the vocational curriculum', in M. Young and J. Gamble (eds) *Knowledge, curriculum and qualifications for South African further education*. Pretoria: HSRC Press.

Gomes, V., Barton, G. Petrie, J., Romagnoli, J., Holt, P., Abbas, A., *et al.* (2006) 'Chemical engineering curriculum renewal', *Education for Chemical Engineers*, 1(1): 116–25.

Hoadley, U. (2006) 'Analysing pedagogy: the problem of framing', *Journal of Education*, 40: 15–34.

Kirschner, P. A., Sweller, J. and Clark, R. E. (2006) 'Why minimal guidance during instruction does not work: An analysis of the failure of constructivist, discovery, problem-based, experiential, and inquiry-based teaching', *Educational Psychologist*, 41: 75–86.

Kloot, B. (2011). 'A Bourdieuian analysis of foundation programmes within the field of engineering education: Two South African case studies', unpublished PhD thesis, University of Cape Town.

Kotta, L. (2011). 'Structural conditioning and mediation by student agency: A case study of success in chemical engineering design', unpublished PhD thesis, University of Cape Town.

Lehmann, M., Christensen, P., Du, X. and Thrane, M. (2008) 'Problem-oriented and project-based learning (POPBL) as an innovative learning strategy for sustainable development in engineering education', *European Journal of Engineering Education*, 33: 283–95.

Luckett, K. (2009) 'The relationship between knowledge structure and curriculum: A case study in sociology', *Studies in Higher Education*, 34: 441–53.

Luckett, K. (2010) 'Knowledge claims and codes of legitimation: Implications for curriculum recontextualisation in South African higher education', *Africanus*, 40: 6–20.

Maton, K. (2005) 'A question of autonomy: Bourdieu's field approach and higher education policy', *Journal of Education Policy*, 20: 687–704.

Maton, K. (2007) 'Knowledge-knower structures in intellectual and educational fields', in F. Christie and J. Martin (eds) *Language, knowledge and pedagogy: Functional linguistic and sociological perspectives*. London: Continuum.

Maton, K. (2009) 'Cumulative and segmented learning: Exploring the role of curriculum structures in knowledge-building', *British Journal of Sociology of Education*, 30: 43–57.

Mills, J. E. and Treagust, D. F. (2003) 'Engineering education – Is problem-based or project-based learning the answer?', *Australasian Journal of Engineering Education*, 8: 2–16.

Muller, J. (1998) 'The well-tempered learner: Self-regulation, pedagogical models and teacher education policy', *Comparative Education*, 34: 177–93.

Muller, J. (2009) 'Forms of knowledge and curriculum coherence', *Journal of Education and Work*, 22: 205–26.

Noble, D. F. (1977) *America by design*. New York: Alfred A. Knopf.

Perkins, J. (2002) 'Education in process systems engineering: Past, present and future', *Computers and Chemical Engineering*, 26: 283–93.

Perrenet, J. C., Bouhuijs, P. A. J. and Smits, J. G. M. M. (2000) 'The suitability of problem-based learning for engineering education: Theory and practice', *Teaching in Higher Education*, 5: 345–58.

Radcliffe, D. F. and Jolly, L. (2003) 'Dilemmas in framing research studies in engineering education', in 2003 American Society for Engineering Education Annual Conference, 2003 Nashville, Tennesee. Available online at www.asee.org/search/proceedings (accessed 13 January, 2014).

Reed, B. and Sass, A. R. (2000) 'Integrating the World Wide Web into an introductory course in mechanical engineering', *Australasian Journal of Engineering Education*, 8: 175–81.

Ruprecht, R. (2000) 'Curriculum development: The whole and its parts', *European Journal of Engineering Education*, 25: 359–67.

Shay, S. (2011) 'Curriculum formation: A case study from History', *Studies in Higher Education*, 36: 315–29.

Smit, R. (2012) 'The recontextualisation of thermodynamics knowledge into science and engineering curricula: The effect of regionalisation', paper presented at the Seventh International Basil Bernstein Symposium, Aix-en-Provence.

Veldman, F. J., De Wet, M. A., Mokhele, N. E. I. and Bouwer, W. A. J. (2008) 'Can engineering education in South Africa afford to avoid problem-based learning as a didactic approach?', *European Journal of Engineering Education*, 33: 551–9.

Winkelman, P. (2006) 'Frankenstein goes to engineering school', *European Journal of Engineering Education*, 31: 449–57.

Wolmarans, N., Luckett, K. and Case, J. M. (2012) 'Investigating principles of curriculum knowledge progression: A case study of design in a civil engineering degree programme', paper presented at the Seventh International Basil Bernstein Symposium, Aix-en-Provence.

Young, M. and Muller, J. (2010) 'Three educational scenarios for the future: Lessons from the sociology of knowledge', *European Journal of Education*, 45: 11–27.

11 Knowledge matters in nursing

Martin McNamara and Gerard Fealy

Introduction

Nursing's struggles for academic and professional recognition have been well documented (McNamara 2008, 2009). A recurring theme in debates concerning the development of academic nursing is disciplinary distinctiveness (Nagle 1999), particularly from medicine (Barrett 2002, Parse 2006). Attempts at temporal demarcation are also evident as a means of distancing nursing from earlier phases of its development (Katz 1969). The content, proper focus and scope of academic and professional nursing have long preoccupied nursing scholars (Donaldson and Crowley 1978). Many contemporary commentators agree that boundaries matter (McNamara *et al.* 2011) and recognise the importance for nursing's disciplinary survival and development of establishing and maintaining strong yet permeable boundaries between it and other health professional disciplines (Meleis 2007).

This emphasis on nursing's 'differentiatedness' (Young and Muller 2010, p. 15), and the notion of nursing as at once bounded and boundary spanning, suggest a shared vision of a future characterised by boundary maintenance and boundary crossing, the third of three future scenarios favoured by Young and Muller (2010) on the grounds of epistemological access and social justice. However, it would be misleading to suggest that agreement exists concerning the future trajectory of nursing as a professional practice and academic discipline. Nursing has perhaps more than its fair share of essentialist fundamentalists (Drummond 2005, Rafferty 1995) championing the fixity and rigidity of boundaries (Cody 2001, Fawcett 2006) but also attracts the attention of those who promulgate 'a spurious ideology of boundlessness' (Muller 2000, p. 5) characterised by 'transdisciplinarity, diversity and plurality' (Holmes and Gastaldo 2004, p. 259).

The debate concerning nursing's 'double-edged dilemma of disciplinary development' (Rafferty 1996, p. 187) frequently generates more heat than light and offers little guidance for nurses' knowledge production, transmission, acquisition and translation practices. Rafferty's dilemma compels nursing academics to construct 'epistemologies of esteem' (Rafferty, 1996, p. 187) while defending themselves from three principal accusations: bringing profane contents into the academy, destroying all that was once held sacred in nursing with vain (in both senses) and irrelevant theorising, and casting academic nursing ever further adrift from clinical practice, which is the ultimate source of its social mandate and legitimacy (Clarke 2006, Thompson and Watson 2006).

Rafferty's term 'epistemologies of esteem' is apt as it draws attention to what is frequently invoked but inadequately theorised in the debate: knowledge. The category knowledge is used rhetorically, its meaning assumed rather than explicated and its 'positive contents' (Elzinga 1990, p. 161) ignored; it is as if knowledge is an empty category, devoid of all substance, that can be reduced to the contexts from which it emerges and in which it is applied (Young 2009). This points to an over or wholly socialised conception of knowledge in which its 'necessary objectivity' (Young and Muller 2010, p. 14) and relative context independence is denied in favour of a preoccupation with knowers and their situated practices (Young and Muller 2010). Much of the debate around academic and professional nursing concerns the discovery, recovery and articulation of the voice of nursing (Meerabeau 2005). However, the focus is on the voice of nurses; that is, on knowers rather than knowledge. Nursing does need to find its voice but, if this voice is to be credible, nursing academics and clinicians will have to listen to the 'voice of knowledge' (Young 2009) and work with the understandings it can provide. A social realist approach takes the idea of the voice of knowledge seriously and offers conceptual and analytic resources to illuminate what is at stake in nursing's struggles for legitimacy.

In this chapter, we consider the relevance for academic nursing of a number of distinctions emphasised in the theoretical literature[1] and explore their implications for the status and trajectory of the discipline. We first discuss nursing's entry to the academy in terms of the disturbance of boundaries between the sacred and profane and go on to explore the relevance of Bernstein's work on singulars and regions (Bernstein 1971, 2000). We then compare nursing and medicine in terms of their processes of regionalisation. Next, we draw attention to the knowledge that is bounded by analysing academic nursing as both a region and a singular. We conclude by suggesting a way forward for academic nursing that involves strengthening it as a region.

Disturbing boundaries: nursing work, nursing knowledge and the sacred and profane

Academic leaders in nursing are constantly challenged to secure their discipline's legitimacy in academic and clinical settings as well as in the wider public sphere. Rafferty (1999, p. 3) believes that nursing has a particular problem in being taken seriously as an academic subject partly because it deals with 'totemically taboo subjects which hardly lend themselves to high table conversation'. Meerabeau (2005, p. 131) agrees that 'much of the knowledge needed for bodily caring is disreputable'. Consequenty, nursing is constructed as a profane presence in academia that disturbs long-established boundaries between the sacred and profane (McNamara 2008). However, it is worth considering the extent to which this disturbance is the result of the structure and substance of nursing knowledge as opposed to the nature of nursing work.

The sacred refers to the world of conceptual relations, comprising the collective representations of a community that have accumulated over time, and which can be manipulated, codified and systematised in the mind, free of engagement in the real world. This capacity to conceptualise allows new possibilities and alternatives to the status quo to be imagined. The profane world is the mundane sphere of practical and direct wisdom, where meaning arises directly out of direct bodily engagement, as in on-the-job knowledge (Muller 2007). In bounded disciplinary domains, custodians 'partake of the sacred' (Beck and Young 2005, p. 185), the field's intrinsic value bestowing on them 'a special significance', a pure identity grounded in knowledge that is 'not ordinary or mundane, but something esoteric' (Bernstein, 1971, p. 215). The sacred and profane co-exist in all social fields and practices; in education, the relative salience of, and relations between, concepts, content, skills and context merit close attention, particularly for professional disciplines (Young and Muller 2010).

In attempting to articulate nursing's sacred, nurse scholars, such as Parse (1999) and Watson (2005), emphasise concepts gleaned from a 'platonic quest for application of abstract theories' (Brykczynski 2006, p.153), derived in the main from the humanities. They aim to establish strong boundaries between their current habituses, capital and practices and those pertaining in the era of the nurse apprentice (Bradshaw 2001). This leads to accusations that nursing academics are motivated primarily by profane considerations of status and reward and that the field of academic nursing is indifferent to the daily realities of nursing practice (Clarke 2006).

These claims invoke the notion of academic drift (Maton 2005): the idea that academic nursing is the creation of aspiring academics seeking to legitimate themselves in academia, and rests on insecure foundations because it is not grounded in a rigorous analysis of the occupational sector from which it derives its legitimacy. Many 'rank-and-file' nurses believe that nursing academics denigrate nursing practice while nursing academics decry the 'long-standing anti-intellectualism within nursing' (Miers 2002, p. 212).

The presence of any subject area or professional practice within the academy is 'the product of history, politics, economics, culture, custom, pressure groups and a good deal of political horse-trading' (Rafferty 1999, p. 3). Social realism provides a socio-epistemic perspective (Muller 2009), recognising that all disciplines have a social as well as an epistemic aspect. Bernstein never suggested that those academics whose identities derived from their 'dedication to the intrinsic value and purity of their scholarly pursuits' were not also always 'implicated (to different degrees) in the "profane" world of . . . educational macro and micro politics' (Beck 2002, p. 619). Fawcett highlights the 'property aspect' (Bernstein, 1971, p. 213) intrinsic to all knowledge claims: a 'profane face [that] indicates their external linkage and internal power struggles' (Bernstein, 2000, p. 54):

> If nursing is to be regarded as a discipline, then there must, by definition, be a distinctive body of nursing knowledge [this] is the only (I believe) justification for schools of nursing and doctoral programs in nursing . . . claims for [its] existence are necessary for political and pragmatic reasons.
>
> (Fawcett 2001)

However, this does not diminish the importance of the epistemic dimension. An increasing number of nurse scholars no longer regard differences in the epistemic power of knowledge forms as an issue that is 'beyond the pale' (Maton and Muller 2007, p. 18), accepting that non-arbitrary limits exist regarding what knowledge can be considered legitimate. Rafferty (1996, p. 187) has called for 'a historical sociology of nursing knowledge' to advance academic nursing while Paley (2004, p. 454) urges the use of quantification for nursing's 'pet projects'; for him, numbers, not words, are the way to advance the discipline. This focus on knowledge is reassuring but requires considerable development. Nursing knowledge is much debated but rarely investigated as an object of study in its own right. This is because nursing scholars have been working with an inadequate theory of knowledge. A sociology of education grounded in social realism offers a set of conceptual and analytic resources with which to conduct a more fruitful inquiry.

Negotiating boundaries: professional knowledge

Complaints about a theory-practice gap are an interminal, divisive and deeply unproductive feature of debates concerning nursing education, research and practice (Risjord 2010). Those who are suspicious of academic preparation for nurses stress the importance of practical experience and laud the practical education of the nurse apprentice (Bradshaw 2001). Frequently, however, there is little attempt to differentiate between practical and theoretical knowledge in terms of their forms or structures or to elucidate the relationships between them. One of Bernstein's significant contributions, of course, was to make visible, and therefore amenable to scrutiny, the distinctions between everyday knowledge and 'coherent, explicit, systematically principled' or theoretical knowledge (Bernstein 2000, p. 157). Social realists recognise that practical experience alone is 'no basis for reliable knowledge or for the curriculum' (Young 2009, p. 201). However, professional practice disciplines must negotiate the space between an academic dimension concerned with largely theoretical knowledge and an occupational or vocational dimension concerned with largely practical knowledge (Shay 2012). As Young (2008) and Muller (2009) recognise, it is in this space that the most interesting and significant challenges for academics arise, particularly for those professing professional practice disicplines.

In a seminal paper, Donaldson and Crowley (1978) argue that academic nursing should be separate from the everyday activities of clinical nurses. Practice is concerned with specific, context-bound, concrete problems, whereas the discipline must embody a knowledge base relevant to all domains of practice. Donaldson and Crowley appreciate that a distinction exists between theoretical and practical knowledge but they fail to adequately elucidate the form and content of nursing's disciplinary knowledge or the relationship between it and practical knowledge. They are correct in insisting on the distinction; what is less clear is what is being distinguished. The structure of both theoretical and practical knowledge needs to be conceptualised if there is to be a meaningful debate about professional knowledge.

The boundary between theoretical and practical knowledge exists because these knowledge forms are structured, produced and acquired in different ways, and judgements as to their validity and utility are based on different criteria (Shay 2012). Theoretical knowledge is powerful knowledge because it grants access to the 'yet to be thought' and the 'unthinkable' and controls 'who may think it' (Bernstein 1990, p. 183). A proper higher education should provide not only 'knowledge of how it is (the knowledge of the possible)', 'the thinkable', but also a sense of 'the possibility of the impossible' (Bernstein 2000, p. 29). Education geared to the minimal training of nurses for 'an assumed practice is just plain bad (higher) education' according to Betts (2006, p. 634) and prevents nurses from accessing the powerful knowledge they need to envision a range of possible futures for their profession within a transforming healthcare system and to resist the ongoing blurring and effacement of health professional roles (Latimer 2000, McAllister 2007).

Bernstein (2000) refers to bounded disciplines as 'singulars' whose 'sacred face sets them apart, legitimises their otherness and creates dedicated identities with no reference other than to their calling . . . singulars construct strong boundary maintenance [and] develop strong autonomous self-sealing and narcissistic identities' (Bernstein 2000, pp. 54–5). Singulars come to be regarded as sacred, things apart, 'freed from the particular, the local' (Bernstein 1971, p. 215).

Professional knowledge entails the converging of singulars to form a 'region' (Bernstein 2000). In this context a region is an assemblage of disciplines brought together to support a domain of professional practice (Muller 2009, Young and Muller 2010). Regions entail a blurring of boundaries between previously insulated domains, such as academia and nursing; between disciplinary tribes, whether hard or soft, pure or applied, each with its own cognitive and cultural style (Muller 2009); and between singulars. Regions must also engage with 'the particular, the local' if they are to support professional practice. Such blurring may disturb existing relations of power and control and destabilise treasured identities. Bernstein (1971) anticipated particular problems 'with the question of new forms, as to their legitimacy, at what point they belong, when, where and by whom the form should be taught' (Bernstein 1971, p. 213).

Bernstein's 'particular problems' continue to trouble nursing. Questions of form, legitimacy, and proper location persist, as we have discussed. That these questions continue to arise indicates that, unlike medicine, the very region from which it strives so hard to differentiate itself, nursing has not cohered into a stable community with a distinct, specialised and identifiable form (Muller 2009, Young and Muller 2010). There are two principal and contrasting reasons for this lack of specialisation, differentiation, cohesion and coherence; first, the way in which regionalisation has proceeded in nursing and, second, the nature and outcome of an opposing process of 'singularisation'. This tension encapsulates the epistemic dilemma at the heart of academic nursing's disciplinary development.

Dissolving boundaries among the health professions

Beck and Young (2005, p. 190) note that the process of regionalisation may be associated with the emergence of 'genericism' (Bernstein 2000, p. 53). Genericism emphasises transferable, core or key skills and competences, such as critical thinking, problem solving, lifelong learning and global citizenship (Shay 2012); these generic outcomes are often referred to as graduate attributes. The focus is on 'trainability' (Bernstein 2000, p. 59); according to Bernstein, however, there is 'an emptiness in the concept of trainability, an emptiness which makes the concept self-referential and thus excluding . . . the identity produced by "trainability" is socially empty' (Bernstein 2000, p. 59). The upshot, as Beck (2002), Beck and Young (2005) and Young and Muller (2010) argue is a progressive weakening and blurring of boundaries within and between labour market sectors, a creeping de-specialisation of higher education and other institutions and a de-differentiation of professions. These trends are certainly evident in the healthcare sector.

The Lancet Commission Report (Frenk *et al.* 2010) argues that the current division of labour among health professionals is the product of social forces, historical processes and cultural values and beliefs, rather than having a basis in any inherent attribute of health-related knowledge. It highlights the fluid and shifting nature of professional boundaries over time as healthcare workers struggle to define and delimit their domains of expertise and spheres of influence. However, in effectively calling for 'the end of boundaries' (Young and Muller 2010, p. 18), the Commission is working with an over-socialised concept of professional knowledge, ignoring the importance for professional identities of a deep, stable, inner commitment to a strongly bounded professional and disciplinary domain (Beck 2002, Beck and Young 2005). The boundaries that the Commission seeks to weaken are indeed partly the product of social, cultural and historical forces, but they are no less real for that; their sociality and historicity do not imply that they are arbitrary (Young and Muller 2010); this is a point that is all too often missed, it is caused by 'knowledge blindness' (Maton 2013) and goes some way to explaining the intense resistance to and ultimate failure of attempts to introduce the sorts of reforms that the Commission advocates.

The language of boundlessness and genericism is everywhere evident in the Commission's report. Institutional reforms entail the full integration of healthcare systems and university schools of health sciences. Instructional reforms include a competency-based curriculum, learning 'empowered' by information technology, task shifting and task sharing, transdisciplinary and multischool approaches and the promotion of a culture of critical inquiry and lifelong learning. The command of knowledge and facts is considered secondary to the acquisition of core competencies such as patient-centred care, interdisciplinary teamwork and socially responsible professionalism. The relegation of the knowledge required to produce experts, 'informative learning', to the lowest of three levels is indicative of the marginalisation of knowledge in favour of 'formative learning', a knower mode entailing socialisation into a set of values required to produce a certain type of professional, and a generic mode, termed 'transformative learning', concerned with the acquisition of the leadership attributes required to produce change agents. The transformative power of epistemically-powerful disciplinary knowledge is ignored; yet it is this that must be put to work if health professionals are to address the critical and pressing challenges that the Commission itself identifies: inequities in access to healthcare both within and between countries and threats to global health security arising from new infectious, environmental and lifestyle risks against a background of rapid demographic and epidemiological change.

Just as élite educational institutions eschew the ideology of boundlessness and genericism (Young and Muller 2010) so too do the established élite professions. Medicine guards its boundaries jealously and has been very successful in preserving strong and secure professional and academic identities. Crucial to medical academics' success in establishing an early base for themselves in academia was their achievement of 'an exceptional measure of collective collegiate autonomy' (Beck and Young 2005, p. 188) over their professional preparation and practice. Medical academics were able to institutionalise and insulate their discipline in professional schools located in universities. Carefully selected medical students were exposed to intensive socialisation providing them with the requisite volume and species of capital to form robust professional identities and habituses (Young 2009). This boundary establishment and maintenance protected academic medicine from profane external 'interference' and 'contamination' (Beck and Young 2005, p. 188). As a result, it continues to attract and socialise élite knowers and to exhibit relatively high autonomy and a high degree of coherence and cohesion. But this is not the only explanation for its success.

Medicine has also built upon the advances occurring in the natural sciences at the end of the nineteenth and throughout the twentieth century, giving rise to the rapid growth of a specialised and differentiated knowledge-based field: scientific medicine. The current status and prestige of medicine is therefore a result not only of its social power and longevity, but also of the epistemic power of the singulars that comprise its region, their integration in the service of a clearly understood 'supervening purpose' (Young 2009, p. 213), a high degree of intellectual specialisation and differentiation (Rafferty 1996) and the capacity to engage in cumulative knowledge-building (Maton 2013). Repeated – and, revealingly, always controversial – calls for nursing (e.g., Paley 2001, 2004; Watson 2003) to build a knowledge base for professional practice analogous to that of the hard applied discipline of scientific medicine is testament both to the success of medicine's regionalisation and the enduring seductiveness of boundlessness and generic modes for soft applied regions.

Boundaries' contents: knowledge matters

From the late 1960s academic nursing was preoccupied by concerns about whether nursing should rely on knowledge derived from practice integrated with knowledge from singulars in the biological, psychological and sociological sciences rather than from a 'nursing-discipline specific' (Fawcett 2003, p. 229) singular styled 'nursing science' (Johnson 1968). Proponents of the former reasoned that as the clinical nurse is concerned with the physical, mental and social aspects of the patient, nursing knowledge should be created through an integration of knowledge from singulars in the relevant fields. According to Risjord (2010), nursing's internal and external relations remained stable when nurse training emphasised the basics of biology, anatomy and pathology. However, uniquely among the healthcare professions, nursing's professionalisation agenda, which began in the early twentieth century, mandated the development of a distinctive body of nursing-discipline specific knowledge.

Alert to both the 'property aspects' referred to above and the legitimacy and stable identities traditionally conferred by singulars, proponents of 'nursing science' argued that if nursing was to be recognised as an academic discipline and granted the right to exercise judgement and decision-making in defined areas of healthcare (Johnson 1968) it must be constructed as a basic science with unique theories at high levels of abstraction (Risjord 2010). According to this view, theoretical development in nursing had to occur independently of practice because current practice was constrained by that anathema: a traditional medical model of nursing.

'Nursing science' styles itself as a 'basic' human science (Northrup *et al.* 2004) with its own distinctive disciplinary paradigms and schools of thought (Barrett 2002); a soft pure discipline, in Muller's (2009) typology, exhibiting all the characteristic elements of its cultural and cognitive style: individualistic, person-oriented, loosely organised, reiterative, holistic, qualitative and preoccupied with particulars, understandings and interpretations. The overarching narrative of 'nursing science' is one of caring, the privileging of patients' and nurses' lived experiences of health, illness and healthcare, and a focus on subjectivities and interpersonal relationships between individual nurses and patients (Nelson and Gordon 2006). In an influential paper, Carper (1978) proposed that the distinct knowledge of nursing is captured in four patterns. The three patterns of 'aesthetics', 'personal knowing' and 'ethics' are presented as deeper, more authentic and enduring bases for nursing knowledge than 'empirics', referring to systematically organised general laws and theories.

According to this view, nursing entails a highly personalised version of knowing geared primarily to the development of a particular disposition. To a large extent, 'empirics' was marginalised and excluded from theoretical developments, resulting in an extreme form of constructivism that reached its apogee in the work of scholars such as Parse, whose 'humanbecoming' theory is concerned with abstract and context-free concepts such as meaning, rhythmicity and transcendence; the following is a fairly typical exposition: 'Structuring meaning is the imaging and valuing of languaging . . . Configuring rhythmical patterns of relating is the revealing-concealing and enabling-limiting of connecting-separating . . . Cotranscending with possibles is the powering and originating of transforming' (Parse 2007, p. 309).

The result is a highly abstract and rarefied 'theory' tending towards the rhizomatic proliferation of double-barrelled gerunds rather than the arboreal integration of dense and parsimonious concepts; this serves to obscure rather than illuminate the phenomena of interest to nursing. Yet, such 'egregious sophistry' (Rafferty 2006) is subscribed to with an almost cult-like fervor and its proponents insist that nursing's knowledge producing and transmitting practices must be governed by such nursing-discipline-specific theories. This is despite the lack of evidence to suggest that the theories are capable of guiding research, education or practice (Rawnsley 2003) or of providing nursing with the epistemic capital 'to promote professional resilience and career longevity ... [and] strong professional identities (Hodges, Keeley and Grier 2005, p. 548).

Even contributors to *Nursing Science Quarterly*, a journal that publishes papers focusing on nursing theory development, nursing theory-based practice and research related to nursing conceptual frameworks, admit that the impact of 'nursing science' on academia and practice has been 'less than compelling' and that the sites of its enactment remain 'disciplinary anomalies, notable exceptions to a medical model rule' (Rawnsley 2003, p. 6). Paley believes that 'nursing science' 'appropriates the words but tends to ignore the theoretical matrix to which they belong, the dense background of argument, experiment, empirical findings ... which give the words their meaning ... nursing theorists believe the words are the matrix' (Paley 2006, p. 278). For Paley, nursing theory comprises nothing more than 'concept piles, stacks of words that can be strung together ... a pick 'n' mix assortment of concepts. Hence the contest to see who can build the biggest heap' (Paley 2006, p. 277). Nelson and Gordon (2006) add that nursing science perpetuates a saccharin 'virtue script', a 'hand-holding', 'dewy-eyed' and 'sentimentalised caring rhetoric' (Nelson and Gordon 2006, pp. 4–5) that marginalises the hard work of bodily care, and conceals 'the scientific and (let's say it out loud) medical knowledge and skills nurses master in order to deliver quality care' (Nelson and Gordon 2006, p. 188).

A social realist perspective permits a deeper understanding of both nursing science's seductiveness and its failure. Nursing scientists' quest for disciplinary coherence and distinctiveness may be understood as an attempt to identify and articulate a sacred singular capable of grounding nurses' academic and professional identities. This helps explain why those who eschew nursing science and 'borrow' theories from other disciplines are denounced for dismantling cherished boundaries and precipitating 'the extinction of the discipline of nursing' (Fawcett, 2003, p. 229). However, the sheer abstractness, obscurity and vacuity of the theories and concepts comprising 'nursing science' preclude their use in research and clinical practice and threaten the entire academic nursing enterprise because they deny nursing the powerful knowledge it needs to realise legitimate practices and identities in contemporary health systems and academia (Nelson and Gordon 2006). A preoccupation with establishing and defending boundaries appears to have deflected attention from what is being bounded.

Against 'nursing science', Holmes and Gastaldo (2004) urge the dissolution of disciplinary boundaries to create a new type of nursing. Nurses, they argue, should reject restrictive and narrow-minded nursing conceptual models, and other ways of developing the discipline, such as nursing diagnosis and evidence-based nursing, that merely ape medicine. Instead, nurses should become 'nomads', dwelling on the margins, bereft of epistemic capital, unconstrained by borders and immersed in 'nursing chaos . . . a brand new and fragmented order, one that will dare to tolerate multiplicities of thoughts' (Holmes and Gastaldo 2004, p. 264). But this, too, is an avowedly anti-knowledge stance.

Caught between the nursing science fundamentalists and the cheerleaders of abject boundlessness, it is small wonder that nursing academics have fragile academic and nursing identities; portray academic nursing as a fragmented field removed from its professional base, and prone to colonisation and subversion by any number of external imperatives; find it difficult to articulate concepts and principles to guide the selection, sequencing and pacing of curriculum content; rarely engage in programmatic research; and struggle to legitimate themselves and their discipline in academia (McNamara 2009).

Conclusions: towards scientific nursing

In this chapter we have used Bernstein's ideas of singulars and regions to illuminate what is at stake in academic nursing's struggles for academic and professional legitimacy. These ideas also point to a possible way forward for the discipline. Attempts to confect a nursing singular have resulted in a most peculiar concoction: 'accumulations of words – detached verbal clusters which are at no point anchored in the world that can be observed, described or measured' (Paley 2006, p. 277). A preoccupation with constructing boundaries at the expense of considering what was being bounded has led to a fragmented and segmented discipline with weak internal conceptual relations and weak external relations to its professional context and, consequently, a very limited capacity for cumulative knowledge-building (Maton 2013).

Muller (2009) points out that, in and of themselves, singulars or regions are neither good nor bad. They are the appropriate form for some fields of knowledge, as the region of medicine clearly demonstrates; but not for all, as the singular of 'nursing science' equally clearly shows. Its spurious singularity ill serves professional practitioners, academics, students and, ultimately, and crucially, those in need of nursing care. In marked contrast to academic medicine, regional-isation in nursing was either strongly resisted or proceeded in the absence of any clear 'supervening purpose' or 'supracontent concept' (Bernstein 1971, p. 217) that might bind diverse singulars together in a new region; this has resulted in a weak region characterised by a high degree of genericism.

Weak regions require strengthening but, as Muller (2009) makes clear, this cannot be achieved by curricular or pedagogic means; a claim that our own research supports (McNamara, Fealy and Geraghty 2010). Curricula based on weak regions tend to be characterised by a carrier bag assortment of 'topics' addressed by means of attenuated versions of disciplinary knowledges, detached from their disciplinary matrices, together with attempts to instil generic competencies and graduate attributes. They may be delivered by teachers who are not specialists in the disciplines being plundered and who are often long removed from the relevant professional practice context (McNamara 2008, 2009). This is a recipe for the reproduction of failure.

Ironically, the way forward for nursing may lie in emulating the field with which it has such a problematic relationship and from which it has expended great effort in differentiating itself: scientific medicine. Scientific nursing, not 'nursing science', offers a possible future for academic and professional nursing. Identifying the epistemically-powerful disciplines required to serve the nursing profession and preserving their logic by maintaining their boundaries is the first step towards strengthening the region of nursing. If we genuinely care about nursing knowledge, this is a worthy area for future theoretical and empirical work.

Note

1   Between knowledge and experience, between theoretical and everyday knowledge and between domains of knowledge (Young 2009).

References

Barrett, E.A.M. (2002) 'What is nursing science?' *Nursing Science Quarterly*, 15(1), 51–60.

Beck, J. (2002) 'The sacred and the profane in recent struggles to promote official pedagogic identities'. *British Journal of the Sociology of Education*, 23(4), 617–26.

Beck, J. and Young, M.F.D. (2005) 'The assault on the professions and the restructuring of academic and professional identities: A Bernsteinian analysis'. *British Journal of the Sociology of Education*, 26(2), 183–97.

Bernstein, B. (1971) *Class, codes and control, Volume 1: Theoretical studies towards a sociology of language*. London: Routledge & Kegan Paul.

Bernstein, B. (1990) *Class, codes and control, Volume IV: The structuring of pedagogic discourse*. London: Routledge.

Bernstein, B. (2000) *Pedagogy, symbolic control and identity: Theory, research, critique* (Revised edn). Lanham, MA: Rowman & Littlefield.

Betts, C.E. (2006) 'Assuming practice amid the culture wars: A response to James P. Smith 28 years later'. *Journal of Advanced Nursing*, 54(5), 633–4.

Bradshaw, A. (2001) *The nurse apprentice, 1860–1977*. Aldershot: Ashgate.

Brykczynski, K.A. (2006) 'Patricia Benner: From novice to expert: Excellence and power in clinical nursing practice'. In A.M. Tomey and M.R. Alligood (eds) *Nursing Theorists and Their Work* (6th edn). St Louis, MI: Mosby (pp. 140–66).

Carper, B.A. (1978) 'Fundamental patterns of knowing in nursing', *Advances in Nursing Science*, 1(1), 13–24.

Clarke, S. (2006) 'Research on nurse staffing and its outcomes: The challenges and risks of grasping at shadows'. In S. Nelson and S. Gordon (eds) *The complexities of care*. New York: Cornell University Press (pp. 161–90).

Cody, W.K. (2001) 'Interdisciplinarity and nursing: "Everything is everything," or is it?' *Nursing Science Quarterly*, 14(4), 274–80.

Donaldson, S.K. and Crowley, D.M. (1978) 'The discipline of nursing'. *Nursing Outlook*, 26(2), 113–20.

Drummond, J.S. (2005) 'The rhizome and the tree: A response to Holmes and Gastaldo'. *Nursing Philosophy*, 6, 255–66.

Elzinga A. (1990) 'The knowledge aspect of professionalization: The case of science based nursing education in Sweden'. In R. Torstendahl and M. Burrage (eds) *The formation of professions: Knowledge, state and strategy*. London: Sage (pp. 151–73).

Fawcett, J. (2001) 'Evidence-based practice'. Contribution to Nurse-Philosophy@jiscmail. ac.uk, 30 June.

Fawcett, J. (2003) 'Guest editorial. On bed baths and conceptual models of nursing'. *Journal of Advanced Nursing*, 44(3), 229–30.

Fawcett, J. (2006) 'Nursing philosophies, models and theories: A focus on the future'. In M.R. Alligood and A.M. Tomey (eds) *Nursing theory: Utilization and application* (3rd edn). St. Louis, MI: Mosby (pp. 499–518).

Frenk, J., Chen, L., Bhutta, Z.A., Cohen, J., Crisp, N., Evans, T., Fineberg, H., Garcia, P., Ke, Y., Kelley, P., Kistnasamy, B., Meleis, A., Naylor, D., Pablos-Mendez, A., Reddy, S., Scrimshaw, S., Sepulveda, J., Serwadda, D. and Zurayk, H. (2010) 'Health professionals for a new century: Transforming education to strengthen health systems in an interdependent world'. *Lancet*, 376, 1923–58.

Hodges, H.F., Keeley A.C. and Grier E.C. (2005) 'Professional resilience, practice longevity, and Parse's theory for Baccalaureate education'. *Journal of Nursing Education*, 44(2), 548–54.

Holmes, D. and Gastaldo, D. (2004) 'Rhizomatic thought in nursing: An alternative path for the development of the discipline'. *Nursing Philosophy*, 5, 258–67.

Johnson, D.E. (1968) 'Theory in nursing: Borrowed and unique'. *Nursing Research*, 17(3), 206–09.

Katz, F.E. (1969) 'Nurses'. In A. Etzioni (ed.) *The semi-professions and their organization*. New York: The Free Press (pp. 54–81).

Latimer, J. (2000) *The conduct of care: Understanding nursing practice*. Oxford: Blackwell Science.

McAllister, M. (2007) *Solution focused nursing: Rethinking practice*. Basingstoke: Palgrave Macmillan.

McNamara, M.S. (2008) 'Of bedpans and ivory towers? Nurse academics' identities and the sacred and profane: A Bernsteinian analysis and discussion paper'. *International Journal of Nursing Studies*, 45(3): 458–70.

McNamara, M.S. (2009) 'Nursing academics' languages of legitimation: A discourse analysis'. *International Journal of Nursing Studies*, 46(12): 1566–79.

McNamara, M.S., Fealy, G.M. and Geraghty, R. (2010) 'Nurse tutors' tales of transition: A clash of legitimation codes'. *Society for Research in Higher Education (SRHE) Annual Research Conference*, Newport, Wales.

McNamara, M., Fealy, G.M., Casey, M., Geraghty, R., Butler, M., Halligan, P., Treacy, P. and Johnson, M. (2011) 'Boundary matters: Clinical leadership and the distinctive disciplinary contribution of nursing to multidisciplinary care'. *Journal of Clinical Nursing* 20(23–24): 3502–12.

Maton, K. (2005) 'The field of higher education: A sociology of reproduction, transformation and change and the conditions of emergence of cultural studies'. Unpublished PhD thesis, St John's College, University of Cambridge. Retrieved from www.KarlMaton.com on 16 May 2005.

Maton, K. and Muller, J. (2007) 'A sociology for the transmission of knowledges'. In F. Christie and J.R. Martin (eds) *Language, knowledge and pedagogy. Functional linguistic and sociological perspectives*. London: Continuum (pp. 14–33).

Maton, K. (2013) 'Making semantic waves: A key to cumulative knowledge-building'. *Linguistics and Education*, 24(1), 8–22.

Meerabeau, L. (2005) 'The invisible (inaudible) woman: Nursing in the English academy'. *Gender, Work and Organisation*, 12(2), 124–46.

Miers, M. (2002) 'Nurse education in higher education; understanding cultural barriers to progress', *Nursing Education Today*, 22(21): 2–9.

Meleis, A.I. (2007) *Theoretical nursing: Development and progress* (4th edn). New York: Lippincott Williams & Wilkins.

Muller, J. (2000) *Reclaiming knowledge: Social theory, curriculum and education policy*. London: Routledge/Falmer.

Muller, J. (2007) 'On splitting hairs: Hierarchy, knowledge and the school curriculum'. In F. Christie and J.R. Martin (eds) *Language, knowledge and pedagogy. Functional linguistic and sociological perspectives*. London: Continuum (pp. 65–86).

Muller, J. (2009) 'Forms of knowledge and curriculum coherence'. *Journal of Education and Work*, 22(3), 205–26.

Nagle, L.M. (1999) 'A matter of extinction or distinction'. *Western Journal of Nursing Research*, 21, 71–82.

Nelson, S. and Gordon S. (eds) (2006) *The complexities of care*. New York: Cornell University Press.

Northrup, D.T., Tschanz, C.L., Olynyk, V.G., Makaroff, K.L.S., Szabo, J. and Biasio, H.A. (2004) 'Nursing: Whose discipline is it anyway?' *Nursing Science Quarterly*, 17(1), 55–62.

Paley, J. (2001) 'An archaeology of nursing knowledge'. *Journal of Advanced Nursing*, 36(2), 188–98.

Paley, J. (2004) 'Response to Watson's guest editorial "Scientific methods are the only credible way forward for nursing research" and subsequent JAN Forum pieces'. *Journal of Advanced Nursing*, 46(4), 453–4.

Paley, J. (2006) 'Book review. Nursing theorists and their work (6th edn)', *Nursing Philosophy*, 7, 275–80.

Parse, R.R. (1999) 'Nursing science: The transformation of practice', *Journal of Advanced Nursing*, 30(6), 1383–7.

Parse, R.R. (2006) 'Editorial. Nursing and medicine: Continuing challenges'. *Nursing Science Quarterly*, 19(1), 5.

Parse, R.R. (2007). 'The human becoming school of thought in 2050'. *Nursing Science Quarterly*, 20, 308–11.

Rafferty, A.M. (1995) 'Art, science and social science in nursing: Occupational origins and disciplinary identity'. *Nursing Inquiry*, 2, 141–8.

Rafferty, A.M. (1996) *The politics of nursing knowledge*. London: Routledge.

Rafferty, A.M. (1999) 'Practice made perfect'. *The Guardian*, 26 January, p. 3.

Rafferty, A.M. (2006) 'Nursing identity and dilemmas of disciplinary development'. *Eighth Annual Public Lecture for Nurses and Midwives*, School of Nursing, Midwifery and Health Systems, University College Dublin, 11 May.

Rawnsley, M.M. (2003) 'Dimensions of scholarship and the advancement of nursing science: Articulating a vision'. *Nursing Science Quarterly*, 16(1), 6–15.

Risjord, M. (2010) *Nursing knowledge: Science, practice, and philosophy*. Oxford: Wiley-Blackwell.

Shay, S. (2012) 'Conceptualizing curriculum differentiation in higher education: A sociology of knowledge point of view'. *British Journal of Sociology of Education*, 1–20.

Thompson, D.R. and Watson, R. (2006) 'Editorial. Professors of nursing: What do they profess?' *Nurse Education in Practice*, 6, 123–6.

Watson, R. (2003) 'Scientific methods are the only credible way forward for nursing research'. *Journal of Advanced Nursing*, 43(3), 219–20.

Watson, J. (2005) *Caring science as sacred science*. Philadelphia, PA: F.A. Davis Co.

Young, M. (2008) 'From constructivism to realism in the sociology of the curriculum'. *Review of Research in Education*, 32, 1–28.

Young, M. (2009) 'Education, globalization and the "voice of knowledge"'. *Journal of Education and Work*, 22(3), 193–204.

Young, M. and Muller, J. (2010) 'Three educational scenarios for the future: Lessons from the sociology of knowledge'. *European Journal of Education*, 45(1), 11–27.

12 Knowledge and teacher professionalism

The case of mathematics teaching

Nick Taylor

Introduction: exogenous and endogenous views of teaching

The term 'teacher professionalism' is generally used in one of two ways in the literature. First, it may be taken to be something that society and the state in particular should grant teachers so that they can get on with their work unhindered by government interference. This is the sense in which Hargreaves uses it in his description of the deprofessionalization of teachers since the late 1970s, when neoliberal reforms began to erode teachers' autonomy of judgment and conditions of work (Hargreaves 2003: 11; see also Apple 1986; Ball 2008; Beck 2008). This voice is present too in Goodson and Hargreaves' seven principles of postmodern professionalism, the first of which is 'Increased opportunity and responsibility to exercise discretionary judgement' (1996: 21). Hyslop-Margison and Sears continue the argument, concluding that the role of teachers in administrating public education, establishing curricular objectives and instructional design is threatened by accountability measures, such as instrumental objectives, standardized testing, and evidence-based practice (2010: 2). This exogenous view of teacher autonomy assumes that the development of a professional approach is dependent on the conferral of autonomous status to teachers by the public in general and the state in particular: without this space teachers are reduced to implementers of a curriculum designed elsewhere, and hampered in the task of elaborating their own vision of good professional practice.

The limits of this view were tested and found wanting by South Africa's Curriculum 2005 ('C2005'), launched in 1998 as the country's alternative to apartheid's Bantu education. The central design feature of the new curriculum was its under-specification of disciplinary knowledge, deliberately providing a great deal of leeway for teachers and schools to develop curricula and teaching strategies suited to the specific context of their pupils. Bernstein (1996) might have predicted that the successful implementation of such a curriculum would exact a heavy price in teacher time, in order to fulfil the intensive learner-by-learner focus required by the C2005 pedagogical approach. This was a price that most South African teachers could not pay, and successive revisions of the school curriculum have systematically amended these elements, most notably by specifying subject content knowledge to a greater degree of detail (see for example, Department of Education 2000; 2002; Department of Basic Education 2011).

A second way of talking about professionalism is exemplified in the work of Abbott (1988), for whom a specialized knowledge base is a prerequisite feature of any profession. Gamble emphasizes the point: '. . . the notion of autonomy is indelibly linked to control of the knowledge base on which a profession's claim to autonomy rests' (Gamble 2010: 13). This may be called an endogenous view of a profession, which assumes that the impetus for professionalization arises from within the occupational field, and results in the formulation of general protocols of practice for operating in the field, which in turn gain public trust through their greater efficacy, compared to any other set of practices. According to the endogenous model, society accords professional autonomy over the standards that regulate the procedures and ethics of practice to a defined group of practitioners because the group possesses a knowledge base that is a more reliable guide to practice than any contending formulations. For Abbott this is abstract knowledge: 'Expert action without any formalization is perceived by clients as craft knowledge, lacking the special legitimacy that is supplied by the connection of abstractions with general values' (Abbott 1988: 103). Putting this more succinctly, Freidson insists that 'The authority of knowledge is central to professionalism' (Freidson 1994: 36).

The point is well illustrated by Goldstein's (2001) description of how, during the first half of the nineteenth century in France, control over the field of psychiatry was the subject of contestation between the medical profession and the church, with the latter not only running its own clerical asylums, but also administering public institutions. What persuaded lawmakers to pass legislation in 1838, which made the employment of a physician in every asylum mandatory, were advances made by the fledgling profession in the diagnosis of monomania. Subsequent decisive moments in the development of psychiatry as a profession were driven by advances in the theorization of hysteria during the second half of the nineteenth century, and of neurosis and psychosis in the early decades of the twentieth. The key move in bringing hysteria into the fold of medical science, for example, was Charcot's demonstration that what was then known as insanity shared an essential nature with a range of other difficult-to-diagnose intermediate pathologies. Through his four diagnostic criteria Charcot exerted '. . . cognitive mastery of the symptom patterns presented by these nervous conditions . . .' (Goldstein 2001: 333). It was this advance in understanding that facilitated more effective treatment and increased public confidence in the profession (Pichot 2000). Of course, psychiatry is the least well understood of all medical specialisations, and cures of many conditions such as schizophrenia are rare. Yet there is generally accepted best practice within the profession and general cognisance of and trust in the expertise of professionals among the public. In the sense that it also works with subjects who are not necessarily willing partners in the enterprise, psychiatry bears a passing resemblance to schooling, yet the two regions of professional activity differ significantly in the degree to which their knowledge base for the derivation of protocols of practice may be characterised as exhibiting what Muller (2009) has called 'disciplinary robustness', a subject we return to below.

What would a professional knowledge base for teaching mathematics look like?

A number of authors writing in the exogenous tradition are of the view that teaching should not follow the other professions in developing a scientific knowledge base. Thus, Apple (2000) has tied attempts to place teaching on a scientific basis to the rise of an instrumentalist discourse, which in turn has been used as a tool to stifle diversity and deskill teachers. Apple argues further that the intensification of teachers' work, brought about by the bureaucracy that inevitably accompanies the systematization of practice in the name of science, has taken the focus off the essential task of fostering critical literacy in students and made the implementation of 'what works' the key focus of teachers' work (Apple 2000: 118–19). Stephen Ball (2008) paints a dystopian view of an all-powerful state driving teachers into continuous self-improvement in the name of greater economy through the technology of performativity, a process that sets what Ball calls the 'tyranny of metrics' against professional judgement, and subverts moral considerations to economic ends (Ball 2008: 53–4). According to Goodson and Hargreaves (1996), teacher professionalism should move beyond attempting to reduce educational knowledge to the level of scientific certainty, rise above 'the recent clamour for technical competency and subject knowledge' (Goodson and Hargreaves 1996: 20) and deal with the more morally-laden and politicized areas of the teacher's work. Sockett (1987) argues that the development of a scientific knowledge base for teaching would deny the contextual, emotional, reflexive and iterative elements that are so integral to teaching done well – in short, it would deny the craft and artistry of the profession (Sockett 1987: 1). Pratte and Rury expand the point:

> We would define teaching . . . as a craft-profession. Unlike the traditional professions, a craft-profession does not rest on a highly formal codified body of knowledge. Instead, competence for craft-professionals is defined in terms of various skills and practices, reflecting a different sort of knowledge base . . . something that they learn by doing and that is experientially learned, rather than acquired in a systematic, highly formal manner.
> (Pratte and Rury 1991: 61–2, quoted in Gamble 2010: 17)

The postmodern far side of this craft perspective on the nature of professional knowledge is articulated by Pachler (2007), who dismisses the 'what works' and 'best practice' agendas as illegitimate importations from an inappropriate paradigm,

> underpinned by an assumption that what works for one teacher with a particular educational biography, values, methodological position, particular

characteristics, working in one specific socio-political context at a particular point in time will necessarily work equally well for another teacher with different characteristics working in a different context, etc.

(Pachler 2007: 255)

The implications of this radical view of teacher, learner and classroom uniqueness is that professional knowledge is more about 'collaborative, enquiry-based' processes (Pachler 2007: 256) and less about a set of theoretical propositions and protocols of practice. For Hargreaves (2003), the sharing of professional knowledge is more effectively done through practice-based forms of 'innovation transfer' (Hargeaves 2003: 50), and less through a codified body amenable to transmission through training. Similarly, for Purinton (2011) collaboration within the profession is key; he exhorts teachers to form 'professional networks of knowledge transfer' (213) through the creation of a system of collegial ties between schools (221).

The reservations of many authors regarding the value of a scientific basis to teaching notwithstanding, others such as Hiebert, Gallimore and Stigler (2002) want to codify knowledge for teaching:

> we recognize the value of teachers' craft knowledge. We now ask whether it is possible to build this personal craft knowledge into a trustworthy knowledge base that can be accessed and shared widely in the profession . . . we propose that professional knowledge must be public, it must be represented in a form that enables it to be accumulated and shared with other members of the profession, and it must be continually verified and confirmed.
>
> (Hiebert, Gallimore and Stigler 2002: 3–4)

The field of mathematics education derives its authority from at least three sources: knowledge of the school subject (disciplinary knowledge), knowledge about how best to teach the subject (subject knowledge for teaching) and knowledge about classroom practice (pedagogical knowledge). Bernstein calls this kind of combination a 'region', where knowledge is drawn from various disciplines and combined to serve a new professional purpose. Regions look backward to the field of knowledge production and forward to the field of practice: 'Regions are the interface between disciplines (singulars) and the technologies they make possible.' (Bernstein 1990: 65).

For Muller (2009) a key variable in characterizing differences between regions lies in their relative degrees of disciplinary robustness. He sees professions like teaching, clinical psychology and social work as being in the process of developing their knowledge bases, aspiring to the stability and autonomy of the established professions, but with a way to go still in terms of their disciplinary robustness. In illustrating the concept Muller (2009) invokes Kuhn's use of the term paradigm, denoting a sharing of beliefs within a scientific field about theory, methodology, techniques and problems. However, the exogenous view to the contrary, even if this is deemed desirable, is it possible?

In what follows below, we will examine these issues from the vantage point of the professional knowledge base of mathematics teachers. Before drawing conclusions about the disciplinary robustness of teacher education as a regional knowledge field, we discuss each of the three components of knowledge for and about teaching mathematics, as seen from a South African perspective.

Subject knowledge

Without subject knowledge the teacher cannot begin. There can be no adequate classroom pedagogy or reflection on and research into teaching without the subject to be taught. This much is agreed, but many questions remain concerning the precise nature of any school subject. First, how does the school curriculum relate to the parent discipline: how, for example, is the school mathematics curriculum derived from the discipline of mathematics? For Bernstein (1990) new knowledge is generated in the field of production. This is where the discipline of mathematics lives and where research mathematicians labour. Mathematics is transformed into a school curriculum through a process of recontextualization. This involves appropriating parts of the discipline and describing the selection in new terms. The result does not necessarily resemble its foundation discipline in all its aspects. In a country with a national curriculum, such as South Africa, formulating the subject curriculum is the task of Bernstein's (1990) official recontextualizing field, which comprises the state and its agents. This has not been an easy task, with the school curriculum undergoing three major revisions since 1994, each of which was accompanied by high levels of contestation (Taylor and Hoadley 2012).

All curricula, to a greater or lesser extent, specify the selection of disciplinary topics to be addressed in any grade, the sequence in which they are to be learned, and the pace with which they are to be explored in the classroom. But school curricula may differ according to the degree to which the topics are explicated. Thus, C2005, the first post-apartheid curriculum formulated the *outcomes* of learning in the broadest terms, allowing space for teachers to customize teaching and learning activities to suit each class (Department of Education, 1995). The realization that most teachers did not have the knowledge resources required to design specific curricula in the way envisaged in C2005, prompted a review of the curriculum in 2000 and the formulation of the National Curriculum Statements (NCS) in 2002, which set out to *specify the knowledge topics* deemed to be worth studying in more explicit detail, as shown in Figure 12.1.

In the interests of providing detailed pedagogical guidance to teachers, the Curriculum and Assessment Policy Statements (CAPS), commencing in 2011, adopted a third approach, recommending particular *sets of strategies* to sequence and pace the knowledge topics, resulting in a ballooning of the curriculum document, from the economical 120-page mathematics curriculum of the NCS for the first nine grades (Department of Education 2002), to the 518-page CAPS curriculum for Grades R-3 only (Department of Basic Education 2011). The very different forms in which essentially the same mathematical topics have been cast in successive curricula for South African schools over the last two decades

LO 1: Numbers, operations and relationships			
AS: Estimates and calculates by selecting and using operations appropriate to solving problems that involve:	**Grade 4**	**Grade 5**	**Grade 6**
	• ... • Multiplication of at least whole 2-digit by 2-digit numbers;	• ... • Multiplication of at least 3-digit by 2-digit numbers;	• ... • Multiplication of at least 4-digit by 3-digit numbers;

Key: LO – Learning Outcome; AS – Assessment Standard. Source: Department of Education 2002.

Figure 12.1 Progression in multiplication through the Intermediate Phase, showing expanding number range.

highlights an important distinction between the discipline of mathematics and the school curriculum. For experienced teachers, whose disciplinary knowledge is strong, the three curricula might be seen as complementary perspectives on the same subject knowledge to be acquired by learners, and the same sets of textbooks would serve all three. In contrast, for teachers whose disciplinary knowledge is weak, there is no distinction between disciplinary knowledge and the curriculum. In such cases, successive curricula might be seen as replacing one another, requiring teachers to learn a 'new curriculum' and to replace textbooks with entirely new ones with each change.

Teacher tests conducted as part of the SACMEQ III comparative exercise (Taylor and Taylor 2013), involving fourteen Southern and Eastern African countries, indicate that the majority of South African teachers fall into the latter category (Table 12.1).

There is widespread agreement among South African teacher educators that the subject knowledge of matriculants entering initial teacher education programmes is problematic. Yet there is no public debate on how to address this fundamental issue, no agreement on the range of topics to be taught within each subject specialization, nor on the depth to which such topics should be known by prospective teachers. For example, a detailed analysis of the SACMEQ test items comprising the topic areas shown in Table 12.1 indicates that the assumption of the test designers is that Grade 6 teachers should be proficient in algebra

Table 12.1 Teacher performance on the SACMEQ maths test (percentage of items correct)

Arithmetic operations	*Fractions, ratio and proportion*	*Algebraic logic*	*Rate of change*	*Space and shape*	*Total*
67.15	49.68	46.51	42.30	56.44	52.39

Source: Taylor and Taylor 2013.

> Joe has 5 fewer hats than Mary, and Lilian has 3 times as many hats as Joe. If Mary has **n** hats, which of these represents the number of hats that Lilian has?
>
> | | | | | |
> |---|---|---|---|---|
> | A. | 3 **n** – 5 | | C. | 5 – 3 **n** |
> | | | | | |
> | B. | 3 (**n** – 5) | | D. | **n** – 5 |

Figure 12.2 Item 30, SACMEQ Teacher Test.
Source: Taylor and Taylor 2013.

to the same level specified by the Grade 10 curriculum in the area of mathematical modelling and techniques involving simultaneous equations, linear graphs, and problems based on two or more linear functions of different gradient. Figure 12.2 below provides an example of an item (item 30) that could be solved by trial and error, but a deeper understanding of which would be facilitated by an understanding of elementary algebra.

Tasks of this kind commence in the early grades, without the algebraic elements present in item 30, where they are solved using trial and error and logical reasoning, with or without diagrammatic representations or proto-algebraic techniques. Unfortunately, many teachers seem to miss the point of these tasks, which is to promote systematic thinking using number patterns, leading to algebraic generalization, representation, manipulation, and the construction of new patterns. Taylor and Taylor (2013) describe a classroom vignette that illustrates the point. Here the teacher is intent on getting to an answer as quickly as possible, to the extent that she provides learners with one of the three numbers in the problem and then sets them the task of finding another, apparently oblivious to the fact that the purpose of this problem is to develop the thinking skills and problem-solving strategies required to find this very information. It goes without saying that a certain sophistication of language proficiency is a prerequisite to making any sense of such a problem.

Maths subject knowledge for teaching

A second set of recontextualizing agents – researchers, teacher educators, expert teachers – perform a second transformation on the disciplinary knowledge: selecting from the discipline of mathematics, from the school curriculum, and from the findings of research into classroom practice, and casting this selection as subject knowledge for teaching. This is the work of the pedagogic recontextualizing field and it is here that professional know-how is codified. This is a relatively young field of study, which is particularly active in mathematics education, although it remains undeveloped and under-theorised (see for example Adler and Pattahuddin

2012). If this kind of knowledge is to provide reliable information to pedagogy – formulating theoretical knowledge about teaching and learning, distilling and codifying experience (Merton 1973), and investigating effective practice – then the profession will need to pursue Hiebert, Gallimore and Stigler's (2002) idea that professional knowledge must be representable in a form that can be shared discursively and practically. It will also need to fit Grimmett and Chinnery's (2009) notion of teaching and teacher education as a profession with a formal, research-based body of knowledge that distinguishes qualified educators from lay persons.

One of the first to give this component of the teacher education knowledge region a name was Shulman (1986) in his much quoted AERA Presidential Address of 1986, when he distinguished between content knowledge, pedagogical content knowledge (PCK) and curriculum knowledge. The first corresponds to disciplinary knowledge while the last, the most neglected in Shulman's view, reflects the teacher's understanding of how the different curricular topics and subjects fit together (laterally) and how they relate to each other at successive grade levels (vertically). Of Shulman's three knowledge categories, it is PCK that has attracted the most attention. This is still content knowledge, as distinct from pedagogy, but focuses on those aspects that are most germane to its teachability.

For Shulman, PCK includes knowledge about the most useful forms of representing an idea, and the most powerful illustrations, examples, analogies and demonstrations. It includes an understanding of what makes a topic easy or difficult to learn; insights into the kinds of misconceptions that students are often prey to; and how these may be overcome. This is the same sense in which Hill and her colleagues use the term content knowledge for teaching mathematics (CKT-M) (Hill, Schilling and Ball 2004; Hill, Rowan and Ball 2005), defined as the specialized knowledge of math needed for the work of teaching.

Hill *et al.* (2005) insist that CKT-M is maths knowledge, not pedagogy. It is the knowledge, or know-how, teachers *use* in classrooms. These authors attempt to capture this kind of knowledge in items designed to measure teacher CKT-M. Hill *et al.* (2005) found that CKT-M is the strongest teacher-level predictor of learner gain scores in mathematics. This research has also established a link between teacher scores on CKT-M items and the quality of instruction, as indicated by the appropriateness of teacher's responses to students and their mathematical errors, the richness of the mathematics taught, and mathematical language used in class (Ball and Bass 2000; Ball, Hill and Bass 2005; Hill *et al.* 2004; Hill *et al.* 2008). Consequently, the authors predict that efforts to improve teachers' mathematics knowledge through content-focused professional development and pre-service programmes will improve student achievement. (Hill *et al.* 2005).

Pedagogy and professional identity

Exogenous and endogenous accounts agree that a fully-fledged teaching profession would contain at least two elements, although they may disagree about their contents. First, a systematic understanding of teaching must constitute the central axis of the profession, whether this occurs as a public dialogue about education within the professional community (Hyslop-Margison and Sears 2010), or whether it takes the form of Abbott's (1988) codified abstract knowledge system. Second, professions adopt a collegial form of organization as the critical point of reference for both practice and the maintenance of autonomy. The collegiate plays a role in the continuing professional development of members and is instrumental in setting and maintaining the standards of both training and practice.

But being a professional is not simply a matter of undergoing training in a knowledge field and belonging to an association. Beck and Young (2005) point to the link between these two elements: '. . . professional training typically involved more than the imparting of specialist expertise; it also involved intensive socialisation into the values of a professional community and its standards of professional integrity, judgement, and loyalty—in other words, the creation of a professional habitus' (Beck and Young 2005: 188). These ideas take us back to Durkheim (1893/1997), who described how industrialized societies are based on a specialized division of labour. Here, individuals differentiate themselves from each other through acquiring the skills to perform specialized functions. Social coherence is achieved through the exchange of labour and the mutual dependence of individuals on each other. According to Abbott, professionalization has been the main route to institutionalizing expertise in industrialized countries (Abbott 1988: 323). Both senses of the term 'discipline' embed themselves in a school subject such as mathematics. When followed in a disciplined way, not only are certain habits of mind and codes of ethics acquired, but the initiate acquires a language and system of thought, an approach to the application of knowledge to the field of practice. As Muller (2009: 214) notes: 'A strong academic identity thus binds the social to the cognitive.'

Afdal and Nerland (2012) interviewed newly qualified teachers from two teacher education programmes: a 'research-based' course at the University of Helsinki, a five-year inquiry-oriented Master's programme; and the 'general professional' programme offered by Oslo University College over four years. These differences are summarized in Table 12.2.

Afdal and Nerland (2012) note several important differences among the six novice Finnish teachers compared with those of their six Norwegian counterparts. Differences with respect to their relation to knowledge seemed to be systematically structured by the educational programme they followed. Generalizing from such a small sample of purposively-selected cases is a risky exercise. Nevertheless, what can be said is that students exhibit different approaches to how they understand the relationship between knowledge and practice, and in the degree to which they draw on knowledge that is relatively robust or relatively more contingent. It is the purpose of professional training to shape such consciousness among prospective adepts. But first, there is a choice to be made regarding the identity to be shaped. An endogenous approach assumes that the answer to the identity question is not arbitrary but that one particular knowledge persona is preferable for the profession, in that it gives adepts a key advantage over rival contenders.

Table 12.2 Differences in students' relation to knowledge associated with two teacher education programmes

Inquiry-oriented Master's programme	*General Professional programme*
Conceptual coherence	Contextual coherence
Specialized discourses of academic disciplines (draws on developmental psychology, theories of learning, curriculum theory and research methods).	Experiential base: trial and error. Teaching is practical, and the knowledge base not very theoretical; teaching as craft.
Emphasis on differentiation, sequencing, formative assessment, and ways of scaffolding the individual learner. Use curriculum theory to reflect on connections between learning content and activities in specific subjects.	Stronger focus on the act of teaching than on student learning processes. Work as a collective enterprise: collaborative work with colleagues.
Strong classification (between disciplinary boundaries) and strong framing (context independence) of knowledge.	Weak classification (divergence among practitioners) and framing (context dependence) of knowledge.

Source: Derived from Afdal and Nerland 2012.

A second small sample case study approach attracts the same reservations about generalizability, but at the same time offers further insights into differences in attitudes to knowledge among South African teachers in two very different institutional settings (Parker 2008). At City University (CU), a relatively well-resourced urban campus, Mr/s X adopts an approach to teaching *subject knowledge* that is very much in the reform maths tradition (see Boaler and Greeno 2000; Boaler 2002), emphasizing the development of conceptual understanding through use of Ball and Bass's (2000) idea of 'unpacking' mathematical ideas through class discussion. It is clear that this is a very time-intensive pedagogy (see, for example, the kinds of discussions typical of such approaches in Brodie 2010) and that, even though the course involves a great deal of contact time, large parts of the maths subject knowledge curriculum listed in the course outline are not attended to in practice, including a number of topics in functions and algebra, calculus and statistics. Mr/s X concedes that the heavy focus on developing conceptual understanding limits coverage and also compromises the development of students' fluency with mathematical procedures. The assumption behind this approach is that immersion of students in unpacking the principles – the conceptual logic – of a few key topics will provide them with the wherewithal to understand the other topics not studied in the course on their own.

As in the case of CU, coverage of school mathematics at Rural University (RU) is limited: trigonometry is not considered at all, while geometry, algebra and statistics are limited to selected contents and do not cover many aspects in the national school curriculum. The approach adopted by Dr A at RU is characteristic of what Bernstein (1996) labelled a performance-based pedagogic mode, in contrast to the competence mode of Mr/s X at CU. Students interviewed identify with mathematics as a structured body of knowledge that they must get to know – it is made up of topics containing both theoretical elements (facts/concepts/definitions/theorems) and established methods for solving problems and procedures for generating answers to standard questions.

In terms of *mathematics education knowledge* (PCK), Parker notes that mathematics teaching as a distinct knowledge domain, and the production of what Ensor (2003) terms a 'professional argot' for developing best mathematics teaching practices, is generally absent from the teacher education curricula at both institutions. Although Mr/s X has a well-developed pedagogical style linked to work from the reform perspective, it appears that her students are given limited direct access to research in mathematics education. At RU Dr A adopts an eclectic approach to subject knowledge for teaching, which is seen as a basket of ideas that may prove useful, and from which each student will have to make a selection, but which does not represent general lessons for teaching. To use Purinton's term, this component all too often looks like an endless array of 'tips and tricks', following the fast and pervasive diffusion of 'fads' (Purinton 2011: 132–3).

On the question of *pedagogical knowledge* Parker notes a wide discrepancy between the two institutions regarding the practice teaching component of the curriculum with a well-developed programme at CU and a very rudimentary one at RU.

Conclusion

What we can learn from these two case studies, and more generally from the analysis above, is that the place to start in improving the whole ensemble of professional behaviour lies in strengthening the *subject identities* of beginning teachers. Placing teacher education in the universities, as has happened recently in South Africa, or placing the qualification requirement at Masters level, in the Finnish case, seem to indicate steps in the direction of stiffening the conceptual spine of professional knowledge, but it is in the content and orientation of the courses that the proof of the pudding will lie, as Afdal and Nerland argue.

At both institutions studied by Parker, trainee teachers did not learn very much mathematics, in terms of topics studied, either because insufficient time was allocated, or because the dominant pedagogy favours studying a few topics in depth and hoping that this provides students with the tools to pick up the rest on their own. On the basis of two case studies, we obviously cannot speculate how widespread these practices are. Our analysis does indicate, however, that, if we agree with Durkheim (1893/1997) that a specialized division of labour is the foundation of a modern society, and if we agree with Bernstein (1996) that immersion in the subject disciplines is the key to specializing professional consciousness, then we should probably agree with Parker that, at least at high-school level, subject knowledge should be taught by subject specialists, professionals whose identities are imbued with the principles and protocols of the discipline.

Regarding the theory of subject teaching, at least some South African teacher educators view research conclusions about teaching either as the truth to be adopted as an article of faith or as a set of contingent hints and tips, rather than part of a field of principled knowledge. The international literature indicates that this situation is not confined to South Africa, as the Norwegian example above shows, and it is clear that the field has a long way to go before it produces knowledge that is a reliable guide to best practice. Ball's call seems eminently sensible for a: '. . . system of design, development, and research that will produce the evidence base and resources to make it possible to accomplish high levels of success in K-12 education' (Ball 2010: 4).

Beck (2008: 121) has argued that because it has proved difficult to claim a distinctive expertise, teaching has long been a fragmented profession, not least because of what he calls teachers' allegiance to competing pedagogic ideologies. This is all too evident, for example, in the special edition of *The Educational Researcher* published by the American Educational Research Association in December 2008 (AERA 2008), where the conclusions of the Final Report of the National Mathematics Advisory Panel and those of its critics provide little basis for a collegial discussion. Wilkinson (2005) explains the consequences of this kind of internecine fighting:

> Members of the education community have not united around any common body of knowledge which they collectively perceive to be essential for teaching . . . [and] given this situation, it is unsurprising that the state and general public do not perceive that a licence to fuller professional control . . . is a plausible policy option.
>
> (Wilkinson 2005: 428)

This quote returns us to the question of professional autonomy with which this chapter began. While the role of the state is important in providing space for teachers to exercise expert judgement, advancing the status of the profession and the quality of practice are dependent on the development of a robust knowledge base that can provide an increasingly reliable guide to practice. This can only arise from within the professional field itself.

References

Abbott, A. (1988). *The system of professions: An essay on the division of expert labour*. Chicago, IL: University of Chicago Press.

Adler, J. and Pattahudin, S. (2012). 'Recontextualising items that measure mathematical knowledge for teaching into scenario-based interviews: An investigation'. *Journal of Education*, 56: 17–44.

AERA (American Educational Research Association) (2008). *Educational Researcher*, vol. 37, no. 9. Special issue on 'Foundations for success: The final report of the National Mathematics Advisory Panel'. Thousand Oaks, CA: Sage.

Afdal, H.W., and Nerland, M. (2012). 'Does teacher education matter? An analysis of relations to knowledge among Norwegian and Finnish novice teachers'. *Scandinavian Journal of Educational Research*, DOI: 10.1080/00313831.2012.726274.

Apple, M. (1986). 'Controlling the work of teachers'. In M. Apple, *Teachers and texts*. New York: Routledge & Kegan Paul (pp. 183–97).

Apple, M. (2000). *Official knowledge: Democratic education in a conservative age*. New York: Routledge.

Ball, D. (2010). Summary of testimony to the U.S. House of Representatives Committee on Education and Labor, May 4, 2010. Available online at http://republicans.edlabor. house.gov/UploadedFiles/5.4.10_ball.pdf (accessed on 15 December, 2010).

Ball, D. and Bass, H. (2000). 'Interweaving content and pedagogy in teaching and learning to teach: Knowing and using mathematics'. In J. Boaler (ed.) *Multiple perspectives in mathematics teaching and learning*. Westport, CT: Ablex (pp. 83–104).

Ball, D.L., Hill, H.C. and Bass, H. (2005). 'Knowing mathematics for teaching: Who knows mathematics well enough to teach third grade, and how can we decide?' *American Educator*, Fall 2005: 14–22.

Ball, Stephen. (2008). 'Performativity, privatization, professionals and the state'. In C. Cunningham (ed.) *Exploring professionalism*. Bedford Way Papers. London: Institute of Education, University of London.

Beck, J. (2008). 'Governmental professionalism, re-professionalising or de-professionalising teachers in England'. *British Journal of Educational Studies*, 56(2): 119–43.

Beck, J. and Young, M. (2005). 'The assault on the professions and the restructuring of academic and professional identities: A Bernsteinian analysis'. *British Journal of Sociology of Education*, 26(2): 183–97.

Bernstein, B. (1990). *Class, codes and control, Volume 4: The structuring of pedagogic discourse*. London: Routledge.

Bernstein, B. (1996). *Pedagogy, symbolic control and identity*. London: Taylor & Francis.

Boaler, J. (2002). 'The development of disciplinary relationships: Knowledge, practice and identity in mathematics classrooms'. *For the Learning of Mathematics*, 22(1): 42–7.

Boaler, J. and Greeno, J.G. (2000). 'Identity, agency and knowing in mathematical worlds'. In J. Boaler (ed.) *Multiple perspectives on teaching and learning mathematics*. Westport, CT: Ablex (pp. 83–103).

Brodie, K. (2010). *Teaching mathematical reasoning in secondary schools*. New York: Springer.

Department of Basic Education (2011). *Curriculum and Assessment Policy Statement. Foundation Phase. Grades R-3. Mathematics: English*. Pretoria: Department of Basic Education.

Department of Education (1995). *Curriculum 2005: Learning for the 21st Century*. Pretoria: Department of Education.

Department of Education (2000). *A South African curriculum for the 21st century: Report of the Review Committee on Curriculum 2005*. Pretoria: Department of Education.

Department of Education (2002). *Revised National Curriculum Statement. Grades R-9 (Schools) Policy*. Pretoria: Department of Education.

Durkheim, E. (1893/1997). *The division of labour in society*. The Free Press reprint, 1997.

Ensor, P. (2004) 'Modalities of teacher education discourse and the education of effective practitioners', *Pedagogy, Culture & Society*, 12(2): 217–32.

Freidson, E. (1994). *Professionalism reborn: Theory, prophecy and policy*. Cambridge: Polity Press.

Gamble, J. (2010). 'Teacher professionalism: A literature review'. Johannesburg: JET Education Services. Available online at www.jet.org (accessed on 14 January, 2014).

Goldstein, J. (2001). *Console and classify: The French psychiatric profession in the nineteenth century*. Chicago, IL: University of Chicago Press.

Goodson, I. and Hargreaves, A. (1996). *Teachers' professional lives: Aspirations and actualities*. London: Routledge.

Grimmett, P. and Chinnery, A. (2009). 'Bridging policy and professional pedagogy in teaching and teacher education: Buffering learning by educating teachers as curriculum makers'. *Curriculum Inquiry*, 39(1): 125–43.

Hargreaves, A. (2003). *Teaching in the knowledge society: Education in the age of insecurity*. New York: Teachers College Press.

Hiebert, J., Gallimore, R. and Stigler, J. (2002). 'A knowledge base for the teaching profession: what would it look like and how can we get one?' *Educational Researcher*, 31(5): 3–15.

Hill, H., Rowan, H. and Ball, D. (2005). 'Effects of teachers' mathematical knowledge for teaching on student achievement'. *American Educational Research Journal*, 42(2): 371–406.

Hill, H., Blunk, M., Charalambous, C., Lewis, J., Phelps, J., Sleep, L. and Ball, D. (2008). 'Mathematical knowledge for teaching and the mathematical quality of instruction: An exploratory study'. *Cognition and Instruction*, 26: 430–511.

Hill, H., Schilling, S. and Ball, D. (2004). 'Developing measures of teachers' mathematics knowledge for teaching'. *Elementary School Journal*, 105, 1; Academic Research Library, 11.

Hyslop-Margison, E. and Sears, A. (2010). 'Enhancing teacher performance: The role of professional autonomy'. *Interchange*, 41(1): 1–15.

Merton, R.K. (1973). *The sociology of science: Theoretical and empirical investigations*. Chicago, IL: University of Chicago Press.

Muller, J. (2009). 'Forms of knowledge and curriculum coherence'. *Journal of Education and Work*, 22(3): 205–26.

Pachler, N. (2007). 'Teacher development: a question(ing) of professionalism'. In *New Designs for Teachers' Professional Learning*. London: Institute of Education Publications (pp. 242–68).

Parker, D. (2008). 'The specialisation of pedagogic identities in initial mathematics teacher education in post-apartheid South Africa'. PhD dissertation, University of the Witwatersrand.

Pichot, P. (2000). 'The history of psychiatry as a medical speciality'. In M. Gelder, J. Lopez-Ibor Jr and N. Andreason (eds) *New Oxford textbook of psychiatry, Vol 1*. Oxford: Oxford University Press (pp. 17–26).

Pratte, R. and Rury, J. (1991). 'Teachers, professionalism, and craft'. *Teachers College Record*, 93(1): 59–72.

Purinton, T. (2011). *Six degrees of school improvement*. Charlotte, NC: Information Age Publishing.

Shulman, L. (1986). 'Those who understand: knowledge growth in teaching'. *Educational Researcher*, 15(2): 4–14.

Sockett, H. (1987). 'Has Shulman got the strategy right?' *Harvard Educational Review*. 57(2): 208–19.

Taylor, N. and Hoadley, U. (2012). 'The evolution of a national curriculum: The case of South Africa'. Presentation to the Seventh International Basil Bernstein Symposium, Aix-en-Provence, 27–30 June, 2012.

Taylor, N. and Taylor, S. (2013). 'Teacher knowledge and professional habitus'. In N. Taylor, S. van der Berg and T. Mabogoane (eds). *Creating effective schools*. Cape Town: Pearson.

Wilkinson, G. (2005). 'Workforce remodelling and formal knowledge: The erosion of teachers' professional jurisdiction in English schools'. *School Leadership & Management*, 25: 421–39.

Index

Printed in Great Britain
by Amazon